What Goes Around
Comes Around

by

Rob O'Neill

Copyright

Labyrinth

The intricacies of life are but common to all:
it is how we untangle these twists
that paints our individuality
in the canvas of destiny.

We can choose to be lost
in the labyrinth of our emotions
or use these trials to harness
our inner strength,
but one thing remains constant in our lives--
we have the sun in our hands.

-Dodinsky-

Contents

Who Would Have an Interest In This Book?
(What You Will Find Within)

• You have an interest in self-exploration; though, ironically, you don't know where to start.

• You've heard talk of the inner journey and feel curious but don't want to get bogged down in complex esoteric/spiritual pathways with conflicting focuses.

• You could wish to consider this the beginning of a spiritual practice or augment an existing practice — but that's not necessary.

• You don't have to be an adherent to any particular spirituality.

• You don't even need to believe that spirituality has a place in your life (and I won't try and convince you otherwise).

• Perhaps, you are someone that has always seen life and your place in it in a particular way and dare to believe something else is possible.

• You have fulfilled a longstanding role(s) in your life, and an ending has resulted (or is getting considered) — what's next?

- I've done this for so long that I've lost myself in it! — Who am I now?

- What is important? (to me) Where do my passions lie?

- Does the idea of being in your heart conjure the realization that it seems like being a tourist in your home town?

Through a personal journey, I used the practice of walking a labyrinth for exploration — it is not necessary that you follow in my literal footsteps (you could — my experience is that it proved effective), but truly, the emphasis here falls on self-exploration.

It is important that what you choose resonates for you and provides you the means and personal space to facilitate reflection and access to your internal world. As such, I recommend that you have minimal to no external distraction.

Alternative activities might include but are not limited to:
- Time alone in nature/the beach
- Walking
- Running
- Cycling
- Yoga

Through my journey, I have compiled a series of questions, which the reader can use for starting points (guidelines). If other questions result (which is quite likely) as you consider these, then, by all means, examine them for yourself — this is your practice.

The questions provided offer suggestions with which to make a beginning. You can ask yourself during your practice things like, "What is it that I need to know about _____?" — In the silence, you may feel surprised at your answer. You will find no right or wrong answers. This offers a personal reflective journey for your expanded awareness. Hold the answers lightly and yourself with curiosity, understanding, and compassion. This is not an interrogation or cross-examination experience.

It may not prove practical (or desirable) to have a journal with you while you engage in your activity — but I do suggest that you have one accessible and, perhaps, allow some time afterward to jot down your thoughts (the answers to your questions) as part of your inquiry/practice.

This, in effect, gives an opportunity to connect with yourself. Though the guidelines are suggestions only, I hope that you will honour yourself with empathy, compassion, and deep listening — the integration of some (or all) of your insights could bring about significant change/transformation in your life.

You have no rules — I would suggest as useful an open mind, a spirit of playful exploration, curiosity, and willingness to embrace the mystery and intrigue that is you.

Labyrinths 101

Labyrinths have been around for over 4000 years. Greek Mythology features a story that centres around a labyrinth built by the architect Daedalus for King Minos of Crete.

Its purpose was to hold the Minotaur (a creature half-man and half-bull — the beast was, eventually, defeated by Theseus from Athens, who killed it).

Theseus received assistance from Ariadne — who gave him a thread (the "clew" or "clue"), which enabled him to get back out.

Daedalus made the labyrinth so complex that he just barely managed to find his way out after he'd built it.

Labyrinths are often thought to be the same as a maze — the modern definition makes the distinction that within a maze lay multiple paths that can take one in a variety of directions. Conversely, within a labyrinth, you find a single path to the centre with no intention to create confusion.

The Labyrinth as Spiritual Tool

The labyrinth is a metaphor for life's journey that provides an opportunity for a direct experience by providing a sacred space within which one can walk from their "ego-self" to that which lies deep within them.

The life of each offers a sacred journey. Along the way, we find constant change offering opportunities for growth, discovery, expansion (of self and what is seen as possible), gaining clarity, and deepening intuitive connections. The journey casts, as the hero, we—the individual—and opens us to ourselves to bring about healing and the reclaiming of our inherent power. Each step will call for courage and fortitude.

Everyone walks on this path and finds him or herself precisely where each needs to be. The labyrinth gives a symbolic representation of this path—an ancient symbol that encompasses wholeness.

Combined within its design, we find the forms of the spiral and the circle, which like life itself, can be seen as both a meandering and purposeful path.

Circles

Circles have significance varied and profound — and, though far more extensive than the scope of this book, some examples include:
- The sun
- The moon
- The cyclic presence of the seasons

The circle can be seen to represent such things as:
- Inclusion
- Wholeness
- Unity
- Cycles
- Completion
- Infinity
- Equality
- Eternal life

The circle is seen, universally, as sacred and divine. It embodies the infinite nature of energy and inclusivity of the universe.

The spiral is the universal symbol for the spiritual journey; it also represents the life force both cosmic and microcosmic.

The spiral has become associated with such things as:
- The feminine as the doorway to creation
- The cycles of:
- Time
- The seasons
- The cycle of birth, growth, death, and rebirth

The cycles of time and nature are the cycles of life.

Long used as meditation and prayer tools, the labyrinth represents a journey into one's centre and back out into the world again.

With only one way in and back out, walking the labyrinth invokes a right-brain experience involving intuition, creativity, and visualization. It is a walk to the centre of your deepest self and back to the outside world with a broadened understanding of who you are.

Introduction

The account you are about to read results from a personal exploration—what may set it apart from other research projects is that I don't claim pre-existing expertise, or education, on the subject matter presented. This being the case, I believe that minimal bias existed to shape and inform the unfolding of my experience. I spent a period of forty consecutive days in compiling the information, which endeavours to chronicle the direct experience encountered each day. The project itself, it's scope and development, all occurred spontaneously—in fact, the day it began, no intent existed on my part to begin such an undertaking—I simply decided to go for a walk one afternoon. In that respect, one could say that the project found me.

As I said, it began with a walk on a beautiful sunny autumn afternoon. I had no particular destination in mind—warm weather of this sort was no longer a given at that time of year, so if ever there were a time to seize the day, this was it! I set out guided by a GPS in the guise of my heart—content to go wherever my feet took me.

Eventually, I found myself in the vicinity of a local Anglican Cathedral where I remembered a labyrinth on the grounds—in the next moment, I had decided I would walk it. I understood a labyrinth to be used as part of a form of walking meditation—my life had become a conscious quest for truth—beginning with myself and then extending to an insatiable appetite for "universal truths." All the former bastions of my identity had now gone—including a seventeen-year marriage, twenty-nine-year career path, real estate holdings, even the last of my RRSPs (retirement investments) had gotten spent to travel to places of personal spiritual significance. All this had taken place within a three-year period of time—I had then returned to my home town of Victoria (having been back about three months at this time from my trip to Europe). The whole time in Europe was accentuated by experiences that proved mind-expanding, to say the least, more accurately mind-blowing—for reasons not the least of which, these experiences were mine, I didn't read about someone else's journey. Such life shaking events would require some processing time to try and determine the implications for my life moving forward—I reasoned a walk about in the labyrinth made for a good place to begin.

I arrived at the labyrinth site and discovered that, in order to walk it, I would first need to clear it off. The newly fallen leaves made seeing the outline of the path difficult. As I pushed the leaves clear with my feet, the notion asserted itself that I take on the clearing of the labyrinth daily (for thirty days—which became forty) and then have a time of walking reflection.

Initially, it occurred to me that I would (at least in part) show up in service of those who walked the labyrinth. I suppose some could have interpreted that I serviced the Anglican Church (given I worked on what I presumed as their property). However, I didn't seek prior approval from the Church, and so concluded that I could claim to serve them. I wondered if my going there daily would draw the attention of Church officials. Many different people witnessed me there daily; however, no one ever asked what I was doing or on whose authority I did it. I had prepared for such an encounter with, "I'm here on higher authority." — I wondered what sort of response that would elicit, and suspected that the parish administration would likely see their organization hierarchy (with he that held the station of bishop) as standing at the pinnacle of Earthly authority and the only one with anything akin to a Divine directive.

Though I attended the Anglican Church in my youth while simultaneously attending a Catholic private elementary school, my journey through life thereafter had formed for me the belief that I need not defer my spiritual authority to anyone. My connection to the Divine remains my own. It occurred to me that this proclamation might either yield me a wide berth (i.e. he's just another west coast eccentric — probably harmless), or perhaps, a net result that I wouldn't care for; i.e. I might find myself contained within a net, with the suggestion my guidance and field research unfold elsewhere. Fortunately, no such encounter occurred — I showed up every morning, broom in hand, and swept the labyrinth, fully witnessed and completely without harassment. In hindsight, it seems to me to beg the question — I wonder where else I could just show up and, randomly, begin a given activity before someone would grow interested (or concerned) enough to ask what I was about.

So, as I stated earlier, I had no previously established practice that I now wanted to share with others and therefore decided to write about. That which became the practice, I arrived at organically — I would even go so far as to say it created itself. I simply followed direction (which included that I would journal each day's experience; the compilation of which would form the raw material to create this book). The focus went from just being there in service of those that walked the labyrinth to consideration for, examination of, and service to The Sacred.

Along with this, though not my original intent, I would come to meet various adversaries and allies on this journey—surprising given I remained alone. So, the day-to-day account includes the various ways I got called upon to face myself and still complete the commitment I had made to myself.

Should you decide to (literally) follow my lead and choose to walk a labyrinth as a contemplative tool for self-exploration, you may come to discover more than the path below your feet.

If your experience proves anything like mine, you may well get introduced to the labyrinthine presence of what the Buddhists call "Monkey mind." First, one thought pops into your awareness, and then like a monkey swinging from branch to branch, one thought generates another and, before you know it, you're in an entirely different tree. (Did I say "tree"? I meant train of thought.)

If you have never done any form of meditation before, then rest assured, this cacophony of thoughts is to be expected. You're not "doing it wrong," and neither mindfulness nor the labyrinth causes you to think more. It is possible that, for the first time, you are being made aware of the never ending volley of thoughts that make your constant companion.

When you become aware that you have booked passage on a run-away thought train, you can bring yourself back to being present by either focusing on your breathing, or each foot-fall as you walk.

With the breathing, you can count ... 1 (on the inhale), 2 (on the exhale), until you reach 10, and then repeat the cycle. Focus on expanding your lungs fully while inhaling, and then emptying them fully when exhaling. Slow and relaxed—don't hyper-ventilate. If thinking resumes—just release it and get back to the breath.

The stepping focus proves much the same. Feel each foot as it contacts the path. Feel the support of the path beneath your foot. Feel the weight exchange while one foot lifts and advances.

Of course, if you utilize your quiet connection time to gain inspiration for the next chapter of your novel, or the song you're writing, then don't throw out creative input coming your way. You could bring a notepad along to jot down ideas, either once you have done or in the moment if you must.

The other thing is, that though not specifically a time for problem solving, don't feel surprised if while observing this time in the silence, answers may just present. So, rather than go with the idea that you will solve a current challenge, release any need to focus on it while you do your practice, thereby creating space for spirit to move.

Walking the Labyrinth (Day 1)

(October 25, 2011)
(Enthusiasm and The Unknown)

I am the Good Shepherd
I am among you
As he who serveth
I am the living bread
I am the true vine

I woke this day with eager anticipation as I prepared to embark on the first day of my thirty-day commitment. I had been around the block frequently enough that I knew all new endeavours began all awash with enthusiasm—I took note both of its presence and of the idea that it would prove short-lived, which appeared stealthily, though it had no difficulty asserting itself upon arrival.

Though there had been considerable time since, I felt reminded of the first day of returning to school after summer vacation—the ease and freedom of the holiday morning give way to a completely different sequence of events. Some excitement grows around a new beginning coupled with some uncertainty, for the same reason—the stepping out into the unknown. To be sure, some form of education would take place with this new endeavour—in this case, with no known outline, and therefore, with no way of knowing what I might learn or the form the lesson would take.

The fact that the autumn day had dawned beautiful and clear contributed to the ease with which I prepared to go — the temperature would feel cool (given it was only 8:00 a.m.), but the sun shone.

I arrived at the grounds of the cathedral with my broom (with which to clear the labyrinth of fallen leaves), my cup of tea, and a gardener's foam kneeling pad on which I would sit later to meditate.

Moments after beginning to sweep the labyrinth, a woman asked me what time the cathedral opened — I indicated that I felt unsure, and that there was, however, a sign posted at the front entrance. She thanked me and wandered off to seek her information, and I carried on with my task. I had the idea that I had come here to serve the sacred (or at least explore it for myself). I was, as it turns out just by being there, in a position to be of service to someone else. If she considered that which goes on within the cathedral as sacred (even if only the peace and solitude inside), then by extension, I had served the sacred already. Of course, she might have just wanted to use the washroom — then again, if one needs a bathroom urgently enough upon arrival, the subsequent relief might be considered a "God send." It has, on occasion, also been known as the porcelain altar — perhaps, not the first thing that springs to mind when one considers the sacred. However, having said a prayer or two there in my lifetime (some might be quick to deem this a complete lack of reverence), just the same, I felt grateful for its presence.

Once again, I considered that I came, in part, to be of service. It seemed interesting to note that it wasn't necessary for me to define the service that would take

14

place—I just needed to remain available to serve. Class in full session and I hadn't even begun to walk the labyrinth yet.

I looked across the grounds to the labyrinth and the beauty of the carpet of autumn colours, which enveloped it, and noted (simultaneously) the fact that it would take considerable sweeping to clear the leaves.

As it turned out, sweeping the labyrinth gave a portal to reflection just as walking would have. I had reached about seventy-five percent completeness with my objective when I became aware of the contrast between the warmth within my body (generated by my effort) and the coolness of the October morning air. My breath turned to beads of condensation upon my beard.

Just then, a fellow that had worked with a leaf blower in another corner of the grounds approached. I wondered if, perhaps, he worked for the city and might harangue me about union job entitlement, or maybe, he worked for the church and would ask me to explain myself, and maybe even stop what I was doing or leave. Well, nothing of the sort happened (interesting that the only place confrontation occurred happened between my ears). Does that make me a confrontational person? Or do I fear confrontation—and if so, why? As I consider the question—an answer occurs ... fear (Fear?) Yes, fear. Fear of not getting what I want or fear of losing something that I have already.

Well, now, what do we have going on here? Conversations with Rob! I've heard that all the answers I need are within—somehow, I hadn't necessarily expected a demonstration. Nevertheless, with no question, the universe provided a plausible answer to my question (which, of course, I remained free to accept or reject—an entirely different distinction from whether it proved true or false).

Meanwhile, back at the labyrinth, the gardener nodded (to acknowledge my presence or perhaps as a good morning). In truth, I have no idea. For all I know, it could have been an unconscious and involuntary tic left over from childhood at which time his older brother and friends convinced him to become the goalie on their dart team.

After this brief gesture, he proceeded to direct the jet stream generated (along with a skull-piercing sound) through the wand of his blower, quickly removing the remaining leaves. He wielded the blower like a Jedi Knight armed with his light-sabre, which he used skilfully to dispatch the forces from the Dark Side.

That imagery soon got lost when the thought arose that he did represent the dark side (well, metaphorically)—didn't he get it? I'd come here to serve and get in touch with the sacred. How could I get in touch with the silence within with all that racket? I felt tempted to tell him, "It's okay. I've got it. You and your petroleum product burning, tranquility squelching, ear drum shattering …"

That mind-consuming rant then got overridden with, "Indeed, the silence has gotten corrupted— might I point out that your perceived adversary wears ear protection—so, even if you were to vocalize your venomous thoughts, then, fortunately, he wouldn't hear you immediately."

And …

"It's also of value to point out that your thoughts are significantly more disruptive to your peace than any mechanical device might seem."

Ouch, that stung a bit, but I had to admit a different train of thought seemed preferable to the potential train wreck my previous thoughts may have created. It then occurred to me that this guy just did his job—who says he didn't hold that sacred? Maybe he had a family at home that he helped support—certainly a sacred undertaking. Perhaps, he simply served the church and held that sacred. Not to mention he had helped me complete my objective—did that have to happen my way? Maybe I should just live and let live, or at least, get over myself.

When he departed, and I prepared to walk the labyrinth. The man had created a margin right the way around the perimeter so that a distinct line appeared where the carpet of leaves ended and a pathway of cleared grass appeared, and then the outer edge of the of the labyrinth. Each contrasting ring comprised different colours and textures and now lay in the form of concentric circles—which, as it happens, looked quite pleasing to the eye. Well, now, the Jedi wasn't such a bad guy after all. Such observation, made in light of new information, allowed me to see the power that my judgments and opinions had on my reality.

Thus far, I have established nothing with respect to the parameters contained within this daily observance. As I walked the path, it occurred to me that I would do so from the labyrinth's entrance to the centre, three times. Once in the centre, I would read and consider the words inscribed on the cathedral wall (see inscription commencing this chapter), and then return the same way I had come in to the entry point. The cycle from entry to centre and back out constituted one complete sequence. Upon reaching the centre for the third time, I would complete a series of Qi Gong exercises I had just relearned and wished to incorporate into part of my daily practice. Each exercise also repeats three times before transitioning to the next.

I can only say that I have a knowing that three makes the appropriate number of repetitions (vs., for example, two or four) and certainly a number which appears frequently when considering the human/spiritual journey. Father, Son, Holy Spirit; Faith, Hope, Charity; birth, death, rebirth; Body, Mind, Spirit; three wise men; and likely, innumerable additional occurrences that I remain unaware of. In fact, for all I know, this same numerical archetype might have influenced the constructs of some of those childhood nursery rhymes—i.e. Row, Row, Row (your boat), Three Blind Mice, Wynken, Blynken, and Nod, etc. As the process is organic and guided from within, I didn't see a need to reinvent the wheel and would trust that direction, such as it lay grounded in wisdom and, perhaps, beyond the limits of my rational mind.

While I attempted to keep my focus within, passers-by distracted me on occasion, many dressed in business attire and, presumably, heading off to work. A discernable sense of self-consciousness became apparent. Did they watch what I did? Unlikely, as they seemed immersed in their own life story, and if they noticed at all, a fleeting curiosity might arise only to once again get consumed by their own stream of consciousness, like footprints in the sand swept by the incoming tide.

I recalled those occasions when I had witnessed others doing Tai Chi or yoga in a public park and felt inspired by their dedication and what appeared to me as ease in following their path.

If nothing else, I took note that I had grown aware of my concern for their concern—its presence didn't prevent me from my intended activity. I came here, after all, to explore the sacred for myself. At times, that would involve the upholding of my intent in the face of lack of interest or approval from others. They walk on their journey, guided by their souls, and participate in determining what it is they hold sacred. I see no need that we hold sacred the same thing at the same time.

After completing my time walking the labyrinth, I gathered my belongings and walked across to the base of a large oak tree on the grounds, where I had the intention to pray and meditate. I began by bringing to mind the ancient Celts and Druidic lineages, which honour my Irish ancestry (on my biological father's side), and for whom the oak tree is held sacred as well. They had a deep reverence for nature and the interconnectedness of all life. This holds equally true for the First Nations people that this land once belonged to and where I now sat and the church had been built.

Given this was an Anglican Cathedral, its historical roots began in England (which represents my biological mother's lineage), a nation that—historically—displaced numerous indigenous people, cultures, and spirituality throughout the world, including Ireland and here in Victoria. Therefore, I had within my biology the history of the oppressor and the oppressed.

How could I reconcile these realities while at the same time attempting to deepen my connection to the sacred on land stolen from a group of people (their culture and all they held sacred decimated)? This made a place of worship erected by the colonialists where, to this day, religious services get held—songs of praise get sung—seemingly completely oblivious to the fact that the edifice that houses their sacred observance now sits upon the desecrated land of another culture. Within the mortar that secures the stone building blocks of its walls, may be contained the blood, if not the spirit, of those that lived there proudly.

I could think of nothing else at that moment than to pray for forgiveness and permission from the ancestors that I be allowed to hold sacred ceremony upon their land. Could reconciliation on any level be achieved, given the proceedings occurred in isolation with me the lone attendee? As an immediate answer to this question didn't present itself, a question formed with a more personal focus. In what ways do I dishonour what others hold sacred? How have I oppressed the sacred in others?

When I got up to leave, I realized that I would need a couple of additional items for tomorrow—some tobacco to offer to the ancestors of the First Nations (and the land), and some incense from Ireland, made from the peat of ancient bogs—a small piece burned to honour my Celtic heritage.

I observed, as the first day concluded, that though no format had existed to begin with, one had taken shape regardless, and all I had to do was show up.

Day 1 Questions
(Enthusiasm and The Unknown)

01) What past activities or jobs, or current pursuits bring up for you the feeling of enthusiasm?

02) What does that feel like to you?

03) Where do you feel it?

04) When (if at all) do you continue to experience enthusiasm?

05) When don't you have this experience and what is the balance in your life currently?

06) Can you hold the energy of enthusiasm if others don't share your enthusiasm?

07) What did you love to do as a child?

08) What dreams did you hold for yourself?

   If not realized so far—would you consider resurrecting them?

09) What would that take?

10) Can you embrace new (previously unconsidered) dreams for yourself?

11) What does the unknown represent to you?

12) Can you (will you) be spontaneous?

13) If you like some structure/framework, could you colour outside of the lines?

14) Are you willing to stretch the envelope?

15) If you have made many choices based on security, can you consider choice based on passion? (Or vice versa.)

16) How do you feel about being a beginner? Not having all the answers?

17) What if you are seen as being less than perfect?

18) Will you start something new with no guarantee of success?

19) What does failure mean to you?

Sample Answers
(from Author's direct experience)

Question 1—What past activities or job, or current pursuits, bring up for you the feeling of enthusiasm?

Many of the activities/pursuits I have done since leaving the nursing profession have felt far more engaging and satisfying to me than my career in health-care. I love fitness, personal development, spiritual growth, and the work of so many in the inspirational/motivational and human-potential fields. I love writing and music, playing guitar and singing, and poetry. I discover now that groups of people exist in the world that work with cutting-edge research that combines science—psychology, spirituality, conflict resolution, and restorative justice, and who hold a vision for and work toward peace (now this lights me up!). I might have never realized any of this if I had stayed in the darkness of my discontent. Just to be clear, I'm not saying that these are the directions everyone should take in their life. This is what I have learned for me, through me. The same proves possible for anyone, as their gifts, passions, and experience reveal themselves and become considered in creating their path moving forward.

Questions 7 & 8—What did you love to do as a child? What dreams did you hold for yourself?

I loved to be in the water as a child (well, any time in my life, as I look back). I became a good swimmer, and living in a seaside city, I had always derived a great deal of comfort from, and felt drawn to, the beaches for long walks and times of contemplation. I remember growing fascinated with the Jacque Cousteau programs on TV. I so loved the old program "Flipper." I recall thinking, back then, that I'd like to work as a marine biologist (well, that didn't happen). I did, however, later in life, take up scuba diving. I don't see myself training for biology now, but I do add my name to petitions and write letters to support movements that strive to protect the oceans and all that make their homes within. Who knows? Maybe, one day, I'll volunteer for a stint on the "Sea Sheppard." The point is, though I haven't realized all my childhood dreams, I can look to them for clues and do some grief work if necessary to resolve any unfinished business around them. They could become the building blocks of new dreams if I still feel drawn to them (it offers an opportunity to engage creativity in incorporating them into the present).

Day 2
(Acceptance)

Upon arriving this morning, I noticed newly fallen leaves on the labyrinth. Even still, it wouldn't require the time or effort necessary for clearing as had the first day. The air temperature felt cooler than the previous day and, though not raining, moisture hung thick and heavy in the air. The rains would come, and it only remained a question of when.

I cleared the path quite quickly, and then began my walk. On this occasion, I took note of the geometrical layout of the bricks, precisely placed to create the round form of the labyrinth itself. Also, I noted the curving pathways within that wound within the circle leading me ever deeper toward its centre.

Then I realized that my walking created the appearance of motion. However, focusing on the bricks became rather hypnotic and, whether I experienced an optical illusion or not, it appeared as though the path itself had become more fluid and had set in motion. For sure, an amusing phenomenon but not an effective meditation focal point.

While I continued to walk, a gentle breeze came up, and leaves dislodged from their places overhead to fall in a variety of flight patterns before making their way around me to the labyrinth's surface. At first, I thought, "What the hell? Hey, I just finished clearing this!" I felt tempted to stop my walk and clear the path again. Then the thought came, "There is a time to sweep and clear, and there is time for the footwork."

My next realization revealed, "If not for the volume in your mind protesting the leaves falling, you might hear each one land."

What was I thinking? While I attempted to connect and deepen my reverence for nature, would its cycles and activities stop at my whim? It invited me to join the dance, not call the tune.

The breeze increased, and the leaves showered downward, some spiralling in aerial pirouettes, and others descending in a zigzag pattern. At one point while standing in the centre doing a Qi Gong exercise, I felt a gentle caress upon my cheek as a leaf had made its way groundward. This brief encounter seemed highly sensuous and felt deeply intimate.

Below the oak tree once again, I offered the tobacco in prayer to the land and First Nations ancestors. And though the breeze wreaked havoc with my lighter, I did manage to get the incense burning.

When I left the site, I stopped to look at the large Celtic cross in the adjacent parking lot—I hadn't noticed it previously. It disappointed me to note that absent were the intricate engraving and patterns that I had seen on many different crosses all over Ireland. Though not familiar with the meaning of the various symbols, they had great significance. This cross stood there like some sort of skeletal remain without heart or soul—form without substance—stripped of its former identity and meaning.

For some reason, this made me feel rather sad.

Day 2 Questions
(Acceptance)

01) What does acceptance mean to you?

02) What comes to mind when you consider the idea of living life on life's terms?

03) Do you believe it necessary to make things happen?

04) How much control do you think you have over external events?

05) How much control do you think you have (or should have) over your feelings/emotions?

06) How are you at allowing others to choose and follow their path without giving advice or opinions about what they should do?

07) Do you see a difference between acceptance and complacency, or apathy or condoning?

08) What does self-acceptance mean to you?

09) Is acceptance a journey (process) or an event?

10) What is it that causes two or more people to view the same event so differently?

11) What would your life need to look like in order for you to feel acceptance?

12) Are you okay with who you are and where you are right now?

13) What feels unacceptable to you? Why? Do you think it will always remain so?

14) What has it taken previously to get from a place of non-acceptance to acceptance?

15) The "Serenity Prayer" suggests the acceptance of that which cannot be changed, and that courage is required to change what can be changed, and the wisdom to know the difference. Consider those three elements: Acceptance, courage, and wisdom

(discernment) as they apply to your life (past, present, and future).

Sample Answers
(from Author's experience)

Question 1 — What does acceptance mean to you?

I have come to believe that acceptance means to me that I am no longer in resistance of what is (whatever that might be). It doesn't mean that I agree with it or wouldn't like to see something else. I can hold a vision of something else and even direct myself toward bringing the new reality into being. The distinction for me is I am a stand for something — not working in opposition to what is. Only ongoing resistance prolongs my suffering. Having said that, I don't necessarily just get up in the morning having attained immediate acceptance. A series of stages exist, much like the stages of grief (i.e. denial, bargaining, anger, sadness, acceptance) that I have to go through, and not necessarily in a linear process. Still, in hindsight, I recognize that I have prolonged my process at times by not being willing to let go (usually of a particular belief of mine) and, consequently, I stayed stuck in (for example) anger.

Now, I'm not making myself wrong or meaning to dishonour anyone else's process. However, I can say that, for various reasons, I have repressed the process altogether, or as already mentioned, stalled it. Maybe, at times, it seemed necessary, and staying angry allowed me to avoid touching the sadness. Do that again and again over multiple life events, and you have a whole different variety of issues. So, I am more thoroughly convinced of the adage, "The only way out is through." Does that mean that the other side will be better than where you came from? Well, not necessarily. Firstly, better is a relative term and truly up to the beholder. I can say that it will be different, and the journey through seems to have proven useful at providing me with tools and awareness that I didn't possess beforehand. So, I am—perhaps—better equipped to deal with subsequent events, as it remains a given that I will continue to get called to try and reconcile my life with Life and the world around me.

Question 3—Do you believe it necessary to make things happen?

I guess I would have to say that the jury remains out on this for me; however, here's where I'm at with it so far. I'm reminded of a situation quite some time ago now, when I used to be someone shy (I mean, if I go back far enough, you might say I was situationally mute—not that I couldn't speak, but much went unspoken and unheard). So, a little older now, and living on my own in an apartment block with shared laundry facilities, I would frequently see the same woman there—now, she was beautiful (of course, we're back in the realm of the "beholder" again) but, suffice to say, she had the physical presence that is commonly held as beautiful.

Again, at this place in time, I had little concept of the idea of inner beauty. All I knew of my inner world in this circumstance was that I felt a little nauseated when I considered any sort of interaction with such a beautiful woman. My story came clear—a woman like her doesn't, would never, talk to someone like me. Of course, I made numerous assumptions here about her and myself. However, my time on the planet at that point had not introduced me to such awareness.

God knows what came over me, but one day, I said something to her (probably something deeply profound and alluring like, "How's it going?"). Sometimes, I wish I had some of that "James Bond," "Top Gun" pilot sophistication or moxy—alas, not so much. To my great surprise, she put down her basket, smiled (oh my God, what a smile), extended her hand, and introduced herself. I thought, "Now what? I don't have the script for this! I didn't see this going this way."

We had a pleasant conversation while doing our respective laundry, and a small piece of my worldview got brought into question, if not changed. (Did we live happily ever after, etc.?) Well, I don't know about her, if you were waiting for the storyline where the unassuming nice guy ends up with the supermodel—not this time. My point is, I had a part in making that conversation happen. It might never have occurred if I hadn't spoken up. My aversion to risk back then saw to it that I didn't get crazy and ask her out or anything. Of course, even if I had, could I "make her" say yes or steer the events afterward?

As for making things happen in general—of course I have a part to play, and need to put certain things in motion, and take some action toward realizing a particular goal or outcome. But I'm not clear at what point I would accept an outcome (especially if not the one I had aimed for). I'm not sure what determines for someone the duration of the applied energy and focus toward a particular outcome. I have begun to think that, for me, in truth, I gave up before a certain goal was met (which doesn't mean it was impossible; for sure, there could be other reasons it seemed necessary to quit—other needs more pressing at the time). What I can't be sure of is whether or not a more resolute desire and accompanying effort might have, eventually, resulted in my reaching these goals. Did I just not want it enough?

Perhaps acceptance in these instances takes the form of, "I gave everything I had at the time, and the process became making peace with the unrealized objective while taking away the insight gained to apply to the next endeavour." I could also say something for the approach toward a particular outcome—I could doggedly adhere to the same strategy without realizing my goal, which could result in frustration leading to abandoning the idea, concluding it unsound, or it could block the realization of an alternative approach that may well have proven the successful path.

Day 3
(Saboteur)

While driving on my way to the labyrinth and doing my best to give my care and attention to this activity, nevertheless, I grew distracted by the Technicolor corridors formed by the legions of trees along the roadside, dressed in their finest autumn frocks.

The sky remained clear—the sun had risen and shone fully visible, as did the last hints of rose-toned shading splashed upon the horizon as the sun clawed its way skyward.

I got on the road fifteen minutes earlier than the previous day and, though I didn't spring right out of bed upon waking, once up, I'd felt eager to get on with my newly forming practice. Practice? Could I legitimately call this a practice, given I had completed just two consecutive days and had reasonable assurance that I would complete Day Three?

Again, I recalled the significance of the number three in scriptural accounts, etc. It even appeared in the music of the western world where the first, third, and fifth notes of the major scale form a major chord or "triad" that is said to be perfect harmonically. Whether there can be any association drawn, I couldn't say with any authority. However, I could say that I felt the flow of enthusiasm. In fact, I'd become so enthused to begin that, in my haste to get moving, I had forgotten the book I'd intended to bring to jot down any thoughts that came through during my walk. Perhaps this pointed to an aspect of preparation, some sort of balance between allowing for the excitement but also staying mindful around what was required to fulfill my intention. The other thing is that I could trust that what needed to get noted from the day's walk would make itself known when I came to write about it later.

I revisited the idea of what I'd embarked upon as being deemed a practice — upon examination, I saw that I had assumptions around the idea (i.e. that it be a long-standing, well-refined observance that an advanced adherent has mastery within, like say, the Dalai Lama). Sure, I had committed to thirty days, but would I make it to the thirtieth? Would I continue to practice any or all of this afterward?

I noticed the self-doubt and perfectionism that attempted to infiltrate and influence my fledgling undertaking. Both felt familiar, and I would see if I could include and observe them — but not allow them to dominate.

So, then, maybe the practice of a practice is still a practice. It's not as though, with time and new information, I might not change this stance — I might even generate opposition before all gets said and done, but for now, I declare, "It is what I say it is."

The idea came to me that the compilation of the musings and insights that I wrote for each of the thirty days could get brought together to form a book. Before arriving at the labyrinth, I received its title: "What Goes Around, Comes Around." (Subtitle: "Around the Labyrinth in Thirty Days.) I like it! Just then, another of the motley crew of detractors that occasionally occupied my mind presented uninvited — "Book? What book? It's been two days — there are two journal entries — you call that a book?

Title? Title for what?—Even if a book materializes, then what? It's a little premature to think of a book, isn't it?"

(Wow, I've got to get this guy on board; he brings me down—clearly, this will require some sort of strategy in order to move forward.)

I considered the feedback of some in my circles with regard to my having an exceptional mind; whether that proved true or not, it seemed to me that, often, the power of my mind gets used to come up with new ways to undermine me and my efforts. There had to be a more effective use of intellect and creativity than that.

It became apparent that conversations with myself would feature in this process, so I offered the following into the mix:

(You know, you raise some valid points—I can tell you have exceptional powers of discernment and analytical thinking, and also an eye for detail. I would love it if you would work with me. I would like to make this project the best it can be. I know you can ensure that nothing but the best will get brought forward. What do you say?)

"Huh?—What the hell? Why, I ought to!"

(Come on; please, I need you.)

"Oh, all right—but it's cold out."

(It's okay; I put on an extra shirt, and there's tea for later—come on, let's go for a walk.)

I had thought the introspection and self-exploration would happen during the walk—but there I stood, getting confronted over something I had embarked upon for myself, seemingly by none other than myself. Suddenly, it felt crowded in the driver's seat.

It also made me mindful that though I made my way to the labyrinth site for what would become the third day of the practice, I could not assume the successful completion of the practice until I had actually completed it. This seemed as good a time as any to interject with the "Serenity Prayer":

God grant me the Serenity
To Accept the Things I Cannot Change
The Courage to Change the Things I Can and
the Wisdom to Know the Difference.

I arrived at the site and, with a quick assessment, observed that it looked as though I had not visited at all yesterday—it appeared completely covered in leaves again. A glance upward confirmed that plenty more leaves remained where these had come from and, of course, even those that blanketed the surrounding area could get stirred and returned to the labyrinth's surface by the whims of the wind.

In that instant, the guidance came—(*You are here, the time is now, and it matters not what you swept yesterday, nor does it matter what you might have to sweep tomorrow. For all you know, you could get hit by a bus while walking the labyrinth.*)

"I suppose it would lack in humility to point out that this incoming wisdom presented in a mixed metaphor?"

(*Yes, it would.*)

"All right, then, I won't mention it."

(*Do you mind if I continue?*)

"No, of course not. Please, continue—after all, I'm just the labyrinth sweeper."

(*You are not "just" anything—and as you mentioned humility, self-deprecation doesn't qualify. Now, to continue, forget about yesterday or tomorrow, and bring all you have to bear — become completely present here and now, and sweep.)*

I swept the surface and felt a certain satisfaction in pushing the leaves aside and revealing, section by section, the symmetrical face of the labyrinth. Just as I had nearly finished, a familiar mechanical wailing broke the silence (well, relative silence, given the proximity of the Cathedral to the city centre). It was "The Return of (My) Jedi."

When he had completed clearing the parking lot, would he join me at the labyrinth? I swept a little faster, reasoning that if I finished the job, he could continue his work elsewhere on the grounds. I had finished just as his machine fell silent and remained so. Then I wondered (again) if he might report my presence to some Church official. I imagined getting asked to leave, and making my stand, defiantly returning tomorrow, getting arrested, and then hunger strikes, news releases, and … and … then?

"Oh, yeah, right — walk the labyrinth!!"

(Indeed, walk the labyrinth. Might I suggest that you rein in that imagination and creativity and save it for the writing? For now, this momentary departure from present reality, though amusing, is not in alignment with your intended objective. In fact, it is counter-productive. Where are your feet?)

"Huh? What are you on about now? They're down there at the end of my legs."

(Very clever. My point is, they are right here, right now. See if you can't keep your mind where your feet are. Step-by-step, left foot, right foot, be here, be aware of each foot contacting the labyrinth surface. Feel the surface with each foot — focus your attention.)

36

While walking the pathway, I became aware of the route—before arriving at the centre, at times, the path wound its way a considerable distance from the centre. Other times, very nearly to the centre. Then it led away again to the opposite side of the labyrinth. At some point, it felt like the path was so convoluted that it appeared as though it wouldn't lead to the objective. However, step-by-step, one foot in front of the other, the path led home.

It proved interesting to note that, at one point when walking from the centre back to the entry point, I had somehow missed a turn and had bypassed half the route. I could feel something off before I saw this as the case. I still ended back at the starting point by following the remaining path.

After completing the walk, I sat under the oak tree for prayer and meditation. While there, a little something fell from the tree (too small for an acorn). I imagined myself to be somewhere in the spectrum between the pre-enlightened Buddha, Isaac Newton, and Chicken Little. I then thought that maybe the tree acknowledged my presence or affirmed its own.

When leaving, I noticed a sign posted near the labyrinth, which read, "Millennium Labyrinth—funded by the federal government and built in collaboration with William Head" (the federal penitentiary). I presumed by this that some from the prison had worked on the project as a community service or work/rehab program.

I sincerely hoped that those involved continued to get acknowledged (and acknowledged themselves) for their contribution to the community and the sacred—and that their lives now reflected this and other contributions they had made, and no longer got informed and influenced (negatively) by the time spent in prison.

Day 3 Questions
(Saboteur)

At the onset of this section, I suggest that you cultivate an objective eye and as much understanding and compassion for yourself as possible while examining this aspect. The intention is not to generate more (or any) self-condemnation, but rather to become aware of the patterns that block our success, with the idea of developing a more powerful approach through insight.

01) Do you finish what you start?

02) Do you have a pattern of unfinished symphonies?

03) External reasons aside, see if you can come up with things you might tell yourself about why you stopped. Are they true? (Not, did your action/inaction make them true.) Were they true to begin with?

04) Can you see that you could have chosen differently?

05) Do you believe yourself worthy of success?

06) What does commitment mean to you?

07) Make a list of commitments you have made and followed through on.

08) Consider commitments that you abandoned uncompleted.

09) What was the difference between what you found in your two lists? (Are there any identifiable patterns in the commitments you left?)

10) Is a commitment to yourself different than one made to someone else? How? Why?

11) Is there any payoff (what do you get) from not finishing what you start? (E.g. Resistance/fear of change; therefore, an attempt to uphold the familiar.)

12) Are you willing to acknowledge that, perhaps unconsciously, you could undermine your success?

13) What could your life look like if you got free of these patterns?

14) If something doesn't go as you'd hoped, where do you look first (to place responsibility)? Inside or outside yourself?

15) What does responsibility mean to you? Do you judge yourself more harshly than you do others?

Sample Answer

Question 1 — Do you finish what you start?

Of course, I have experience with beginning something and seeing it to completion. Upon deeper examination, I find many examples of projects that I have started but not finished, or an idea that never got off the ground. I can't say whether any of these ideas were good or bad, as they never got extracted from the realm of visions and subjected to the effort it would take to make them real. Perhaps the quality of attention, energy, and focus has more to do with an idea (dream) getting realized than concluding that the idea itself lacked something. (I'll say that is the case in my experience and leave you to determine that answer for yourself.)

Some of the ways that I discovered I have acted more in opposition than supportively in my endeavours are:

- Fear — this can produce a huge barrier, and can take on so many forms (though, I suppose, at the end of the day, it's still fear). I will distinguish some of these for the purpose of assisting others to identify them ...

  Fear of failure.
  Fear of ridicule (criticism).
  Fear of looking bad.
  Fear of change.

- Procrastination — which looks like waffling, engaging in some other completely unrelated task, and creating busyness that generates the illusion of productivity or taking on so many projects, classes, book studies, and commitments that I'm either overwhelmed or ineffective at most or all of them. There is a feedback loop that can prove either supportive or non-supportive. In the case of smaller, manageable goals, incrementally attainable, I have the experience of more or less on-going success, which can help to maintain inspiration and momentum. Conversely, if I take on too much, leading to overwhelm or inability to focus, then success can get compromised, which in turn undermines enthusiasm. If this becomes a longer-term pattern, confidence and self-esteem can get affected.

Now, keep in mind that these self-defeating patterns are not pre-meditated. I don't get up in the morning and lay out a plan to undermine my success. These patterns remain unconscious and, therefore, can go undetected until I subject myself to some honest scrutiny.

Why would someone sabotage his or her success, you might ask? Well, in my case, it had to do with unconscious beliefs with regard to worthiness and confidence. I don't suggest that these are necessarily present for the reader, but simply point at a place to look. If they are present, however, my experience is that some form of inner healing work is called for, as these unconscious beliefs become insidious and powerful. So much so, that they wreaked havoc repeatedly on my view of the world and my place in it.

The clues for me (in hindsight) were the ideas that the world, or my job, my partner (something outside myself) always did to me. Someone or something had to get held responsible for this, and it sure wasn't me! Needless to say, a need existed for me to journey with responsibility/accountability and learn what I had responsibility for. Equally as important, I had to learn what wasn't mine.

I have encountered many strategies for goal-setting and prioritizing, and while they are effective systematic approaches, my experience says that unless some of the unconscious beliefs, emotional wounds, and old ideas get brought to light and released, success can still prove fleeting. These unconscious energies have a great deal of power, some of which gets lessened through awareness; otherwise, it's a bit like baling faster is the answer to a leaking boat—wrong: the answer is to plug the hole.

Day 4
(Teachable)

I got up and prepared for my morning practice even earlier today. I couldn't attribute this to enthusiasm; though I don't feel resistant to the idea either. It's more that enthusiasm stepped from centre stage and joined the chorus line so that its voice could still get heard with focused listening, or otherwise get lost in the mix. Some of the other voices, which could even be considered melodic when taken alone, proved, in fact, dissonant to that which had sung as lead vocalist. However, with the right direction, I could restore harmony. Who or what, then, would stand in the role of choir director? I recognized it would remain necessary that I show up—at the same time, I also seemed to operate as the source of the most inharmonious of voices.

The night before, I had gone out with some friends, and the evening went fairly late, and this contributed to the morning inertia. I felt aware of some fatigue. It would have proven too easy to roll over and go back to sleep. Though I had not yet established that I would always take this walk in the morning, I had come to know that it proved effective to begin the day with some sort of centring activity, something to set the tone for the day. For me, this has come to involve some observance of prayer and meditation (a growing, changing practice in its own right). It represents my effort to establish a relationship with, and a connection to, that which I often refer to as God.

It remains way too easy to end up spinning off into the activities of the day, or even the ruminations of my mind if I don't give this observation priority. My personal journey with this alone had gone from no observance at all (or even the notion that I would practice it, or find it of any use) to sporadic attempts, followed by periods of no practice. This evolution led to a daily practice (with the odd hiccup), which if nothing else, demonstrated to me the need for continuance (as I grew aware through contrast of its absence).

I do not advocate this for anyone else—though if you're curious, you could, as a former mentor of mine used to suggest, "conduct the experiment." I don't advocate a particular form or pathway but will say that my experience showed me that the observance offered an effective way to ground and centre myself going into my day.

I could still honour the intent to make this a daily practice by going later in the day. For today, I resolved to adhere to the morning start and notice the mental gymnastics that occurred—for example, "I'm too tired." I could still do the walk and have a nap later today if necessary. Even taking this internal discussion into account, I still got out of the door half an hour earlier than any start time so far.

I arrived at the labyrinth and decided that before entering and sweeping, I needed to take a moment to remember why I'd come here. Something had invited me to show up here, and while some consistency seemed warranted, I also remained open to in-the-moment guidance. I let go of any preconceived ideas of what this was all about or having it become dogmatic.

So, I stood on the walkway at the entrance to the labyrinth, placing my hands together in prayer position, first at my bowed head, and then brought them to rest at my heart, followed by a bow. The hand gestures, along with the affirmation "Namaste," communicate acknowledgement and reverence for the light of Spirit in another. In my martial arts training, it was customary to bow before entering the training "dojo" to pay homage to past masters. In this case, I honoured the spirit of those that had walked this labyrinth before me (perhaps some among them had attained mastery of themselves upon this very path). I also recognized the spirit and soul journey of those that laboured during the construction of the labyrinth—each brick put in place by hand, anointed with the sweat of their brow, that I might now place one foot in front of the other and, step-by-step, walk toward myself. Could the labourers themselves be considered without also recognizing those in their lives that supported them and held them and their wellbeing in their hearts? And what of those that organized and financed the project?

My thoughts returned, once again, to the countless others that have walked this labyrinth—what truth revealed itself for them? How did that effect their lives and how they showed up in the world? Is it possible that the collective consciousness of those that have gone before me have called me to this spot to take up the torch on the next leg of this ethereal relay?

Last but by no means least, I considered my ancestors and their traditions, and the ancestors that once occupied these lands and held them sacred. Both the land and the people must have inclusion and recognition. Where did the idea come from to do this? Why would I assume it as mine?

I got adopted at birth—raised in a family that wanted children—but just the same, I then became subject to the influences of the embodiment of their lineages—was I now getting called through the lineage of my bloodline? I may never know the "truth" around my ancestry—I have met many members of my mother's side of the family and know from records that my father came of Irish ancestry. No one from my mother's family seemed willing or able to shed any further light on the identity of my father. In my heart, I feel drawn to indigenous teachings around spirituality (which, I suppose, could come from my Irish ancestry, which has a history of earth-based cultures deeply connected to the land [pre-Christianity]). Were there any link to First Nations in my bloodline, I may not get afforded the hard evidence. Instead, I got offered the leanings of my heart, which I endeavoured to trust and follow but found tenuous at times).

The family that I had met, certainly, all appeared Caucasian, which for me, raised the question, if any First Nations connections existed, would that get revealed within family circles that hailed from times and places where there existed obvious advantages to being white?

Of course, I can't ignore that I don't live in a vacuum—while I might say that I don't practice or overtly perpetuate racism, I remain unsure that whether, or if indeed, anything I do will promote healing. Maybe to become aware makes a beginning. I can't, however, identify through my actions, past or present, that my contribution is complete or nearly enough.

I mentioned the resonance for me with indigenous spirituality—I have had the honour and privilege to sit in various sacred circles. Each experience affirmed itself and called for more. Did this mean that I had an ancestral link? I couldn't say. Is it possible that the universality of the wisdom itself speaks to some part of me, perhaps that which so doggedly seeks truth and recognizes this as a viable path? Even if any of this held up—given the history of colonialism and the systemic abuse of the indigenous cultures—drawn to it or not, as a white person, can I claim heart path or passion without revisiting the "sins of my fathers"? Can I embrace these paths and teachings without traumatizing those individually and collectively working at reclaiming their identity and birthright? It is not my intent to injure or behave disrespectfully.

I then offered the following words in prayer, "I am sincerely sorry for what my ancestors visited upon the indigenous peoples of this land. I regret anywhere in anyway, in my present life, conscious or unconscious, that I have not been part of the healing or have, in fact, perpetuated the existing violations and trauma. In many ways, my walk through life is not working—I believe that the ancient wisdom and teaching hold for me the key to my right relation to the world. There are probably more reasons for you to say no than to say yes—would you, please, teach me anyway?

It is said that when the student is ready, the teacher will appear. Who is to say what form that teacher will take? I work at being open. I have been

48

introduced to the idea that things are not always as they appear (sometimes in quite dramatic demonstration). This meant that the shaping of my life, moving forward, remained shrouded in uncertainty.

Meanwhile, I considered the blessings I felt honoured and privileged to have received. Such as participation at sacred gatherings in ancient stone circles. I had visited tombs and the sacred sites of some of the ascended masters and gotten invited to take part in ceremonies with First Nations pipe carriers. In my heart, I feel deeply grateful (even more so in hindsight). I'm sure I received far more than I managed to contribute. Though not in the physical presence of those teachers—do they now continue to walk with me? Perhaps the lessons continue to download even now.

So, there I sat beneath the majestic oak tree, seeking direction—pondering the teachers in my life and how I would go about deepening my connection to the nature-based paths. Who, then, would teach me? Could it be possible that the ground I sat on, the tree I sheltered under, and the leaves that I swept, did just that?

I opened my eyes from my meditation and lay on the ground. Directly in front of me, drifted a beautiful black feather that I'm sure wasn't there when I first sat down. Now, did this give a sign that my questions had gotten heard, or a test to see if I'd paid enough attention?

Day 4 Questions
(Teachable)

01) Do you believe the old adage, "I learn something new every day"?

02) Who have become some of your most valued teachers so far?

03) What qualities did they possess that proved most effective for you?

04) What conditions must be present for you to learn?

05) Do you know your learning style?

06) Have you considered the idea of an inner teacher? If not, would you feel willing to explore the possibility now?

07) Do you feel confident in what you know?

08) Do you feel willing to explore the possibility that what you think you know isn't the last word?

09) Do you believe there is a great deal more that you could learn?

10) Are you aware of a vast body of knowledge available that could be called "don't know, what you don't know"?

11) What does being open-minded or flexible mean to you?

12) Consider another couple of old adages: "You can't teach an old dog new tricks." And "A leopard doesn't change its spots." — Do you believe them to be true? For you?

13) What would become possible if they proved untrue? Do you have the willingness to find out?

14) How do you feel about becoming a beginner again in certain areas of your life?

15) What does it mean to you to ask for help?

16) Can you say, "I don't know" and be "teachable"?

17) Even if you have lived/worked in a role that involves teaching, guiding, or counselling for quite some time—do you believe that you can still become the student? Do you believe your student could be your teacher?

18) Are you aware of the natural world and what it holds in terms of lessons?

19) Do you see life itself as something to be endured, or a vast teacher?

20) Identify for yourself people that you admire (past or present)—what could they teach you about the potential direction you might take within your life?

Sample Answers

Question 11—What does being open-minded or flexible mean to you?

In my earlier life, what I thought of as open-minded or flexible might be thought of as wishy-washy. I thought myself easy-going when, really, I often compromised what felt true for me. At the same time, I had many beliefs and mindsets indicative of considerable rigidity (i.e. "I'm this way—not that way." And, "No way I'd ever do that."); you get the idea. As well as the known (conscious beliefs), I'm discovering innumerable unconscious beliefs as well. What I want to illustrate is that, though it's not necessary for someone to change everything about themselves, if, across the board, I won't let go of some old ideas, then nothing much can change.

Even in my present life, I can see my lifetime of rigidity embodied (literally) in my physiology as I incorporate a yoga and Qi Gong practice into my life. I can say that incremental changes take place (cultivated for me through further development of consistency and patience), but can't give you an end result, as it's not over.

I used to argue vehemently to uphold my point of view (I am learning that I have come from a place where there was either right or wrong, which left little room for the view of someone else or something outside of the views of either of us). I've had some rather severe consequences come home to roost as a result of this "my way or the highway" stance. The good news is that it has (and is) made me more teachable. For one thing, I consciously work at embracing the grey zone. Things are not always (if ever) either black or white. This would be akin to the Buddha's "middle road." I don't suggest that anyone immerse themselves in Buddhism (unless you feel curious). The concept proved useful for me—living in the swings between extremes definitely didn't serve me anymore. The Buddha himself gave up extreme forms of ascetic practice popular among some of the most ardent spiritual seekers. His departure from the "discipline" got frowned upon—nonetheless, through following a path outside the accepted practice of his peers, and maybe of his own conception or, perhaps, through his personal guidance, he reached success beyond his wildest dreams.

This, for me, demonstrates the vast wealth of life-changing teaching available. However, as the saying goes, first the student must be ready. If I, for example, had held to an attitude such as, "What has some sort of Eastern world religion got to do with my life … blah-blah-blah," then I may not have had the change of perspective I wanted (and needed). And, I can assure you there would have been a time I would have said something close to or exactly like that. The world has opened up for me (as I open to the world)—this is my experience. Again, I will say it is not necessary that you specifically seek answers through religion or spirituality (as happens to be one of my passions), but I can assure you that metaphors (teachers) are available in many forms. I suspect that the intelligence of life itself can select the perfect teacher(s) for anyone. It also makes my experience that this occurs only relative to my willingness.

Question 12—Consider another couple of old adages: "You can't teach an old dog new tricks." And "A leopard doesn't change its spots."—Do you believe them to be true? For you?

For me, neither of these prove true—likely the only variable would be my willingness to change. My life gives a testimonial to the possibility of change, which, of course, remains subject to change. I have gone from a place where significant change felt necessary to save my life—recovery from addictions to where I'm at now, which is a sincere desire and deep passion to continue to embrace transformation in my life and play a part in teaching its accessibility to others. This journey represents twenty-five years (at the time this practice began—2011) of my life—during which time, I have had numerous teachers. Had I refused to change or denied a need for change, it's questionable if I would have had the additional years of life. And if so, they certainly wouldn't have been of the same quality.

Now, I know that no two people experience change the same way, and whether it is invited consciously or thrust upon you unexpectedly, or even "forced" through circumstances out of your control, it can feel challenging. It can also feel exciting, refreshing, and energizing. I guess, because of what could be said to be a rather dramatic change in my life (of course, others could say dismissively that I just never should have gone down that road in the first place), I strongly value human potential and believe people can become so much more than their history. I also believe that, where possible, the environment created needs to be one supportive of the process of change. My growing realization being that it was up to me to create that environment through, for example, the people I associated with. Not that anyone else is obliged to wait for me to undergo the changes.

I have come to realize that willingness to change is also of deep importance—that many things aren't as permanent as they might appear. I might have to give up some of what represents a current reality in order to pave the way to transition. And though some of what I needed to let go of was material in nature, there is also that which is more an internal process involving beliefs and reasons that change isn't possible. Fair enough, there might be some things that are, indeed, the way they are. What I want to say is that I found value in not being too quick to adopt this mind-set.

The other thing I learned about myself and change is that I can believe I want something to be different in my life, only to run into habitual ways of being and believing that I had set up to avoid the discomfort of change. Fear and resistance reared up in the face of the unknown, and discomfort with being a beginner again, not to mention impatience with my learning curve, and the hesitancy to ask for help. So, many forces seemingly external exist, and more truthfully, internal that make remaining unchanged seem like a good idea. It would seem, over time, this creates a discomfort of its own. Therefore, the motivation for change can be that the discomfort of not changing can override (become more dominant) than the discomfort (fear) of changing. The prevailing "Aha" here for me was that to grow/expand (fill), I would first need to empty.

And to empty, I would need to have the willingness give up (let go). This might sound easy; however, I discovered that I possessed a grip of steel, which needed coaxing in order to soften.

Day 5
(Centring/Emotional Mastery)

I awoke from a fitful sleep at what I first thought was 6:30 a.m. I dozed a while longer, and then glanced at the clock, which read 6:30 a.m. again/still? Bewildered and rubbing my eyes, trying to integrate myself fully into waking consciousness, I wondered if I'd experienced my private version of the movie "Groundhog Day." (To carry the reference forward from the early 90s, the same repeating theme occurs in the 2014 movie "Live, Die, Repeat.")

Once I established that the power remained on and the clock functioning, I concluded that, due to my near-sightedness, the first time I'd looked at the clock, it had actually read 5:30 a.m. and now, one hour later, it was, in fact, 6:30 a.m.

I didn't jump right into action; instead, I rehashed a conversation on the phone from the previous day with a female friend. At times, this interaction became quite heated and, overall, had seemed an extremely emotional ride. As I lay there in bed, I realized that I felt wrung out (rather like a hangover)—for me, we had reached no resolution during this discussion—there I lay like a warrior abandoned upon the field, bleeding from multiple wounds, some inflicted by my perceived adversary, and some likely inflicted by myself.

I raise this matter because, believe it or not, it has relevance to my morning walk. I found myself entertaining the idea that I could forego my walk. I lay stewing in my juices and realized, "I don't feel like doing it." There I found myself, at Day Five, and

Day Five might not even happen. Of course, the day itself would transpire—a look out of the window indicated that a beautiful day had commenced— bright blue sky, sunny; however, there existed upon my inner landscape a weather front that, in that moment, didn't look so bright.

I considered the Serenity Prayer, one of the many tools I had become familiar with on my recovery and healing journey. The ideas held within it have deep meaning and sweeping application upon life's circumstances. And, though it won't necessarily bring immediate relief, I say it anyway. To prove of any use at all, then first, I must remember the use of the prayer, and then I must use the prayer.

I arrived at a pivotal shift in perspective, recognizing and acknowledging the presence of these feelings of melancholy and asking could they be allowed while at the same time upholding my intention to walk the labyrinth? I knew those feelings; I also had an awareness that continuing to feed these emotions with what amounts to self-defeating thoughts, could and would become a justification to take me out. So, what if I were to go, anyway?—Could I take the blues for a walk? I felt almost sure that I wouldn't feel any worse for going. I felt equally sure that the sacred, in this case, some part of me, would get dishonoured if I didn't go. I could, reasonably, allow for a goal to change, or something coming up to postpone a commitment; however, these feelings would not become that reason, at least not today.

I arrived at the labyrinth and set about sweeping when I came across a maple leaf bigger than a dinner plate. It occurred to me that nature grew this to just the size and proportion necessary to fulfill its purpose. This happened within the timeframe (the seasons) required for this to occur, and even in the twilight of its life (well, at least, in its present form), it remained brilliant as its life got laid down for the continuance, the ongoing cycle of life itself. I collected the leaf, thinking at the time that it would, somehow, preserve this experience—this journey within the labyrinth.

As I walked, a crow landed on a limb of a nearby tree and called out. Though unfamiliar with the specific attributes of this animal messenger (as seen through the *animal medicine paradigms), still, I wondered, "What are you trying to say to me, my raucous friend?" I continued my way around the serpentine curves of the labyrinth path when the thought came to me, "Speak up and speak clearly— regardless of whether others agree with what you say, or they feel annoyed at what gets said—speak anyway." I don't suggest belligerence or behaving in a disagreeable manner. The ability to speak respectfully and with grace may well carry an unpopular message far further than if delivered in anger. While I considered this, the crow flew to a second location, and then a third, all the while continuing its incessant cawing. Now the message coming through told me that it remained my responsibility to see to it that I get heard (and not just by raising my voice). The crow relocating itself told me that I could consider different perspectives, either trying to see things differently or seeking to try and understand the perspective of the other person.

I left the site, having completed my morning practice, and considered how often I had thought the sound of the crow's voice just noise. Now, I stand in awe of its capacity to make its presence known and have a renewed respect for the power of the voice. It raises a question for me, "In what situations do I surrender my voice? When does my truth go unspoken and, therefore, unheard?" Finally, considering my brush with self-sabotage earlier this morning, I realized that none of this would have occurred today if I didn't first show up.

*Early shamans were mystics, magicians, and scientists. They spent time in nature, studying animals, and learning about them to more fully awaken their power and more accurately interpret their messages. (Taken from: "Animal Speak" — written by Ted Andrews.)

Day 5 Questions
(Centring/Emotional Mastery)

01) What is your current level of awareness with regard to your feelings?

02) What impact (if any) does the state of your inner world have on your ability to effectively operate in the outer world?

03) Can you maintain an inner calm (peace) while subject to external stimuli? (Did you know that it is possible?)

04) Does someone else's bad mood or upset mean that you have to get upset too?

05) What strategies do you have currently to deal with feeling down?

06) Can you do what you set out to do, even when you don't feel like it? Is this even possible?

07) Do you have any awareness of the connection between what you think and how you feel?

08) What does it take to restore a sense of inner peace for you?

09) Do you know where your emotional wounds lie and what triggers you?

10) Do you take responsibility for your feelings?

11) Do you feel comfortable expressing your feelings?

12) Do you feel comfortable having someone else express their feelings with you?

13) Should feelings get expressed?

14) What does inner peace mean to you?

15) Is there more to inner peace than keeping the peace?

16) Is "peace at all costs" too much to pay?

17) What is your experience with emotional honesty?

18) Have you heard of emotional intelligence?

19) Is emotional awareness equally important for men and women?

Sample Answer

Question 10—Do you take responsibility for your feelings?

I may end up addressing some of the themes in more than one question as I address this one—which, if nothing else, gives the reader a more comprehensive overview of where I am coming from.

When considering my emotional awareness, I'm happy to say that I have experienced significant evolution, which in hindsight, began from limited emotional balance and even less emotional connection. I felt amazed upon embarking on self-development courses such as anger management, assertiveness training, various communication courses (and the list goes on), and receiving lists of feelings. I could hardly believe that such a broad spectrum existed. Given that my experience seemed to consist of a swing between angry and numb, variances included despondency and melancholy. Of course, I did have occasional intervals of feeling happy—sometimes, I would allow some excitement (however, this I usually restrained, as my prevailing belief held that to welcome excitement was only to invite disappointment). I had no idea until later in my life how much I had repressed most all of my emotions in an effort to avoid the more painful feelings (neither did I know that you can't selectively repress, or if you can, I couldn't; I just stayed repressed).

As to my emotional state, as it related to my performance, well, for example, if I initially felt any enthusiasm, I found it difficult to sustain. A funk brought on by an event unrelated to my commitment could send me reeling, and consequently, whatever I had set out to accomplish could get interrupted if not abandoned. Interestingly, the emotional upheaval might not have gotten brought about by a challenge with the undertaking itself—more often than not, there could be an incident perhaps involving someone else in my life, and the resulting emotional upheaval and negative spiral became insurmountable and somehow the reason to derail myself.

I discovered that I often lacked much in the way of any significant separation between myself and the person with whom I interacted. This increased markedly with significant others and resulted in what seemed inevitable, that if they were down, then so was I (or, I felt somehow responsible). As a result of my discomfort with my emotional landscape and lack of separation, this mostly resulted in my trying to change the experience of the other, or what amounted to a lack of regard for what they felt, preferring that they would cheer up so that I would feel better.

As with any journey, it's not enough just to know where you want to go—you must also know where you are to begin with. That particular leg of the self-discovery path was sometime in the making—first, I had to find myself in it, which meant recognizing that the problem didn't exist exclusively out there somewhere.

As I said, I might jump around somewhat—so, with regard to inner peace, I have seen (and, of course, will continue to see) quite the evolution. The way I once carried myself in the world comprised of underlying beliefs like, "To get along, you go alone."

And, "Don't rock the boat." ... "I'm easy going and flexible." ... "Go with the flow." None of these concepts are wrong, necessarily, except if they become cover stories for, "I fear confrontation." Or, "I'll get hurt."

At some point, my world view said that confrontation resulted in someone wins, someone loses, and losing invariably brings about pain. So, avoid confrontation, thereby avoiding pain, and resulting in inner peace. I had no idea that healthy relating meant that conflict was a given, or of the possibility that conflicts could get negotiated without creating suffering. I became hyper-vigilant at sensing when tensions or emotions went on the rise and "got out of Dodge" (flight), attempted at times to shut the other person down (fight), or said nothing—believing that such silence registered my disagreement by not upholding the view getting expressed (freeze). All of the aforementioned happened in an effort to keep the peace; none of which proved successful. After all, it's difficult to feel good about avoiding a situation or not speaking (either way, it entails an abandonment of self—which, I can assure you, can erode inner peace most effectively). Whereas with the "fight" example, I may have experienced a momentary sense of "victory", i.e. "sure told them," but this resulted in either regret after the fact, with thoughts like, "I wish I hadn't said that" (especially if this were someone I would see again regularly). The other possibility necessitated that I could sustain the "righteous indignation" but, in this case, I have come to realize that if I still ranted about this incident well after the fact, it certainly couldn't be deemed as resolved. More likely that I continued to justify my actions to defend, and that, at some level, I didn't handle this as well as I might have. This, too, I must acknowledge, doesn't lead to peace either.

Day 6
(Authenticity)

This morning, I felt a bit harried. Not only did I need to get my morning practice completed, but I must do so in time to arrive at the first rehearsal of a choir getting put together for a Christmas performance — the rehearsal started at 9:30 a.m. Now, while I do enjoy singing, I have mixed feelings about this business of singing in a group. Perhaps an odd time of life to feel so concerned about self-realization, but I do struggle with my voice getting lost in the crowd. And, though I haven't held much in the way of affinity for, or a sense of connection to, the crowd for a large percentage of my life, I must confess, the ways I have chosen to express this have largely proved counter-productive and, at times, extremely self-defeating.

I continue to hear from a wide variety of sources of the power of living in the day (even the moment), and that right here, right now, there exists infinite possibility. If so, does it matter how old I am now, or what I have done (or not done) in the past? What, exactly, defines who I am in the world, and is the die cast? Well, for starters, I have held beliefs about myself and the world (I wasn't born with them, so is it required I die with them?) still held firmly in place. As well, memories of past experiences, and fear that the pain of those past experiences might get re-experienced, triggered by present endeavours.

One could say that I have developed the habit of defaulting to these parameters, which, frankly, boils down to developing the habit of continuing to practice that which places various limitations on how wide, deep, and diverse the experience of my life could be. An example of how this might manifest in my life could be, let's say, I believe I am not a writer—that would pretty much herald the end of the story where writing is concerned. Upon closer examination, I might ask, "What are the composite elements that would define me as a writer?"

If I think I must earn my living writing, that I must have a publisher, that I must have been published, and there need be critical acclaim—well, frankly, I can feel the terror mounting as I write this—I might not get out of bed, never mind write.

Conversely, if none of the aforementioned criteria became a concern or, at least, got reduced to a more manageable proportion, then at anytime while writing, I would be a writer. So, for now, I will lay my concern for Pulitzer Prizes and book tours aside and embrace, "I write, therefore, I am a Writer!"

I ask myself what exists at the root of all this for me—is it just some ego-driven neediness to be noticed or part of the universal need for contribution? I don't know how the lives of others go, but it seems to me that life (or, perhaps, my resistance to it, and what it wants to teach me) provides me with a rather reliable set of checks and balances—like I'm allowed to run free, seemingly without restraint—free-will reigns supreme and then, one day, boom, consequences (not punishment), and with them a further glimpse at humility (which, I suspect, in itself could provide a lifetime's worth of teaching).

Maybe if my need to get heard and recognized got met in other areas of my life, it wouldn't seem such an issue here. I do recognize the beautiful harmony when a multitude of voices joins—I not only hear it, I also feel it.

This individuation was supposed to happen during adolescence—for me at that time, I became lost in the energies of misdirected rebelliousness, a stranger to myself, allowing my life to get shaped through appeasing my fears in the eyes of resignation. I'd like to think (in fact, I choose to believe) that what now occurs is, indeed, a profoundly transformational spiritual awakening, and not just the realizing of arrested development (which is an eloquent way of saying immature). Perhaps the latter must be accepted and embraced as part of the realization of the former. I could just deny it, but it remains present just the same.

Incidentally, this idea of spiritual awakening might conjure for some notions of other-worldly, mystical, or magical transcendental experience; at times, it has seemed all of that. At other times, it has felt chaotic, unsettling, disillusioning, heart-breaking, bewildering, and downright painful. However, they do say, "In order to make an omelette, you must break a few eggs." And, "That which doesn't kill us makes us stronger." Just how close must you get to death to attain this newfound fortification?

Also, I have become familiar with the concept of losing myself in something bigger than myself. And, earnestly, I try to find the middle road in this regard. I want my life to matter. I want to make a contribution to something meaningful, to make a difference—I wasn't born to come and be like everybody else (I don't believe anyone was). Each is meant to make their unique contribution somehow. We eke out what that personal path is, and then either find the power, passion, and perseverance to walk it, or fall to the wayside and get consumed entirely by the beast of conformity. I don't want to be always isolated and alone, but neither do I want to blindly follow a group anywhere.

Don't get me wrong; I don't advocate that the way will be discovered by following me; after all, I'm sure there are many that would look and say, "I don't like where you are." (Let alone where you're going.) So, where am I? At fifty-two years of age, I remain single (divorced) after a seventeen-year marriage. I left fulltime employment with no desire to work any further in a twenty-eight-year career. I have invested immeasurable energy — blood, sweat, and tears into spiritual development, completed an epic travel odyssey through six European countries (at considerable financial cost), and here I am, alone, walking in circles around a labyrinth (yes, I am aware of the irony). Mind you, instead of thoughts just going around in circles, they now wove to unfold the contents of this book. Will anyone ever read it? Damned if I know!

Where was I? Oh, yes, two cycles through the labyrinth, and one to go.

A light drizzle fell today — just a mist, really, which reminded me of the mists that hover over and envelop the bogs in Ireland — huh, maybe the labyrinth acts as a portal? I acknowledged myself for coming here today, even in the rain, and despite additional commitments and emotional upheaval.

As I continued to walk, I noticed the minister out walking around the perimeter of the cathedral — I supposed he prepared for observing the sacred according to his beliefs, or maybe he made his grocery list. Had he ever walked the labyrinth? Did he wonder if I'd ever gone to Communion? How would his communion differ to my current exploration and experience? The word "communion" has come to mean a particular religious sacrament. The root of the word "commune or communing" is defined as:

1) The sharing of one's intimate thoughts or feelings with someone or something, esp. when the exchange is on a spiritual level.

2) Feel in close spiritual contact with.

Right here, right now, all these criteria seemed satisfied. I felt deeply connected to the labyrinth and the process of the walk, as well as connected with the land and trees. In the presence of the edifice of Anglican Christianity, I considered the teachings of the man, Jesus. I held with reverence the sacredness of what went on within its walls for those that attended, though I didn't embrace the theology personally. I connected through my heart. Could there exist any deeper communion? Any relationship more intimate than the realizing, connecting, and honouring of my heart? Could the leanings, urgings, yearnings of the heart be anything less than the Divine? When I considered the innumerable things that I had worshipped in my lifetime, I wondered if any one of them (or combination thereof) had proved adequate to compensate for ignoring my heart? Is the heart not the most worthy of altars at which to worship? Conversely, what are the ways and means that we commit desecration of this altar and the connection to human suffering?

So, yes, I had received Communion at the Anglican altar—would I ever return? Doubtful, and for sure, not today. I walked toward an entirely different form of communion, one that will still involve people and further define the difference between dependent and interdependent.

For now, the time had come to sit in meditation—the oak tree provided shelter from the rain—and I began with thanks and blessings for the sacred oak.

Day 6 Questions
(Authenticity)

01) What does authenticity mean to you?

02) Have you considered what might comprise your authentic self?

03) How might some of your relations change if more authenticity were interjected?

04) Are you satisfied with the current degree of authenticity in your relating?

05) Does your life path feel congruent with your values?

06) Have you ever done an inventory of your values?

07) What changes (if any) might be necessary to reflect your current values?

08) Are you willing to represent a different perspective where a group consensus exists? If not, why not?

09) What are your views with respect to conformity?

10) Do you place equal value on your uniqueness and that of others?

11) At what point do social conventions such as manners or political correctness result in erosion to self (and therefore to relating), thereby inflicting or, at least, upholding damage to the relationship?

12) What do you know of, or what do you believe to be true, about a heart-path?

13) Have you ever heard of heart intelligence?

14) What is your experience with following your heart?

15) What part (if any) does your heart play in your decision-making?

16) Do you listen to your heart?

17) Do you believe it has anything to tell you?

18) What does "To thine own self be True" mean to you?

19) What is your heart song?

20) Have you shared it with the world?

21) If not, are you now willing to do so, and what will it take to make it real?

Sample Answer

Question 3—How might some of your relations change if more authenticity were interjected?

The first relationship that changed significantly was the relationship with myself. Though maligned, dismissed, and pigeonholed as merely a mid-life crisis, the idea of finding (knowing) yourself, I've found vitally important. Socrates once said, "The unexamined life is not worth living." In the context of this question and my interpretation, I see that, to the degree I didn't know myself, the resulting disconnect ensured that a lasting contentment remained elusive. As this lack of knowing also proved foundational in the formulation of my choices (including the relationships I formed), I discovered that they developed with incongruence and lacked authenticity—how can I tell you who I am if I don't know myself? Another consequence of this lack of self-awareness is that many of my needs would go unspoken for, unaddressed, and therefore, unmet. One other thing; as I didn't have the awareness to source my frustration, then frequently, someone else wore it.

Another manifestation of inauthentic living that I discovered was a behaviour that I could liken to the chameleon. So desperate came my need to "be part of," to feel connection, and so uncertain did I feel with regard to my sense of self that I would find myself with people and in circumstances that, suffice to say, were not a good fit. It involved considerable angst to learn to say that tiny but powerful word "No." I suppose, in a roundabout way, it showed me who I was by growing clear on who I was not—but not necessarily in the way I would advocate others to discover for themselves.

The other side of that coin is that it can feel just as challenging to say "yes" to those opportunities that might well lead to amazing experiences and changes. Of course, it's not just a matter of saying yes, as I must continue to say yes even when I say no, such as in the face of circumstances and realities that might tempt me, where I have to retract the yes and go with a resounding no.

It is this self-knowledge, this comfort with self, that can become pivotal in how "I" shows up in the world, and which becomes the basis for forming relationships, choosing vocational paths, hobbies, and virtually all aspects of my life. The distinction becomes, "Are these various facets created with honesty, integrity, and authenticity, or with self-deception?" Such deception becomes the foundation for a life built like a house of cards, which, as you can imagine, is rather vulnerable when the ground begins to shake.

Day 7
(Tenacity/Surrender)

The first week into this commitment and I can't imagine getting to Day Thirty. Obviously, this line of thinking doesn't embrace the concept of "One Day at a Time," and, "Carpe Diem," or, "There is only this Day," or anything of the sort. Life away from the labyrinth has included an emotionally tumultuous period within a friendship/relationship, which has brought up some sadness and pain. While some of these feelings may be attributable to the current circumstances; much of it likely comes from old repressed feelings, triggered by the relationship or, perhaps, the healing work and processing getting done on issues around abandonment, self-esteem, and the opening of the heart to giving and receiving love.

Today felt as though I had walked a labyrinth-like pathway into the very core of my heart and discovered relics in the form of old hurts, regrets, and traumas that I had never allowed expression. Whether I saw through these hurts or hyper-vigilantly tried to protect against further hurt, I just felt raw. The status of this friendship, presently unknown, made me feel very much alone. Nothing bad or wrong about this—it was, after all, often the case. I always walked the labyrinth alone, but in this particular instance, I felt so alone, disconnected, and lost—not hopeless, but certainly some despair.

The tears flowed freely as I walked—no flashes of inspiration. No revelations. I appealed to God for answers, "Please, give me direction. What is your will for my life? Is there anything besides pain on this heart's journey?" (I know there is — how quickly we can lose perspective when navigating the river of sadness — more so when the river plunges one over the falls and into the abyss of grief).

Though, to continue with the river metaphor, one is best served by not struggling against the current (not resisting what is and allowing it to be). The trip upon the river will take the time that is naturally required to travel its length — no short cuts. Though one may disappear below its surface from time-to-time, with trust and abandoning the struggle, a return to the surface is, largely, assured. Said another way, "This too shall pass," (which even when one knows this or hears it from a well-meaning second party, it can seem abysmally ineffective).

(I need answers, damn it!)

Not one of my more eloquent prayers. I have come to believe that sincerity defines a cry for help, not sentence structure. It is also my experience that I open myself to *Any* answer (not just what I want to hear). Selective listening can pass right over the answer I seek. No answers seemed to be forthcoming.

(All right – all right, I give up. I'll just keep walking!)

One foot in front of the other. Maybe, in some moments, that becomes all that I am capable of and all that is required. Perhaps, a miracle unfolded when, despite having no good reason to do so, I kept right on moving. Life itself dictated the marching orders. It doesn't matter if it doesn't feel right — you can quit as many times as you want in your mind, just as long as you keep moving, one foot then the next and repeat. Maybe this offers an aspect of what self-love looks like — to do what you need to even when no one's looking, and no one exists to applaud. Still, from God knows where, comes the impetus of left foot, right foot, to me, from me—with love. I still have no idea about Day Thirty; however, I completed Day Seven and made Day Eight, therefore, more likely to occur.

Day 7 Questions
Tenacity/Surrender

01) What comes to mind when you think of the idea of surrender?

02) Is there any difference between surrender and quitting?

03) How do you distinguish when to continue and when to surrender?

04) Have you considered the two might happen simultaneously?

05) Does surrender imply to you an act of courage or cowardice?

06) Were you encouraged or discouraged from being wilful as a child?

07) Can you distinguish between when tenacity serves you and when it doesn't?

08) Are there times when direct and sustained uses of the will are required?

09) Surrender = conscious choice (and, therefore, a decision implying an act/action), or do you see it as passive inaction?

10) How have ideas like, "Never give up," and, "Nobody likes a quitter," influenced you?

11) Can you think of examples both when you quit too soon or hung on too long? (What did you learn from these situations?)

12) What do you tell yourself about your ability to stay the course?

13) If "never give up" is your mantra—would you feel willing to consider when letting go might prove beneficial? Now? Are you willing to be willing?

14) Consider the following ideas: "Go with the flow," and, "Trying to push the river." How did each play out in your life?

15) Have you (or are you willing to) examined the constructs of your habits, thinking, and beliefs as the potential limiting factors in your life?

16) "My way or the highway"—path of strength, or self-constructed prison?

17) The serenity prayer suggests, "Accept the things I cannot change," and, "Courage to change the things I can," along with, "The wisdom to know the difference." Consider each passage as it may pertain to your life—in your journal, reflect on your present view of these ideas(for or against).

18) Could this prayer contain useful strategies for anything you currently struggle with in your life?

19) Are you open to praying?

20) Do you accept that the resistance to what is creates the discomfort/suffering that we experience?

Sample Answer

Question 1—What comes to mind when you think of the idea of surrender?

Well, let's face it, culturally, not much positive attention or emphasis gets placed on surrender. So, I have remained steeped in the same presentation of such concepts for most of my life, along with most everyone else. This, in itself, begins to open the conversation, providing an example of an "old idea" or belief system that might require revision (certainly, I have found it necessary). This remains an idea that I wrestle with when a new set of circumstances presents.

I grew up watching T.V. and movies where all the surrendering that happened represented defeat (which, of course, had a strong association with weakness/losing). Think about it; was the one waving the white flag ever portrayed to embody any qualities that looked attractive? No, the idea of surrender has, largely, been given negative associations. Expressions such as "Do or die," and, "Take no prisoners," and, "Death before dishonour," (ideas coined during warfare), carry with them a virtuous connotation, and the same consciousness has found its way into day-to-day living, whereby non-military members of our modern "civilized" society embrace these maxims in their personal and professional interactions.

The same mindset gets reinforced in the sports world where the most aggressive players receive all the attention and accolades. Now, I don't mean that times and places for a tenacious approach don't exist, but merely trying to distinguish that while at times "staying the course" etc., is the desired approach (in some cases necessary for survival or success), not all situations and interactions have survival at stake. To then utilize strategies that resist what is, and are defensive/offensive in nature, proves both inappropriate and ineffective.

I offer these reflections as a person who has behaved in just the ways I have described. Consequently, this is not just philosophical speculation but my experience. Aggressive/defensive behaviour, typically, will elicit a similar or escalated response. To resist the realities, at any given time, seems only to create further suffering. It doesn't mean either ignoring the reality or condoning it — surrender can occur even while taking action to create change. It's an internal process (an important distinction, as it is continually associated with quitting and losing, thus making it a tough sell). Even so, it is counter-intuitive (i.e., to succeed, one gives up).

I have come to realize that a great deal of energy has gotten lost (or misdirected) trying to force results or changes where I had no power (or business) asserting myself in the first place. The idea that you can't push the river gives a useful metaphor to remind me to look at a given situation (and myself) and ask, "Does the situation need to change, or does how I relate to the situation need to change?" So often, I observe something and draw a conclusion, which may or may not be an accurate assessment of the event; either way, there have been circumstances in my personal life that I have thought the worst possible reality that could occur, only to find out some time later that, in fact, this was the proverbial blessing in disguise. Therefore, if I can misread an event in my life, how can I possibly "know" what is good or bad for someone else?

I simply don't have the perspective required to know what choices someone else will make given their present circumstance. I don't know where they've been or where they're going, and I can't even say whether the seemingly most disastrous outcome is, for them, a necessary part of their curriculum. I don't like to see others suffer—I also realize that I have, ultimately, created suffering for myself in trying to help someone else avoid their suffering. (In hindsight, my motives proved misguided—I wanted to feel better about myself and win approval of another by rescuing them. The end result? More suffering for them and me.)

Where surrendering is concerned, my greatest challenge lies in the ability to let go of my expectations of a particular outcome. If my motives remain clean and clear, then perhaps my continued representation of what I believe to be true, expressed through my unique voice, are in themselves the rewards. The outcome is none of my business.

Day 8
(Non-Attachment)

Not only had Day Eight become more likely, it had now, as they say "entered the record book." While I made reference to previous days of this journey, I decided to put the large maple leaf (which I collected earlier) back where I found it. It occurred to me, who am I, to interfere with nature and its cycles? The lesson lay within the observance that the trees discard what they no longer require for the approaching season of their lives. They don't lament, "Oh, these leaves are so beautiful; I must hang on to them — I know winter is coming, but I just can't part with them — or, I might need them for something; I better hang on to them." No, they know inherently that to prepare for the beautiful new growth that will present in the spring, they must let go of that which they nurtured all through the previous season. Then the emptiness of the winter season gets embraced, during which the intention of growth of the season to come rests, already present, just waiting for the perfect union of nature's elements to coax them into being.

What a powerful lesson held within this idea. How often do you hear someone saying something like, "Oh, I couldn't get rid of such and such that belonged to my Auntie Em, and it reminds me of her,"? Meanwhile, if Auntie Em could intercede on the matter, which she may well feel willing to do if invited, she might say something like, "Oh, honey, get rid of that old piece of crap. I gave it to you because I didn't want it cluttering up my living room.

Your uncle won that in a draw at the Legion, and I could never get rid of it while he was around. Search your heart, and that is where we remain connected until we meet again. If you want to keep it, keep it, but not in my name."

Truly, my attachment presents for examination here—as though having that leaf pressed in a book would, somehow, preserve the memory of this journey. I suspect the legacy of this walk will prove far more profound than an artefact sitting on a bookshelf that, perhaps, I will stumble across one day and then wonder, "Where did this come from?" And if I happen to remember, "For what did I keep it?"

How much simpler might my life become with less stuff? I have made an effort at various times to purge that which has become superfluous—to keep my participation in unbridled consumption in check. I have gotten steeped in this consumption consciousness my entire life—it now, along with many other "dictates," has come under my scrutiny to determine where I stand on these matters. I consider the impact on the planet, which must get pillaged continually for the raw materials to continue to produce the new products that feed the insatiable appetites of fashion or have me, continually, compete like some sort of neurotic gladiator to own the latest in home furnishing or electronic gadgetry. The collective adversary being none other than the "Joneses." I don't even know these people. Have never met them. Why then, do I knock myself out to engage in this? I don't (at least, not when I'm practicing being more mindful). I withdraw from the competition—Joneses, whoever you are, I declare you the winners. By all means, do what you will; whatever floats your boat, but I'm done.

Of course, like much in my life, this remains a work in progress—as I mentioned earlier, I stayed three months in Europe last year (and lived out of a backpack the whole time)—I let go of things I'd brought along (some of which had commanded significant retail value when I'd purchased them) and things I seemed to think I had to have at one point in the journey, and then received the awakening experience of carrying these "treasures" on my back. I soon re-evaluated each item in that pack, becoming like some sort of bohemian Santa Claus "gifting" items to people in train stations or leaving them behind in hostel rooms.

The concept of "baggage" became all too real when I considered it in terms of physical weight upon my back. And, the more I let go, the more I could experience that glorious sense of freedom. To carry on with the metaphor, I have personal experience with the ways my life opens, and how much more becomes possible, without the burden of continuing to carry a particular set of beliefs (or, at least, becoming willing to try something different even in the face of the old belief). In fact, the aforementioned trip would make a fine example. I had never, until then, done anything of the sort.

The other side of the metaphor opened up when I found it, upon returning from my trip, challenging to adjust on many levels, not the least of which when I stepped into my one-bedroom condo and looked around. The amount of stuff there left me overwhelmed, and I had to ask, how much of this is necessary? I had none of it with me for three months and didn't require or miss it. Still, realizing this, I didn't get rid of all of it either — I did take a bunch of clothes to a drop-in centre where those that live on the street gather, took bags full of stuff to the thrift shop, and donated dozens of books to an organization that teaches people to read.

I hope the legacy of this walk will become far more profound than a leaf in a scrapbook that would grow meaningless soon after its collection. My aim is to forge a deepening connection, an expanded relationship with the insights made available to me — I know, at some level, the walking of the labyrinth will affect and inform my walk in my life.

Mother Nature had proven generous overnight, and not much in the way of leaves had fallen. Thus the clearing of the labyrinth turned out relatively quick today. Of course, the volume of fallen leaves had nothing to do with concern from nature for my workload — it just happened to be how it unfolded on this occasion. I remained well aware that more or less leaves falling had absolutely nothing to with me; though, my metaphorical reference to "the Mother" did seem to reflect that I'd made it personal — in this case, more a literary device to convey my story. However, it merits asking the question, in what areas of my life do I take things on and make them personal?

I noticed debris of another sort on the labyrinth today. Cigarette butts and the screw-on metal caps from some type of alcohol bottles. Also present upon the path, a small pool of human sputum/saliva. (Of the three, I find the latter the most offensive — not from a critical/judgmental standpoint, but even after years of nursing, this particular substance seems visually and viscerally repulsive to me.)

I considered the stuff scattered upon the surface that I had intended to use for an exploration, observance, and serving of the sacred and pondered what, if anything, it meant to me. It raised for me the question of desecration. I could take it to a place where I perceived the site had been defiled; i.e., my observance could no longer take place here until (though I hadn't been granted such "power" by any external authority) it had become, once again, consecrated. I reckoned that, as this made my practice, the authority lay within me, and the consecration then looked like me sweeping the labyrinth, as I had done all along.

Still, I would like to consider this idea of desecration. I don't wish to vilify anyone but, rather, recognize the debris as an inconvenience, actually no more personal than the leaves. The desecration I speak of is that the individuals themselves ingest these toxic substances. If it were to be seen only at the level of the site itself, it could invite a vastly different conclusion than if the desecration is seen and understood to be those involved defiling themselves and the sacred (life itself) within themselves.

This is not disrespect for the Church or the labyrinth or nature or me, and what I decide to deem sacred (although any of these perspectives remain possible—and I could run with any one of them)—largely, this represents a disrespect of the individuals for themselves. There is present, for each, unimaginable pain, from which they seek temporary relief. Though called "partying," there is nothing truly getting celebrated (most likely)—even while the pretence presented. Self-hatred seemed present that would deepen with each subsequent desecration. In light of this perspective (which, incidentally, I gained through personal experience, not academic conjecture), it becomes possible to generate more in the way of tolerance, patience, and compassion. Still, at times, my patience wears thin and, frankly, I have become the desecrator of that which is sacred to another. Flooded with emotion and a lack of consciousness for the needs of the other person (in those moments), I have reacted, blindly pursuing my agenda (ironically, not my needs) without grace or sensitivity. Seldom, if ever, do my true needs get met through this behaviour.

As I walked the labyrinth, I saw that it represented — from its outer perimeter to its centre — a journey from outside myself, where I interacted with the world and others in it. By then following a pathway, which I could see winding through my thoughts and feelings, I arrived at the core within, where a selection of the spectrum of universal human needs sacred to me exist. I don't know that it matters how these particular needs became important to me — the fact is, they exist within me, and to ignore them extracts a significant cost to self. To place the burden of responsibility upon others to meet these needs is misguided and, ultimately, ineffective. Therefore, I become both steward and benefactor of these needs, and the experience of wellbeing when they get met.

Perhaps this is the altar I should kneel in front of and worship as sacred before any other.

Day 8 Questions
(Non-Attachment)

01) Do you own your stuff (material belongings) or does your stuff own you?

02) Does your stuff determine who you are? Your personal value?

03) Beyond the time and physical effort involved to clear your living space—does the idea of getting rid of things cause you stress?

04) How much energy do you suppose you expend, obtaining, maintaining, sustaining, and feeling concerned about your stuff?

05) Does your living space represent what you need for yourself or what is required to house your stuff?

06) Could you be okay in the event of a fire that destroyed all your stuff? (Loss/grief not withstanding.)

07) What of your story (your opinion, beliefs) about yourself, people in your life, and world events—can you hold space for opposing viewpoints?

08) What lessons can you observe/learn from nature about non-attachment (detachment)?

09) Do you see for yourself any relationship between attachment and suffering?

10) Consider the idea, "A person is wealthy to the degree of what they can do without."

11) Are all your thoughts true?

12) Do your feelings need to determine the quality of your day?

13) It's easy to appreciate the physical weight of any given object — what about emotional investment, beliefs, and expectations, do they have "weight"?

14) As a practice, would you consider detachment beneficial?

15) Consider the various roles you play (have played) in your life — do any no longer serve you, but you find them difficult to release?

Sample Answer

Question 1—Do you own your stuff (material belongings) or does your stuff own you?

With respect to general rules of engagement in our Western consumer culture, I own what I have, with the exception of the bank-held mortgage on my apartment. The relationship I describe with regard to owning (and the associated belongings) entails how much energy in the form of concern/worry that I invest in my stuff. Is the living space free of excess clutter, allowing freedom of movement and a feeling of openness and spaciousness? For me, I have at times felt as though my stuff held me hostage. Slowly and insidiously, things accumulate—I suppose, at some level, I have a need for order and harmony (which extends to my living environment). It is my experience that more stuff does nothing to increase my level of peace or sense of freedom. Quite to the contrary, the opposite seems to prove true for me.

Not until I noticed that when I got rid of things I experienced enjoyable feelings such as ease, did I question this relationship. Yes, I found at times some feelings of hesitation, but that came more from the effort required to clean out the garage or spare room or to organize a closet. Invariably, it felt good when I'd done. I experienced disappointment if the thrift shop wouldn't take something I felt intent on getting rid of, or if stuff still sat on the table when the garage sale had finished (not because it didn't sell but because I didn't want to bring it back into my space).

Now, I don't suggest neglecting your belongings—that just results in unnecessary deterioration and premature replacement. However, I do question the point of having something if I become more stressed about wear and tear instead of just enjoying and appreciating whatever it is I have while I have it. I appreciate the Buddhist perspective on impermanence, which reminds me to feel grateful for what I have in my life because, sooner or later, they will be gone. In this respect, it is more accurate to consider that which I have as being on loan (which doesn't begin to address the planned redundancy of many things these days). I don't feel compelled to upgrade. Usually, I don't have comprehensive fluency in the features of the current gadget, and so the marketing and hype to promote the "new & improved" doesn't impress me, as I don't enjoy the learning curve of trying to figure out the myriad functions. I'd rather go walk on the beach or in the woods.

Then there comes the letting go of attachment, which can get put to the test when considering letting go of something or losing something unexpectedly. For example, I now have the latest Mac laptop upon which I continue with the writing of this book — this comes not as a result of my believing my four-year-old Mac inadequate, but rather as the result of the previous computer getting stolen. Admittedly, the sudden thought that the entire draft of this book (plus dozens of poems I had written) were all on that computer, initially felt upsetting. However, I moved through that quickly enough and acknowledged that writing offered an important form of creativity and expression for me, and then decided another computer was a requirement.

The old computer got stolen from my car (so, I learned a thing or two about the many ways of being that didn't serve me particularly, and that had contributed to the theft happening). This also meant that the wireless modem/back-up drive remained in my home. And, checking with the dealership what this meant, I found that once connected to a new computer, it would restore everything on the drive up to the last back-up, and so, I retrieved all my writing intact (a valuable testimonial to backing-up). Ultimately, this situation felt more of an inconvenience than anything else. I could have made the whole thing considerably more unpleasant if I had remained angry at the thief (or myself) or wallowed in self-pity at the injustice, etc. (I am no stranger to either of these mindsets.)

At other times in my life, I have simply given up. Before the successful retrieval of my writing, I had let go of the book, as it previously existed. (I did still have the original hand-written journal entries with which to begin again.) It would not have found rebirth in the exact form as the first version — it would be what it would become. If I'd held rigidly to the need for it to be *only* what it had been, I might not have found the willingness to begin again. As it turned out, I released the form and decided that the work would continue — newly. It involved the price of a new computer; however, my vision to be a writer and the realization of this particular book (in some form) over-rode any attachment to my stories of how that would not be possible.

Day 9
(Intention)

I got to the labyrinth site earlier than any day so far—not, however, because I'd brimmed over with enthusiasm. No, "restless," "irritable," and "discontent" made for my companions this morning. I could include impatient as well. I had posed upon the universe all matters of existential questions. Of course, the impatience came due to the answers not coming in a timely fashion—which, in case you didn't guess, would be on my schedule. Now, I admit that sometimes I talk when I should listen (this could well happen more often than not), and I have come to realize that, at some point in my early life, I took on the idea that what I had to say held no value. Additionally, I had a fear of criticism or looking bad if I did speak up. The end result—I surrendered my voice. It would seem in compensation that, sometimes, the pendulum had swung to the other extreme, and I monopolized the conversation (both relishing in getting heard and afraid I would leave something out and get exposed and criticized for not knowing what I talked about).

Then there come those occasions when I listen but don't like what I hear; for example, the answer is no or not yet. So, really, what I speak of is illuminating my need to exercise more patience and acceptance—to live contrary hasn't worked. Well, that's not entirely true, if what I'm trying to do is to continue to stoke the fires of discontent, then to continue without changing anything would prove highly effective. If I choose inner peace instead, which I do, then impatience and resistance will most certainly be counterproductive. It's revealing to realize that though I identify ways of being, such as peace, as being important to me, yet upon an honest look, I discover myself busy pouring my energy into ways of being not in alignment with that which I value.

"Embrace the mystery," and, "Things are not as they appear," are both ideas that come at me from a variety of sources (which increases the difficulty of ignoring these suggestions). I have elevated pride and obstinacy through the stratosphere (which, as it turns out, introduced me to the concepts of humility, open-mindedness, and willingness), not how I would suggest that you learn these qualities—less painful ways exist. However, as they say, when the student is ready, the teacher will appear. One of my teachers has arisen within the consequences of my self-will.

I must clarify that I don't mean because many people parrot the same thing. Rather, it means it's right (the contrary often holds true). In this case, the suggestions I received came from different people and sources, but the same message came through. I can hear the argument, "Still doesn't mean they're right."—Correct, and I can, and probably will again, make them all wrong. However, the distinction for me is that I make an honest self-appraisal and sincerely wish to make a change. (If I don't want to change something, I can keep doing the same thing. If I say I want to change something but keep doing the same thing, then the result will remain the same—no change.)

So, at the labyrinth, I took a step toward embracing the mystery (of life) and said, "Okay, now I've done this, can you tell me what it will look like?"

Amazingly, an answer came — (*Actually, no. That is why it's called the mystery, and besides that, what do you want it to look like?*)

"Huh — want what to look like?"

(*Your life — life has many mysteries (including your life) that may reveal themselves over time and, in some cases, maybe not during this time. Still, you yourself define what your life is about, either consciously or unconsciously. ... What do you want? What do you want to do?*)

"It's not that easy," I argued. "You make it sound as though anything is possible!"

(*No one said it would prove easy — but it is simple — the fact is, anything is possible.*)

"But, circumstances don't always allow ... and I tried one time ... and, oh my God, the result was horrendous."

(*Well, you have effectively shown how infinite possibility can become severely limited — but none of that means anything is impossible, just that you have various challenges to work with to bring what's possible into being.*)

"What if I fail to do what I dream of doing?"

(*You speak of failing as though a one-time event permanently determines an outcome — is this true? A better question would be, what price do you pay for not doing what you dreamed of doing?*)

"Well, yes, I have tried various things in the past that didn't work out, and so I abandoned the idea. I thought that to dream is to invite disappointment — better to go with the sure thing."

(*How's that working for ya? Are you not sad that you have dreams that you've abandoned? It could be said that your strategy to avoid disappointment has actually created disappointment. If, rather than giving up on your goal, you had applied yourself again after the first failure, how do you know whether or not you might then have found success?)*

"Uh, well, I guess I don't know that—I just changed my mind."

(Yes, you could see that as true. However, here's what happened: You gave an outcome (fears and beliefs) more importance than your dream. The idea/dream had nothing wrong with it. You, for a variety of reasons, gave up on making it a priority. You said yourself, you chose to go after the sure thing. The safe choice might provide some sense of security, but truly, that is just an illusion, and even while that lasts (as it is temporary at best), it can't possibly feel satisfying if it in no way falls in alignment with what you have in your heart.)

"Well, now I feel like a failure for both quitting and failing to realize my dream."

(The intention here is not to make you bad or wrong. This is just what you did—it would be helpful for you to redefine failure. It simply means a desired result didn't get achieved. It certainly doesn't mean that you should quit; nor does it mean that you are a failure. It just means that, if the goal continues to be your goal, then a new approach may be needed to see it to completion. If, in your mind, you run thoughts that make yourself wrong and bad, or worse, thinking that you are the failure, then understandably, the energy will not be there to continue your pursuit. All those low-vibration thoughts and beliefs are not conducive to creativity or enthusiasm. They will, indeed, take the wind out of your sails.)

Huh, interesting conversation. I have to admit, these ideas rang true for me. I considered their source (and the labyrinth metaphor) from outside to in, then from the centre and back again to the outside. It is of myself I asked these questions (not the universe), though the universe could be said to exist within me and, in turn, I within the universe — no separation. Of course, knowing this doesn't pay my mortgage, which is not the point of my existence, but it does make it more comfortable. I have heard of "a spirit of living truth" within me (in fact, in everyone, not just me). Did I have my conversation with this spirit? If so, how could I distinguish this from the "voice(s)" that, for example, might say, "Oh, sure, another piece of that chocolate cake would be fine, and I might as well finish off the ice cream along with it, then it will be out of the house." More questions!

Once again, I noticed the presence of these various emotions and thoughts to abandon my commitment. What, then, from within myself, in the face of emotional turbulence, orchestrates quitting? Something ultimately beneficial to me would get abandoned (ironically, in this case, the morning practice with the potential benefit of calming and centring would be worth adhering to when I feel all this upheaval). It's easy (well, easier) to sit quietly when I feel calm already. The real work comes in trying to maintain or return to peace.

Who's side am I on, anyway? Clearly, my thinking is not always supportive or constructive and not helpful in meeting my goals (or needs).

So, instead of sitting at home brooding, adding to my already uninspired emotional state by beating myself up for not following through, I took my angst for a walk. During which, I became aware that the tail wagged the dog, by which I mean, my emotional state mastered me (rather than the other way around). My thoughts did nothing to turn this around; in fact, they fuelled the funk. I watched such thoughts, as I'd only gotten halfway through the first time around the labyrinth — still two more rounds to go (like this were some sort of race), and then I had the Qi Gong plus the meditation. (I pondered the notion that I'd grown agitated about the prospect of meditating — rather funny, really). Can't you just hear the conversation? ... "I'm going to blast through this meditation so that I can hurry home and get back to worrying and generally creating more suffering for myself with my thoughts." This negative self-talk needed to get put in check. I didn't want to ignore my feelings, but neither did I find it helpful to spiral further downward.

Back to the practice — slow the pace, focus on each footstep, feel each foot contact the surface of the pathway, just as one foot lands, the other pushes off. Inhale ... exhale, one breath at a time, the air flows in cold, and then exhales warmed to body temperature. The trees exhale, I breathe the life-sustaining oxygen — I exhale carbon dioxide (the waste product of my metabolism now gets taken in and processed by the trees). I noticed my desire to stop and pick up the maple seed pods on the labyrinth surface that I'd missed when sweeping. Instead, I brought my attention back to the breath — (*Let Go; it's perfect as it is.*)

While I sat under the oak tree afterward, I noticed that someone had left some unshelled peanuts (I guessed for the squirrels). I felt grateful that my seated position placed me where I could see and be reminded of the sacred balance and interrelationship of all life on Earth. On my way to my car, after completing for the day, I saw a squirrel carrying an acorn. I tried to tell him about the peanuts under the oak tree; however, I feel unsure that he got the message.

Day 9 Questions
(Intention)

01) What does intention mean to you?

02) Do you give your intention any degree of priority?

03) Intention: Does it determine outcome or describe the current plan until something better (or different) comes along?

04) Is intention a declaration or a loophole?

05) Is there only one way to fulfill an intention?

06) Is challenge indicative that intentions were misguided?

07) Do you trust yourself to follow through on your intention?

08) What does failure mean to you?

09) Is failing the end of an intention?

10) Could failing form part of the process of realizing an intention?

11) What is the relationship between trying, intention, and failure to you?

12) Does intention mean something more definite than trying?

13) If you tried and failed, does that define intention? (I.e., that was my intention, but it didn't work out.)

14) Could a sustained intention stand in the face of a failure? Repeated failures?

15) Can you make a distinction between feeling the disappointment of failing and considering yourself a failure?

16) What does realistic mean to you?

17) Have you considered the impact that being realistic might have on your joy, passion, hopes, and dreams?

18) If, upon examination of your life, you find realism a limiting factor (an elaborate excuse), could you redefine it to outline a manageable approach to realize the intention?

Sample Answer

Question 2—Do you give your intention any degree of priority?

Question 13—If you tried and failed, does that define intention? (I.e., that was my intention, but it didn't work out.)

I have to say that, often times, my intentions rang hollow—of course, I could look and listen around me and convince myself I was no different than anyone else. After all, innumerable people speak of the pointlessness of "New Year's Resolutions" due to the rapid rate at which they get broken. The first thing for me to recognize is that I continually looked to validate my actions (or inactions) by what others did and said.

What would it feel like, for example, to be in a group where everyone exchanged stories of giving up on one thing or another, and I interjected, "That's not my experience. Frequently, I complete what I set out to do." Of course, first of all, it would need to be true (and it's not as though it's an outlandish claim—in general, many people do manage to do this). Deeper examination discovers that a need for acceptance and to fit in lay behind this behaviour. I could trace back wounds to a time in junior high, and though I had the ability to achieve high marks, I lacked the belief in myself necessary to ignore the ridicule directed my way for doing well. So, I dumbed myself down, trying to win acceptance (one of many strategies aimed at gaining approval. Unfortunately, this never did win me the coveted acceptance and, while attempting to avoid the pain of rejection, I created more pain for myself through under-achieving and not realizing my potential, but the realization of this came many years later.

The thing with these strategies devised early in life, the patterns and associated underlying issues, if allowed, could dog me for my entire life. If I believe of myself that I'm not one to finish what I start, then a good chance arises that I'll live that as though it's true.

Another consideration is that it doesn't matter if I set out a goal (or intention) if I don't give it serious priority. Nobody else can carry it out for me—many may consider my endeavour ludicrous, unattainable, unrealistic, or unimportant (the list could go on indefinitely). Once again, I find myself faced with a need to believe deeply in myself (and what it is I do).

The other definition of convenience I have applied to intention is as follows, "Well, yes, that was my intention, but it didn't work out." Now, while that might hold truth in some cases, there are times when, while plausible, this is more accurately an excuse. If I had some measure of enthusiasm for something and, perhaps, experienced some difficulty or frustration; instead of deepening my resolve, I abandoned ship (in other words—quit), then that would make me at that time a quitter. Phew, there, I said it; glad that's over with. Now, I realized a couple of things for myself about some of these incompletions—they were, in fact, part of the process of searching for and discovering where my passion lay—I could eliminate these as possibilities. I didn't have an ongoing interest, so I could take what I learned and move on.

The other thing I learned was that passion, interest, and enthusiasm don't mean that challenges won't appear. Where those three exist, they can help to facilitate continued effort toward the goal in the face of challenge. Without them, it might become difficult to direct sustained energy if the motivation is only, "I should," or, "I must," or even, "I'm afraid if I don't."

Day 10
(Moderation)

I rose even earlier today—not due to agitation this time; I felt energized and ready to begin. I got up early enough to fit in a short yoga practice and still walk out the door sooner than any day so far. The yoga routine remained short, in part because I am a novice, and also, it had been a while since I'd done any on a regular basis, and so I wanted to ease my body into it. I am one given to extremes, all or nothing. In this case, that might look like I get excited about bringing a yoga practice into my life, and then, next thing you know, I've lost perspective. My participation then takes on a mindset that if a little is good, then more has got to be better.

To further the yoga example, I ended up taking on too much too soon, and in some cases, ended up injured. Yoga detractors speak of the risks of the practice, and I would assert (for me, anyway) that the practice offers a beautiful spiritual path and inner journey. At no time did anyone tell me, "You have got to get yourself into that pose." The body, in part, is the master/teacher—if I honoured it as such, I would ask, "This is what I propose. How do you feel about assuming the following asana?" If I then tuned into my body, a reply would render through, telling me what it felt ready and willing to do in the moment. It may respond with a further opening over time if requested gently, and then again, the answer today might be, *"No, this is it."* I believe injuries occur when I ignore the body's answer and demand that it push further.

This does not hold sacred my body, or the practice of yoga (especially if I were to insist that yoga caused my injury). I believe that it would fall more in keeping with the heart of the practice if I honoured myself instead of becoming consumed by comparing and competing with others in the class—all the while generating thoughts of being "less than" (i.e. if I can't do what they can do). I would let go of concern for what "they" are doing, and find contentment in my practice. What if, on the request of the instructor to assume a particular pose, I checked in with myself, and my body said, *"Not today"*? At that point, my practice is to honour me and stand in that. At the same time, I would observe the volley of thoughts going on with regard to my image management and become further informed of their presence. Which, do you suppose, would offer a practice more appropriate for spiritual and character development? Push myself to the point of injury, or have compassion and understanding for where I'm at, and exercise some self-control over my thoughts and emotions?

Again, yoga is not my problem, this is self-generated, in the yoga class, or in the gym or at the 10 km run, or in the workplace. As you can see, I have used a wide variety of external means to hide from myself, which also includes compulsive spending, eating, and on and on it goes. I should emphasize that none of these pursuits are inherently bad—in this case, it is the way I engaged with them that proved counter-productive to my wellbeing.

I could write a book about this way of thinking—come to think of it, I suppose in part, that is what I'm doing now. As I walk a labyrinth, exploring the sacred and practicing an activity that in itself might be described as grounding or centring, perhaps this conjures the image that I am some highly-evolved being—well-versed in the disciplines of spiritual practice. This, somehow, elevates me above my human condition—oh, at times, how I wish this were so. (Allow me to bring my feet to the ground.) Yes, I am deeply interested in spirituality. As mentioned, I came to embark on that path twenty-five years ago through recovery from alcohol and drug addiction. In total, some fifteen years of my life that I spent in what began as what I jokingly referred to as better living through chemistry; culminating in the abyss of my private hell of oblivion and depravity.

Still, I must remain mindful that my spiritual path is not allowed to become my identity—I remain cautiously optimistic that if I keep the right perspective, it may continue to reveal for me who that is, but not without marching me through who I have been, what I have believed, how I have behaved, and what I told myself to continue to do what I did. Whatever spirituality might represent to anyone else, I must be clear, I don't speak from any high moral ground. Addiction represents, at best, an attempt to produce a feeling of euphoria that doesn't seem possible through natural means. At worst, it was suicide on the instalment plan and, once the pain reached a certain level, the focus of life became ending it. Another day on this side of the dirt only serves to reinforce just how utterly cruel the universe seems.

I had hoped that when I got clean and put the plug in the jug, it would spell the end of addictive and compulsive behaviour. As I outlined earlier, I have come to recognize in hindsight that the insatiable maw of addiction has not a discerning palate and sees almost anything outside of itself as one big smorgasbord. The premise is that, somehow, I'm broken and just not okay in the world—can't even begin to be at home in my own skin—I have pain (don't know I have pain, would deny I have pain, and yet act out in the world in an attempt to avoid painful feelings or create more desirable feelings like, say, excitement). Along the way, I create circumstances that produce more painful feelings that, of course, must be avoided at all costs (oh, what a telling statement that is—heart and soul become the currency of addiction for the tyrannical creditor).

The myriad of ways I have run from myself (which includes physical running—a healthy pursuit of wellness some might say). Have you ever heard of the "runner's high"? It doesn't mean that everyone that runs is an addict (though there are many in those circles that I have heard say, "I'm addicted to running—but it's a healthy addiction!"). If they merely express enthusiasm inaccurately, that's one thing; otherwise, no "healthy addictions" exist. Combine this with emotional eating, and my weight has yo-yoed up and down (how clever and insidious this addiction is—no secret, exercise is touted as part of any healthy lifestyle—and I need to eat). However, when I eat to stuff my emotions, and then run to further manage my emotional landscape and my expanding waistline—not so healthy. Not to mention the number of running related injuries I sustained, again by too much too soon, or not taking a day off to allow my body to recover.

At one time, I had the magazine-cover physique, which frankly, proved of no consequence while I died inside. Spending money, which many quip is just a little "retail therapy," became the polar opposite in my case. If one were to use the model of my being the adult (caretaker/parent) of my inner child, then my child never stopped wanting, and my parent rarely said no. I can honestly say I love music—and spent countless amounts of money on guitars (my instrument of choice). I had eight of them at once (I must make a distinction between legitimate collectors or musicians that play a variety of musical genres and, therefore, require different guitars for the appropriate sound, etc.). Alas, in my case, I had many different guitars—none of which came cheap, and I even took lessons from a couple of different instructors at the same time. "Oh, ya, they teach different styles." Although true to a point, does that reflect now in my guitar playing? Not so much. Couldn't I love music and listen to the radio? Hell, no—I found it necessary to spend hundreds and hundreds of dollars on CDs, and still have a cabinet full of them (and I've gotten rid of dozens along the way). It's all about the hunt (the mind boggles when I consider what calibre of musician I might have become if I'd spent as much time practicing my guitar as I did researching new ones and trolling through CD stores). I have CDs I don't even know I have—for sure, I have some in there that I've never listened to.

Much of this out of control spending, etc., happened during my marriage—needless to say, it negatively impacted our financial standing. I always found money for what I wanted, but it ended there.

For the most part, I worked in health care—union job, and therefore, a reasonable wage—but without question, I lived beyond my means.

You might think this would bring the practice to a screeching halt—not so. In this day and age, innumerable financial institutions seem only too willing to give you credit—it's too easy. I sat what amounted to the pretence of a qualifying interview, just a formality in reality, and in no time, I could shop 'til I dropped. Is there anything more aptly suited to someone given to compulsion and impulse than credit? Fits like hand in glove—no need to walk away and think about it, save for it, or budget. Instead, you see it, want it, and have it—that simple. (Instant gratification addict utopia.) Did I appreciate anything acquired this way? Who said appreciation even became a consideration?

Did I think all this stuff made me who I was? I never thought it through then, but in retrospect, yes. The irony of much of this behaviour is that, outwardly, no one would have batted an eye—to some, I might have appeared as someone with diverse interests. I worked at an honourable job and, of course, of paramount importance to many, I supported the economy. I bet that plenty of workaholics grace the covers of some of those glossy entrepreneur magazines.

One might wonder if this recovery journey has yielded anything worthwhile—believe me, sometimes I wondered that myself. Given the frequently held view on addicts, reflected in statements like, "He's just a waste of good skin and fresh air," (which, incidentally, I quote directly from a previous co-worker in health care), then this stigma produces a major stumbling block to seeking help. What I can say from my experience is that what I would have described as contempt for me as an addict, stemming from society (in other words, outside myself) was, in fact, no less upheld by myself, toward myself. That's not any easy thing to come to know. It has proven, however, one of the portals to my freedom.

The key lay in my need to find my way through these wake-up calls. For the truth to set me free, I must recognize it, then find the willingness to own it and let go and move on. Hatred (this applies whether directed outwardly or toward myself) is not an energy conducive to healing and personal growth. This might seem self-evident. It can, however, prove surprisingly insidious and lurks within, despite my insistence to the contrary. Denial makes for both a protective device, which serves and provides a benefit, but once it has outlived its usefulness, it can then become detrimental.

Though I can't begin to know for sure, I have to believe that every minute of my life has been necessary to bring me to right here and now. From here, I can express from the perspective of observation and insight into my life. I didn't wake up one day with the ability to see the entire truth of what had gone on in my life; it has been a process— breaking through the layers of denial. Does it matter that I didn't just overdose years ago? Would it have made any difference in the greater scheme of things? I don't know. I have to presume that if I were meant to go, I would have. It goes far beyond (for me) dumb luck. It proved rare that I didn't consume combinations of drugs and alcohol that should have been lethal, and yet, here I am. (At one time that would have fed my deluded sense of immortality; however, now all that remains is a nodding acquaintance with humility.)

For many people, they may refuse to get beyond morality and, therefore, discredit everything I say when they realize where I have come from. I'm here to say that, without doubt, I take responsibility for a great many acts that I am not proud of. That I can speak frankly about them now represents a journey out from under my shame—a walk that continues with each word on this page. I anticipate the wrath of many. Day-by-day, perhaps minute-by-minute, I move toward the realization of enough love for myself that I dare to believe I can endure the judgment of others as I tell my story. To begin with, it's doubtful that the hatred and contempt from anyone else could match that which I have harboured for myself. Perhaps that in itself made a necessary right of passage to turn this train-wreck of a life around. I'm not alone in this (addiction) if even one person exists that I can reach—literally, right off this page—and take their addiction-ravaged heart in my hands and show a way out. It doesn't have to end this way. Look at my life. If it can happen for me, it can happen for anyone. My history will become of value, and the risk and fear of judgment, inconsequential.

Will I ever become a paragon of virtue? No. However, I also seek freedom from my perfectionism, which would have me believe that I don't have anything to offer until I become perfect myself. Can you see where that becomes another self-defeating loop? If I can accept that it's possible to learn from mistakes—that failures, rightly examined, become the stepping-stones to success and, as such, elements of an enriched life, then I ought to be a scholar by now, as God knows, I've made no end of mistakes.

Socrates said, "The unexamined life is not worth living." My life would seem to affirm that this rings true. My reason supporting this comes down to my complete blindness, at times, to the ways I have participated in the creating of pain for myself and others, and therefore, the fact that I just keep right on doing it. Even the beginning of becoming conscious around this behaviour has turned into a justification for me to wallow in a morass of self-pity and shame, which is not the emotional underpinning of effective decision making. From here begins another cycle of: Experience pain; run from pain; choose pain (or, at least, circumstances that will lead to pain and feed the consciousness of victim—until such a time as I see my part and take responsibility for my choices, behaviour, and life).

Upon examination, I have come to recognize that the hole in my soul was my story around getting given up for adoption at birth—this is in no way meant to read like a cry for sympathy or pity. As far as I can tell, this is my "Alamo," and all my "demons" are cloaked in the fabrics tailored by this event in my life. I don't deny that I have free choice throughout my life; however, I had no idea that I exercised this power of choice while influenced continually by this age-old pain.

Some aspects of my personality, I crafted just to protect against rejection and, equally unconsciously, I brought no authenticity to the way I showed up in

116

relationships—my truth goes unspoken, and indeed, abandonment occurs—that which I perpetrate on myself. I'd have to say that I universally feared rejection, i.e. by both men and women, but women figured uniquely on my journey. Throughout my whole life, a relationship has gone on with the one woman I never met, in an attempt to meet unmet needs for love and acceptance (oblivious to the fact of how little I had for myself). My personality became warped for the purpose of winning the approval of women. Add to that an emotionally immature belief that love and sex were one and the same, and I can't honestly lay claim to anything akin to the expression of healthy sexuality. This would include everything from compulsive to, at times, obsessive, as well as illicit and illegal (by which I refer to "escorts"). I feel painfully aware (now) that there were others involved—I regret deeply the part that I played in perpetuating their pain—the whole what goes on between consenting adults alibi, absolutely doesn't wash with me (for me). It's not clear what I can do to make amends or restitution at this time—a bare beginning is for me to continue to do whatever it is I need to do to heal, so I no longer participate in perpetuating more pain in the world.

It would seem that, driven by unconscious beliefs, I have found it necessary to ease my pain (frankly, without any awareness that there was pain present, or that what I did had anything to do with avoiding it or bringing on more). Constantly, I sought something outside myself to try and distract me from, or resolve, this pain. I had a hole, and filling it required "more" (more of what?—you might ask)— anything, really. I could try and justify/minimize my behaviour by saying that at least the fix wasn't this or that. Truly, just a lame attempt to feel better by trying to rise above those that have behaved that way. But, in all honesty, where this behaviour has taken me and the people I have had a part in hurting, including myself, is far enough. I have objectified other human beings; using them to, ultimately, avoid looking at myself—my compulsive behaviour has, in turn, fed their addictions and plays a part in the pain they endeavour to avoid. I have never been one to overtly speak in terms that would reflect an attitude that poorly reflected on, in this case, women. Just the same, my behaviour has not been congruent with who I say I am—who I sincerely want to be. I accept full responsibility for my behaviour and, as such, continue to seek the help I need for liberation from the shell game of cross addiction—that help is spiritual.

So, I neither judge those caught in these cyclic (what can be self-destructive) ways of being—but neither do I want to bring any further variety of the ways of experiencing them into my life. Nothing short of the root causes behind this disconnected way of being in the world will suffice. It has been said that it takes more courage to face one's self than to face an army of one thousand men. Now, I can say those are no longer mere words on the page; the truth held within is becoming part of my personal experience.

I arrived at the labyrinth site while it remained quite dark. I reckoned this wouldn't interfere with sweeping the leaves clear. The chief critic within felt concerned that the lack of light would lead to my missing a few leaves or seed pods.

(A little pep-talk seems required here — it is my intention to clear the surface to the best of my ability at present. Therefore, any debris left behind will be due to lack of light, not lack of diligence on my part. It will be perfect in its imperfection, hmm … maybe there is no "lack of light" here, after all.)

I felt lighter in spirit when framing the situation this way.

I completed the sweeping, and then wondered if I would manage to see the pathway well enough to walk it (the bricks that delineated the actual route had only a slightly different colour than the pathway bricks). I considered that I could do the sitting meditation first — though, so far, there had been a sequence within this morning practice — it felt interesting to notice my awareness that I felt some concern when considering changing it up. Nothing I did there occurred in a particular order because of some principal of practice — that was just how it had unfolded so far.

I had not taken into consideration that, though the practice stood at only ten days old, I had carried it on as the season of autumn advanced. I started earlier in the morning, and in two days, the clocks would turn back one hour, all of which meant it got darker at the same time of morning that I'd shown up.

I noted that an element of the dogmatic had crept in — would it make sense to cling to the sequence of events if in doing so, I couldn't see the path I wanted to walk? I could start bringing a flashlight; maybe, I'd switch it up tomorrow just to keep it fresh. I could just walk within the confines of the labyrinth without worrying about the pathway (colour outside the lines, so to speak). The sun would still rise, regardless.

I created this—where did the rules come from—there's a part of me that gets excited about some creativity/flexibility (others might call it bending the rules). All at once, I saw that rigidity might affect the organic nature of this practice. Did I need to apologize for breaking rules that I had made?

I then considered that, perhaps, rigid adherence didn't necessarily honour the sacred or make the event sacred—it would appear to be an ongoing dialogue (wow, I'd better keep building those listening skills so that I don't miss anything).

As I set off on my walk, the daylight infused the darkness slowly, and with mindful observation, the path became visible. The light made the path visible through the darkness. I found nothing present in the dark that gave a true obstacle. The light made this clear. In the dark, and within the shadows, existed distortions—once the light focused upon the dark, the obstacles vanished. The path, I could see as a metaphor—with the darkness representing all the wounding, fears, and mistaken beliefs that have resided in my heart, denied the light of truth. My shame, the walls of the prison I built for myself. Through a crack in the wall, the light shone upon the interior—darkness yielded to the ongoing invitation of the light. I walked to become aware of the sacred. I set down my judgment and recognized life as sacred; all life, including mine. I walked step-by-step toward the light—mine is no longer the unexamined life, but a life worth living. Through the darkness, the light allowed me to see with the eyes of a man with worth, and so I kept walking.

The gradual infusion of light not only revealed the beauty of my surroundings, as the dazzling display of fall colours became more visible, but also the trees appeared to become more animated in their presence. Seemingly, doors of invitation opened, offering the choice, "You can look at the show from the sidelines or join and become one with the show." The former would offer an impression of the show while the latter offered direct experience.

As it turned out, I learned that nothing on the path would prevent the most profound connection with and to the journey. The most formidable obstacles existed within myself.

Day 10 Questions
(Moderation)

01) What do you believe about more is better?

02) Consumption—to fill legitimate needs or satisfy competition?

03) If you believe we are in competition, what would determine when you feel as though you have won?

04) What defines for you enough?

05) Are you aware what you give up in some areas of your life to have more of something else?

06) Can you see any relationship between continually wanting more and suffering?

07) Could you be okay with less?

08) Is it possible that less is more?

09) Though you may well say, "Everything in moderation," is this truly the defining principle in your thoughts, beliefs, and actions?

10) Do you relate to "full on" or "full stop" or "feast or famine"? Have you considered there might be an alternative?

11) Have you ever experienced a positive outcome from too much? (I.e. eating, spending, working, exercising, etc.)

12) Identify for yourself areas of excess or inattention (neglect).

13) Consider the strings on a guitar—if too loose, they are ineffective, and conversely, if tightened too much, they will break—how does this analogy apply to various areas of your life?

14) At times, it might become necessary to moderate—find moderation. If, for example, one area of your life has become severely compromised, it

may require considerable energy directed that way to restore balance. What parts of your life call for your attention?

15) Have you ever considered that your wants/desires may be a source of discomfort?

16) What if instead of the popular marketing mantra "Super-size it," you instead chose to "Minimize it"? Do you feel willing to conduct the experiment?

17) If you are considering a change in your life, are you able to think in terms of small, incremental shifts?

18) Can you see where too much too soon has been detrimental to your success?

19) Reflect on the following: Too much thought without action—too quick to take action without any thought. Either could be seen to be ineffective—dig a little deeper; what might be under-lying causes for either pattern?

Sample Answer

Question 1—What do you believe about more is better?

Question 6—Can you see any relationship between continually wanting more and suffering?

I can't say that I ever consciously believed or would have stated the position that "more is better," but I certainly lived my life as though this were true. I remember a friend's dad once saying to me, "The winner is the one with the most toys (or the most expensive toys) before he/she dies." I understood this, at least in the context that he made the statement, but I never embraced it as a value system—it didn't make sense to me. Nonetheless, as I said, I consumed and accumulated with reckless abandon at various times in my life, despite never formally declaring that I had entered the "competition."

Waking up to myself and what drove me has happened as a gradual process (although, at times, some shifts in awareness had been far-reaching, intense, and rather sudden). I would say the process begins with a willingness to look at myself and be as honest with this inquiry as possible. It would seem the answers would come as long as I remained willing to keep asking the questions—the process over time has been about learning to ask a better question. No question = no answer (I should add that it has, largely, proven ineffective to direct my questions continually outside myself).

Through this process, I came to some awareness about what I valued, how I behaved, and whether the two could get reconciled. I won't pursue an "anti" (consumption, capitalism) position here; my focus is on the idea of moderation, which you may decide has application across the board (or not).

With respect to "more is better"—I can say more exercise, which is generally considered to be a good idea, doesn't necessarily prove true (too much and I can end up run down and susceptible to sickness or injury). If I begin a new workout routine too aggressively (ambitiously), I can end up so sore, and the whole idea can seem misguided (not a strategy to encourage program adherence).

Who hasn't sat down to a holiday dinner or attended a potluck (which includes all these delicious choices)—a little of this, a little of that, and before you know it there's a mountainous plateful? Each mouthful is, in itself, a delight for the taste buds, and yet, twenty to thirty minutes after finishing, you have the feeling of being kicked in the stomach, perhaps some gastric distress, and the rise of a stupor-like state. How can this be?—It all tasted so good—got prepared with loving hands, and shared in delightful company. Answer ... too much!

In this journey of discovery, I have learned that the object consumed or pursued is not problematic—it is the strategy itself that more is better. For me, I came to recognize that the hole I attempted to fill was insatiable. There seldom came a point in time where I could just believe that all was right with my world. There would always occur to me to be more of something I already had or a need to get something, or somewhere else, and then it would be okay. This constant projection of enough or okay as being out there somewhere made it impossible to enjoy the present, and what's more, it fed a chronic state of discontent.

Day 11
(Inner Guidance)

The trend toward earlier starts shifted today, due to a combination of getting to bed a little later and an overall increase in activity (exercise) in the form of both a walk around a local golf course (a rather hilly 3.5 k.m. of trail) and a visit to a recreation centre for a gym workout (steam, whirlpool, and sauna to follow). The result? I slept in; didn't even wake up until shortly before 8:00 a.m. All the ruminations yesterday regarding early morning visibility had now become a moot point, as full daylight had arrived.

As I tried, hastily, to get myself out of the door, I realized, "What's the hurry? I'm walking in circles around my apartment—forgetting things. Why not just slow down, breathe, and get there when I get there? Not to mention the irony of rushing to get to my meditation practice. Maybe I'll be more effective getting there if I could first be here!" What was going on for me now? I noticed that I'd made myself wrong for sleeping in. That's where I needed to begin again. Instead of criticizing myself, I could have understanding and compassion. I could give myself credit for the start up of a new fitness commitment, and acknowledge the increased activity as good for my body, but also one that created some fatigue, and that proper rest is also integral to wellness and self-care.

This undertaking proves multi-faceted with respect to focus. The "what" that this is all about continues to present newly. I hope the realizations and illuminations will become expansive for me personally. By no means do I want it to end there. I truly aspire to have the written account serve others as a form of inspiration/encouragement and something that allows them to take time to examine for themselves what they consider sacred in their lives. And to then determine what would be required to have it become present more consistently — if that is not already true for them.

I have no wish to present as the one with "the answers," rather through sharing my journey, I hope to demonstrate (guide) each to the guide within him or herself, to search their heart, and answer its call. For sure, the journey to my heart has revealed some tender places, and some downright painful ones. Still, the release and healing are, in turn, shifting the perspective with which I see myself in the world, allowing more to become possible. While continuing to follow my heart has involved facing my fears and a commitment to a more openhearted approach to living, it seldom seems dull and frequently challenges my personal status quo.

What I have experienced in my life with regard to "playing it safe" is that, in an effort to avoid the potential hurt, the result is the creation of a more chronic form of discomfort, which I would describe as flat-lining through life. I suppose it is not unlike a financial investment — a small investment in a low-risk vehicle might produce a return but, likely, won't take your breath away. I don't advocate recklessness, but a half-hearted investment in life will return in kind. Much like preparing for a New Year's celebration with a box of discount fireworks lower priced because they had previously gotten wet. Come midnight, the fuses can get lit, and they may snap, crackle, and pop, but the anticipated show might just disappoint.

The idea and experiential evidence of a heart engaged feels both attractive and exciting to me. That there be more people in the world living that way, and have an ongoing connection with all these open hearts, would seem to describe Heaven on Earth.

Would this morning walk accomplish this transformation for me? This I knew so far, I had nobody telling me I should do this each morning (not even me – I chose to follow the guidance of my heart in carrying this through). That connection is indescribable and irreplaceable and can come from nothing outside of myself. No one stood at the labyrinth waiting to applaud me when I arrived. It remained an act of love.

I now combine that with a love to write and a vision that what touches my heart will, sometime, touch the heart of another – though, in truth, the final outcome remains unknown. For today, I committed to an authentic account of the journey.

Day 11 Questions
(Inner Guidance)

01) What do you know about (and/or believe) intuition, gut-instinct, and heart path?

02) Do you have the willingness to explore these qualities as those that could help determine your unique path?

03) Have you experience with a hunch that you followed with favourable results? How about one you ignored that you wish you had listened to later?

04) In the case of either previous example, do you recognize that you have powers of perception beyond what your mind can determine?

05) What are some of the barriers that might influence your ability to access these faculties? (I.e. Western World emphasis on the mind, women more intuitive than men, fear of being seen as indulging in woo-woo?)

06) Do you listen to your heart?

07) Can your heart be trusted?

08) Do you believe that your mind knows best?

09) Have you ever examined your choices re: career path, etc.? If so, how much do you consider your heart desires, and how much gets influenced by "I should" (or, perhaps, someone else's "you should")? — In other words, influence of *your* mind or *group* mind?

10) Did you receive encouragement when younger to trust your instincts?

11) How willing are you to stand out from the crowd? (To determine and live into your authentic self?)

12) Do you make time and space for quiet contemplation (be it meditation, walks in nature, or journaling), a chance to connect with your inner guidance, and wisdom/discernment?

13) Can you allow for the realization of your guidance (despite misgivings from your mind) or dismissive reflections from family, friends, and society?

14) Do you believe that you can find all your answers within yourself?

15) Do you acknowledge and value your unique gifts, experience, and interests as integral elements of your purpose?

16) How can anyone else call your dance when they are unable to hear your fiddler?

17) Is there some cause, project, or hobby that frequently impresses upon you that you have yet to pursue? (Do you ever hear yourself saying that "someone" should do something about this?)

18) Do you not only say, "There's got to be a better way," but you *know* there is?

19) What brings you joy and delights you, makes your heart sing?

20) Could heart dis-ease, heart attack, heartache, or a broken heart be brought about by ignoring what your heart tries to communicate to you?

Sample Answer

Question 6—Do you listen to your heart?

Question 19—What brings you joy and delights you, makes your heart sing?

Question 20—Could heart dis-ease, heart attack, heartache, or a broken heart be brought about by ignoring what your heart tries to communicate to you?

Quite a number of years ago, I found myself one of dozens of people in attendance at a speaking event/book launch conducted by a motivation/inspirational author/speaker. I only remember one thing he said during the whole presentation, which went something like this, "I don't think there is anything sadder than the number of people who pass from this world without ever having sung their song."

My experience of that statement felt as though he had stood on the platform with a crossbow and fired its projectile directly into my heart. Was this individual uniquely powerful to have made such an impression? I'd say no more so than anyone else. In this instance, he acted as the messenger. Perhaps the same statement had impacted others, and maybe other things he said proved of more significance to different individuals.

All I know is that, as I sat there with my former wife and a few friends, if I were to die that day, his words would make the true summation of my life. In that moment, the defining impression came not from the need to create a legacy but because I had become profoundly present to the pain and sadness in my heart. It would take many years to come before I developed the awareness to see that this pain began with the deprivation and estrangement I had in relation to my heart and that, further to that, I acted as the gatekeeper who kept it imprisoned and remained the only one who could act as caretaker and liberator. No one else could facilitate the physical manifestation of, and give voice to, my heart. At this particular point in time (in my mind), the heart was a physical pump—the whole idea of emotions and connection thereto baffled me. And, like so much of what I didn't understand or experience at this time, I proved quick to write it all off as nonsense. I had no knowledge of repression (even though I'd become a master of it). At once, this guy made what to many might have seemed hollow words feel emotional and profound. (Though no way would I allow that to show at a public venue.)

As for listening to my heart, a long-standing journey continued that I would describe as heart-centred (which I would liken more to the path of the "Heroes' Journey" than the romanticism conjured by some representation of "follow your heart" doctrines). This path offers a full-spectrum, emotionally multi-dimensional experience of life—Technicolor versus grey, and marked by sensational myopia.

If we look at the origins of the word courage, it lends some additional context: Middle English (denoting the heart as the seat of feelings) from the old French corage, -"cour" = "Coeur" (French for heart) from Latin cor "heart."

Hence, one can be said to have "great heart" to describe their courageous character. I would say it also takes great courage to connect with and heal in order to develop a great heart, and then be led by it. Interestingly to me, while I have seen myself as doing "what is necessary" from the reflections of others, I'm told that I possess great courage. So, my suggestion is, don't feel surprised if courage becomes available to you, proportionate to your needs and in forms you may not recognize or be quick to acknowledge.

What then of the relationship of heart conditions? While I am no expert, my experience shows that, certainly, there is considerable heartache present when engaged in activities or relationships that are incongruent with the truth of who I am. The relationship that suffers most greatly is that with self. As I have said, I can develop rather complex ways of ignoring the pain; however, at best, it just delays the inevitable. I can run, but I cannot hide. Does following your heart ensure fame and fortune? No. I feel convinced, though, that to engage in your heart path brings its own reward, which may not take the form of the widely held views on success. Intuitively, I suspect that the long-term ignoring of my heart must always leave me longing—and I don't see how that couldn't impact all other aspects of self, including physical health.

Certainly, I have only just scratched the surface on this subject. If you have an interest in further exploration, then I suggest additional reading and such topics as heart sciences (Heart Math), the heart, and spirituality.

Day 12
(Possibilities)

I had observed the day before (while sitting under the oak tree where I do the sitting meditation) that the small pile of tobacco that accumulates from my daily offering to the ancestors of the First Nations had gone completely. This seemed strange to me; the grounds didn't get cleaned that thoroughly (of, for example, leaves), and this little pile seemed inconspicuous. Though I hadn't tracked it specifically, I did habitually drop it in the same spot and, even given wind and rain, usually, some sign of it showed the next day.

At first, I wondered if someone might have watched me during my observances and, after I'd gone, examined the site and decided what I'd done was, somehow, a desecration of what they held sacred and, therefore, did a clearing. When I considered this, I noticed agitation rise within. I then considered that, even were this true, it had nothing to do with my practice being "more sacred" than someone else's. How interesting the emotional response I'd experienced when thinking about a mere story (someone clearing my offering) that I had not a shred of evidence to support the truth of it. Even if my story proved untrue, to become aware that I created stories and then carried on as though they were real, gives a useful awareness. Even if this particular story translated into real life, if I give my offering in an honouring way, with reverence for what I'm doing, then the "truth" of that would communicate energetically — the ceremony and sacredness conveyed and upheld by my intention—the tobacco remaining (or not) becomes of no consequence.

What is worth noting is this business of fabricating stories. How does that affect my interactions and relating to others? If I react to what someone says, believing it to mean whatever I have interpreted it to mean, without checking with them to see if they intended such—it becomes as though I have the conversation without them even participating. Which means that they could get blind-sided by my reaction (to my story) that had nothing to do with what they had communicated. In that case, they wouldn't know what had hit them. Do I interact with others this way? Without question, it happens. Perhaps, now that I have a nodding acquaintance with this dynamic, I might catch myself in it more often—but room for improvement remains.

I had also noticed that the peanuts someone else had left had gone—maybe the squirrels had eaten or collected them and used the tobacco for their nests. Then, as I wrote this, I wondered, did someone else sit there, have a snack, and roll themselves a cigarette? Clearly, these or an infinite number of other possible realities could hold some reality, none of which could I verify without witnessing for myself. I would better serve myself by saving the creativity and stories for my writing. Maybe that's what the squirrel sightings had been about; to draw my attention to my mind-works. Just as I had witnessed them jumping frenetically from branch to branch in the trees, so my mind jumped from the generation of one thought to another, none of which served any purpose with respect to staying in the moment. Most certainly, they brought a departure from the sacred space of the still/peaceful place within.

I found it interesting to observe how the thoughts created emotions, which then generated more thoughts, which brought a more intense emotional response. The escalating cycle took on a life of its own. In this case, everything took place while I remained alone—as fruitless as I know it is to blame another for my feelings, even if I'd wanted to in this instance, I had no one present onto whom to shift it. In effect, I'd triggered myself. It came as somewhat of a surprise that my mind had desecrated the domain of my inner peace. I saw clearly at that moment how these thought processes affected the relationship with myself and also how the same mechanism operated and projected upon others—even those closest to me. When seen in this light, I realized, nobody had a chance to get seen any other way than the way I expected to see them, based on the constructs of the thoughts necessary to uphold my story.

How limiting this thinking could become to others. How it could limit the possibilities in how I related to people. Also, I became aware of spaciousness—a sense of choice and freedom that become possible if I'm the creator of the story.

Day 12 Questions
(Possibilities)

01) Is anything possible?

02) How do you suppose what you believe impacts what is possible?

03) We live in an infinite universe — have you considered what effect the constructs of your mind have with respect to imposing limitations on possibility?

04) Is everything you believe true? How do you know?

05) Take an example from your life, something you see as being "just the way it is" — consider, what else is possible? What makes what is true for you, "more" true than alternative outcomes?

06) Do you presume to know all there is to know about the people in your life? How about yourself?

07) Can you hold a space for possibility with yourself and others?

08) How does resignation affect your ability to embrace possibility?

09) Do you have painful events from your past that continue to inform your willingness to consider possibility?

10) Are you willing to let go of the pain from the past to explore possibility?

11) Are you willing to consider the possibility of letting go of your pain?

12) Have you ever considered the effect your personal narrative has on your ability to see clearly?

13) Do you see yourself as the author/creator of this narrative?

14) Even if the events are accurate, need your response and perception continue unaltered?

15) Why might you want to limit what is possible?

16) How much energy do you suppose you expend looking for evidence to uphold your story?

17) Wouldn't it be more accurate to qualify much that is considered as "impossible" with "so far"? Rather than too readily resigning yourself to presuming it as impossible.

18) If not an innovator on a worldwide scale — what life-changing innovation is possible for you?

19) Will you embrace your possibility even if you must do so alone?

20) Is there any difference between "possibility" and "maybe"?

Sample Answer

Question 1 — Is anything possible?

Question 6 — Do you presume to know all there is to know about the people in your life? How about yourself?

I suppose for much of my life I have thought largely in terms of the impossible (and where I didn't actively engage in those thoughts, I behaved in ways that upheld my limited worldview without conscious intent to do so). I think, now, at best, that creates the illusion of impossible and facilitates a resistance to change — it doesn't determine the possible. Certainly, as long as I believe something to be impossible in my life, less likelihood remains that I will allow myself the experience. Even still, possibility might well prove more about belief and concerted effort toward a particular outcome to bring something into being that didn't exist previously than whether it was possible in the first place. Conversely, I can't ensure something is impossible just by denying it (i.e. I don't believe myself or anyone in my life will get touched by cancer — so, therefore, it won't happen).

I believe that it is possible for me to uphold ideas not even in my best interest and, in doing so, stand in the company of those having an alternative experience and continue to maintain that it isn't possible for me, and even cast doubt on their truth. In contrast, I have had innumerable experiences that I believe became possible from a willingness on my part to staying more open, which seemingly had an effect like placing a key in a lock — aligning the assorted tumblers and opening a door to an entirely different perspective than I had ever believed possible. Admittedly, this did at times, disturb, as the shelter of my limitations afforded me a degree of comfort. This expansion had the effect of making real for me the sort of experience that I had heard from others (verbally and in written anecdotes) but which remained overshadowed with my doubt and scepticism until it occurred to me directly. I found this both thrilling and disconcerting, as it brought home the realization that if these things were, indeed, possible, then what else might also prove so? Also, however, it brought home the need to more deeply accept responsibility and accountability for the limitations that I enforced upon myself.

Very little is possible with respect to what I can know about another or even someone of themselves, especially if they adhere rigidly to the idea that all there is to know, they already know. Take the analogy of holding a full cup of tea on my lap and requesting additional tea be added to the cup—very quickly, I would come to realize that hot tea overflowed into my lap. Why? The cup is full, and no further room exists. So it is, on occasion, with my mind. No room for new information. Sure, ideas get held within the collective that "a leopard doesn't change its spots" and, while throughout its lifespan it is a leopard, I don't think the implied message rings entirely true. Yes—one day to the next, the leopard is spotted—however, like many other animals, they shed their fur, which subsequently gets replaced—perhaps even over the course of a lifetime, comparative photos might reveal different patterns of spots at various stages of maturity. Nonetheless, change occurs.

Without question, I can say that, once I commenced on the path of self-discovery and healing, many things were not as they appeared. It is absolutely possible to believe that I know something as true about myself, but when subject to honest scrutiny, something else reveals itself. Interestingly, when I experience these various shifts in my perspective about myself, people and situations outside seem to transform. Once I accept it as truth that I can change, it then follows that so can others. If this is so, how can I say that I know all there is to know of a person?

I don't like to get stereo-typed (or pigeon-holed), yet I have done just that to others—presuming to know them based on previous judgments and assessments (whereby I haven't always elicited the verification of the other party before drawing my conclusion). Where this is the case, others have little opportunity to be anything but blank screens upon which I project my imagery. It is not relating at all, more like dictating. Absent has been curiosity/inquiry, openness, and mystery/discovery. I feel grateful that my viewpoint has become subject to expansion. At times, I experience regret for those in my life at a time when both they and I got held captive by the limitations I imposed. Of course, they would have had their "movie" running too.

It strikes me as interesting when I consider how frequently I have so adamantly upheld a version of reality or a likely outcome, particularly where my life is concerned. How was it that I held to be true, out of all the infinite variables, such limitation? How could I be so sure? The truth of the matter is that, often, I didn't give such matters a great deal of consideration—if any at all. It just wasn't possible; end of story! What I gained in exchange for this certainty was no need to risk failure or looking bad or humiliation. I also held myself to false beliefs, an artificially low ceiling of achievement, and the obliteration of reaching my potential. Coming to know this has created some freedom, but not without the need to feel a little sadness and grieve at how this impacted my life.

Day 13
(Trust)

Well, I showed up today—I suppose that is worth acknowledging. I don't know that I expected any stark realizations at this point, and it's not as though I had ever clarified what the objectives of this practice might be. I have no way to know where will go, so how, then, would I recognize when and if I arrived? No distinguishable signposts mark the way.

So, I could say that though I don't know where I'm going, I'm not lost! If I don't know where this might lead, I could be right on track with regard to where I'm at in the process and where it will take me—though, I must say, I find it disturbing, this sense of a lack of knowing and control. I could make this a problem, try and get back in the driver's seat, but I suspect some benefit comes in exercising trust and staying open to guidance from the process itself. So, here I am—right where I'm supposed to be— squarely upon and moving on down the road.

My original "plan" dictated that this practice occurs over a period of thirty days. Today, I received that, in fact, it will cover forty days. In my mind, where all gets reduced to that which seems reasonable and logical, I had already found the thirty-day framework daunting, so how would extending it to forty days prove helpful?

When the idea came up, it reminded me of biblical references—firstly, the rains in the story of Noah's ark falling for forty days and forty nights. A possible metaphorical/metaphysical interpretation is that of being far from visible land, and the need for the development of the inner resources necessary to go the distance. Secondly, the story of Jesus spending forty days alone in the desert.

Without having some sort of empirical evidence, I got the sense that the forty days represented an incubation period of some sort, and/or a time of spiritual initiation. These remained personal, intuitive interpretations, which I happened to believe showed the intentions of the teachings. As I had no precedent in my life, there came the need to employ a leap of faith with regard to what transpired here. This gave rise to my scepticism — faith? In what? To what end did this pursuit direct? There also occurred the not nearly as profound, but nonetheless, present question — why should I? What an interesting convergence of realizations, I'd become aware of at that moment. At this time of my life, I'd reached around about what some deem as "middle-aged," and sought to embrace the mysteries of life, the universe, and my part in it. However, what aspect of myself had stepped on the field of possibility to receive the guidance but a defiant child? Perhaps, in light of that insight, I could rule out (for the time being) a call from the U.N. begging me to undertake the role of world spiritual leader.

It did seem possible that this period of time in my life proved akin to preparing (ploughing) the field and planting the seeds. To continue with this metaphor, I recognized that while I had already looked over my shoulder at the one row I had walked (impatiently expecting to see already the fruits of my labour), I had begun to realize that the whole field had, in actual fact, become overgrown with weeds, which needed to get cleared. To put this into perspective, the farmer doesn't judge the field as bad or wrong, just that weeds exist. Rather, he/she accepts that work needs to get done to prepare the field for optimal growth.

To return this enquiry back to the realm of the sacred, I recalled that this morning undertaking got conceived by me (or through me) for me. No one asked (or told) me to do it, and no one cared if I did it or not. As an aside, I had a book in mind but had no idea if anyone would buy it (let alone read it). Could I find within me that which is the continued reason for (and perhaps is fed by) my upholding this commitment, not for the approval of others, not for the completion of a book (commercially viable or not), but just to honour, as sacred, something that had been taken on just by me for me?

I guess I shall find out.

Day 13 Questions
(Trust)

01) Do you consider yourself a trusting person?

02) Do you consider yourself trustworthy? (Not just to others but to yourself.)

03) Do you need to have all the information necessary to start something?

04) How able are you to go with the flow?

05) If presented with the opportunity to join an adventure for the afternoon with no further information, how likely is it that you would participate?

06) Would you step up for something (fill a vacancy) on the spur of the moment, never having done the task before? ("It's easy; we'll talk you through it!")

07) Do you believe (trust) in the unfolding process of life (the universe)?

08) Do you believe that no matter what, you will be all right?

09) Are you inclined to think, "I haven't done it before, but how hard can it be?" Or something more like, "I don't think I could ever do that"?

10) Think of experiences where you needed to trust and felt delighted with the outcome.

11) Think of experiences where trusting didn't result in an outcome you saw as favourable.

12) How do the outcomes of the past continue to affect your willingness to trust in the present?

13) Is a lack of trust limiting you in any of the areas of your life?

14) Are you willing to trust again? What would it take?

15) If past hurts exist, connected to trusting, are you willing to heal them?

16) Can you conceive of possibilities beyond the framework of your beliefs? (In the world and, in fact, for yourself?)

17) Can you trust your inner guidance/gut-feelings? If so, do you pay attention to them?

Sample Answer

The themes from a few of these questions, I touch on here.

This idea of trust presents the prospect of a rather extensive inquiry. For the sake of brevity, I will state up front that this will, by no means, offer a complete address of the subject.

I would say that hurts (real or imagined) and concern for my getting hurt again impacted an aspect of my ability to trust. Further examination reveals that it has less to do with trusting others, or events/circumstances, as it does with my ability/willingness to trust myself.

Repeated patterns around committing to a project, pursuit, or event and then bailing out, if done frequently enough, undermine my ability to trust myself. It sets off an inner dialogue and belief system that I don't keep my word, or that I never finish what I start.

Simple real-world examples of taking small personal risks can, incrementally, give me the experience of victories. This, in turn, builds trust. Trust in myself, trust in the process, and trust in life. Showing up and taking on what lies in front of me to do demonstrates that I can trust myself to do the necessary to take care of myself.

Again, with practice, I can learn to listen for, and to, my inner guidance; trusting that my highest good will get upheld.

I can practice letting go of expectations and attachments to outcomes. I can practice having little or no knowing before stepping out and learn to trust that I can handle whatever comes up along the way.

Notice the frequent use of the idea of practice. This implies and allows a trust to develop that, during my ongoing practice, I will relax my critical eye and self-persecution and acknowledge that I have courageously stepped out into unfamiliar territory, and if undesirable outcomes occur, I can both adjust accordingly and trust that I will exercise self-understanding and compassion. This could be said to be the practice within the practice.

Day 14
(Exploration/Expansion)

Thus far, it hadn't become clear to me whether I had received any discernable benefit from this morning practice. I couldn't claim attainment of emotional equanimity; on the other hand, however, I hadn't allowed the often-varying emotional upheaval I had experienced during this morning commitment to take me out either.

When I considered a previous state of being whereby I'd experienced little variance emotionally and would have felt hard-pressed to identify such feelings, even if I'd noticed, not to mention the awareness that my emotions varied and, at times, sat in the driver's seat, then I saw some measure of progress.

Even then, when I saw a hand-out from the Non-Violent Communications work I had practiced that listed examples of the spectrum of emotional flavours, it amazed me at the range, and led me to wonder how I got to that stage of my life with so little awareness.

It seemed a bit like my tongue-in-cheek synopsis of the education boys and girls must have received as children on the colour spectrum. My theory posits that boys were given one set of coloured pencils or crayons, and girls an entirely different set. I drew this conclusion from listening or trying to participate in adult conversations where colours got discussed and where I saw purple, but they told me it was fuchsia or, perhaps, violet, and maybe even magenta. I saw red, but, "No, my friend, it's crimson," and, "Wow, look at how blue the sky is," ... "Actually, it's somewhere between teal and azure." About then I would clamber for some form of stable ground and declare, "Well, at least I know that couch is beige." The reply, "Sorry to inform you, that's taupe." Frankly, I don't even think that's a real colour—I've gotten dragged through enough furniture stores to observe a wide range of colours that garner the hue of taupe—probably something someone came up with in marketing to put the coloured furniture with a dye lot, and an error got made (i.e. what the hell colour is that?—Ah, just call it taupe, mark it down a hundred bucks, and they'll think they're getting a deal!).

My point is that I must have gotten roughly the same emotional and colour palate in my education, which consisted of the primary colours (tangerine is a fruit, the colour is orange, and I realize that's a fruit too; in my world, oranges are orange—tangerines are orange, too, but they're not oranges—it's quite simple, though I'm not sure why apples, then, are not "reds," and bananas "yellows"). I might have to spend a great deal more than forty days in the labyrinth to determine that.

To add to the perspective-altering events of the last six months, I spent three months overseas in Europe (for the first time in my life). I visited seven different countries (including two that I only "visited" long enough for flight or mode of transportation transfers). The original intended destination was Ireland, which held the opportunity to participate with a group of people (internationally diverse) in a spiritual transformational workshop. In addition to this, I had come to explore my roots. My biological father came of Irish ancestry, so I would set foot on the homeland of my ancestors (which, in itself, gave a mind-blowing/altering experience). Through an administrative error on my part (or, perhaps, other powers came into play), I missed (by four hours) the opportunity to extend the return date on my flight, which meant I forfeited my return ticket but also that I remained relatively free in Europe with no return date. I then found myself in a position to (more or less) live in the moment and go where I felt drawn with next to nothing in the way of an itinerary.

I went to additional healing circles (in two more countries), visited sacred sites of personal significance, and attended two yoga retreats in Italy. All the while, people, opportunities, and circumstances presented in the most amazing ways. The most significant difference for me came in the fact that the events that unfolded appeared like those I had read of in inspirational books or heard others talking of. However, this actually happened to me, in my life—even as it occurred in the moment, my mind scrambled to make sense of what had happened. Life-long paradigms and belief systems crumbled before my eyes, both intriguing and bewildering, as well as extremely destabilizing. How could I reckon with such a thing?

Well, I'll tell you what this space cowboy did—certainly, I rolled with it while overseas, even though I felt dumbstruck on too many occasions to recall numbers, as I stayed too busy experiencing it to think much about it. Let me tell you, though, since coming back and trying to reconcile what I experienced, with long-standing beliefs and life experience and the current realities, I felt bewildered, to say the least. It gave a bit of a conundrum—my life could never be the same; however, I felt unsure of how to live in the new presentation.

I suppose it boiled down to realizing and then becoming more skilled at managing my fear of change or, perhaps, more accurately, letting go of further limiting beliefs that stood in my way of showing up fully and completely as the person I suspected had waited in the wings to make his debut.

Since coming home, my heart had gone from the peaks of love and elation to the abyss of abandonment—all in the course of a two-to-three-month relationship. I don't even think that is normal—whatever that is. As it happened, this personal melodrama overlapped a period of my current morning practice. Which had, in part, given me the opportunity to practice the exercise of continuing to put one foot in front of the other (literally) without (and, I emphasize *without*) ignoring the feelings and emotions associated with the crisis in the other areas of my life. A few precedents exist whereby turmoil of this variety brings the endeavours of others to a grinding halt.

I felt bewildered as to where to take my life vocationally while, at the same time, feeling the stress of being out of work. I had attended another transformational workshop, an ongoing study group (12 steps), and of course, the meditation itself (around the labyrinth and afterward), which all served to deepen this relationship with self and the inner world, which in many ways, had become more familiar to me than the outer. Of course, as this process unfolded, the self-knowledge that became available, I would rather have observed in someone else. Still, without facing the truth, those attributes that sullied my attempts toward excellence would continue to do so.

At times, it seemed that I would welcome the return of the self-assurance of unconsciousness. I knew this held no truth (or possibility), as I could not unknow what I had come to know, and to try and turn the other way would only create further suffering. It would bring a living hell without the protective shroud of denial, which meant that I must seek my bliss somewhere other than my ignorance.

As I continued to walk the spiral path of the labyrinth, I observed some newly released leaves making their descent to the path ahead. Each leaf (as well as the small-winged maple seed pods) engaged in some variation of a spiral flight path as it made its way toward the ground. It reminded me of the "Triple Spiral" found carved on the monolithic stones on ancient structures in Ireland. Some conjecture suggests that this might symbolize Birth, Death, and Rebirth. The ancient cultures in existence were said to have a deep connection and reverence for nature.

Infinite examples of this cycle of death and rebirth occur in the natural world, upon our planet, which we can see as a microcosm within the macrocosm of our universe and galaxy. All of this occurs within infinite additional galaxies, extending endlessly; the continued cycles of rebirth unfold ad infinitum. So, too, countless examples of the spiral appear throughout the natural world—many shells once the home of some of the ocean-dwelling invertebrates, and the shell carried on the back of the snail. Picture walking outdoors at just this time of year when a seemingly random breeze picks up fallen leaves and swirls them in the air before allowing them to return to the ground. Observe the way in which water exits from a sink or toilet as it disappears down the drain. We can go from the micro—the helix of human DNA—to the macro—the heavenly bodies seen through high-power telescopes or satellite images, and all configured in the form of a spiral.

Back here on planet Earth, I continued upon the spiral pathway of the labyrinth. Each outward step led me inward, where feelings presented, some sadness at a relationship changing (the cycle presents—birth, death, rebirth), and beginnings which could lead to endings leading again to new beginnings. The transitions didn't come necessarily so linearly and tidily on the inner landscape—I felt the loss of letting go of a vision that would not get realized, as well as the pain experienced from the illusion that love was lost, and the suffering created by attachment to the form of the relationship rather than the endless presence of love. Still, acceptance makes for a process instead of an isolated event. Likely, I could lessen the duration if I could return to trust and faith sooner. That which had been remains complete with no need to hang on. I had to make room and trust that the best was yet to come.

I'd become aware that today's walk had taken me spiralling within far beyond the current hurts, and the pathway led deep within my heart, which had served to warehouse many long-repressed feelings. Therein lay some of the errant code that I had placed upon the hard-drive of my unconscious, and which continued to steer my choices in the present. Dare I go there? It would seem I'd said yes to some process that had led me here—very likely prayed that this be so (though I'd qualify that by saying I didn't fully appreciate what I had asked for or what it would entail).

So, just as the smoke spirals from within the burning bonfire, I reckoned this journey toward greater self-acceptance and love would involve the unraveling of, and the death of, parts of the old self. The fires of purification and transformation had ignited from within. I visualized the loving energy of the earth itself entering through my feet as they walked the path—the energies spiralling through my being. That which no longer serves must get released—the skin of the proverbial onion peeling off in spiral layers and getting thrown upon the fire. All that remains is the spiral trail of smoke and ash returning to the heavens.

Before the Phoenix can rise, signifying rebirth, there first comes a death—from within the fire transformation—that which was, becomes ashes to ashes, dust to dust.

Day 14 Questions
(Exploration/Expansion)

01) Do you believe yourself to be naturally curious?

02) Does how things work interest you?

03) How about, why are things done a particular way?

04) Does the next corner on the road or the horizon inspire curiosity?

05) Do you enjoy trying new foods, meeting new people, or having new experiences?

06) What comes up for you when you consider self-exploration?

07) Could it (self-exploration) feel as intriguing and exciting as other forms of exploration?

08) Have you ever examined your beliefs, behaviours, and ideas? Where did they come from? Are they true? What makes them so?

09) How able are you to be with differences?

10) Do you believe that exploring yourself can lead to expansion?

11) Are you aware that there might be uncharted territory within yourself?

12) Have you ever done a comprehensive list of personal attributes?

13) Do you know yourself beyond the physical?

14) What does spiritual exploration mean to you?

15) Beyond missing the familiarity of home if travelling, can you embrace the different lifestyles, cultures, food, and worldviews?

16) Do you see exploring as being about finding something new or something familiar to you?

Sample Answer

Question 8—Have you ever examined your beliefs, behaviours, and ideas? Where did they come from? Are they true? What makes them so?

I remember, quite some time ago, I had gotten introduced to some of the ideas from "A Course in Miracles." Specifically, "Would you rather be right, or would you rather be happy?"

With very little consideration, I replied, "I'm happy when I'm right." That, indeed, gave a reflection of my consciousness at the time. As I consider that now, this wasn't just a belief in the need to be right; I also had a deep concern about being "wrong" (that side of the coin didn't become apparent to me for quite some time to come). The thing I came to realize about this propensity of avoiding getting it wrong—and the corresponding need to get it right—is that it meant it didn't take much of a stretch to self-righteousness as a way of being. After all, I was right. Once there, inappropriate use of, for example, anger became readily justifiable and rationalized—what a slippery slope.

So deeply entrenched had this either/or, right/wrong thinking become, that it became detrimental to relationships of all kinds. Of course, I didn't have the monopoly on it, but still, it proved necessary for me to see how it operated in my life. This model got impressed upon and reinforced early in life with rewards for good behaviour and punishment for bad. Then on to school, pass/fail for those that got it consistently right, and the honour roll. Yet, for those that didn't necessarily thrive in that system, there came solitary confinement in corridors or cloakrooms or, perhaps, humiliation in front of all your peers as you attempted to demonstrate your interpretation of algebra on the chalk board. Collectively, I'd say that gives a strong motivation always to be right.

This gives just one example of some personal exploration work I have done. Something else I had to come to realize along the way was that it is not helpful to judge what I discover about myself through the same "right/wrong" lens that in the previous example I had found to be a roadblock in my life. The point is to root out that which no longer works—not to punish myself for what I find. I can assure you that further self-admonishment is counter-productive—at least, that's my experience. So, I would encourage anyone taking on this practice to have compassion for themselves along the way.

I've found it so revealing, this business of examining my beliefs (not always a joyful ride), but nonetheless, expansion is made possible as I re-evaluate and release various limiting beliefs. It's useful to know where they came from (not for the purpose of blame but understanding). Do I still believe them? Why do I choose to continue to believe them? What am I afraid of that would make holding on seem like a good idea?

Day 15
(Simplicity)

Before rising from bed, I became aware of the sound of the first of the morning commuters, as one of the city's cross-town thoroughfares ran right past my bedroom window. After listening more intently, I recognized the sound of tires on wet roads and determined that it either had or continued to rain. Certainly, it would be my preference that the rain would subside; however, the practice would go on, rain or shine.

As I pulled out from my underground parking, the current weather status soon clarified—on went the windshield wipers.

I considered my good fortune, as I had left behind a warm apartment, gotten into a vehicle (with heated seats, no less), freely choosing to expose myself to the autumn weather as part of a personal inquiry. I remained well aware that some would have spent the night trying to stay warm and dry night after night, as they eked out their survival, living on the street. Very little separated my reality from theirs, and certainly, I didn't think myself better than them. I feel unsure that the average person realizes how rapidly they could find themselves in that circumstance.

If the illusory security of employment or health (or both) disappear, then these things don't prove as robust as we might have thought. I neither considered this alarmist nor pessimistic. I'd had some time to examine my identifying with the work I'd done and the impact of a considerable period without paid work. It gave a challenge to separate my personal value from my work in this North American society, but I believed it vital in terms of personal spiritual development. We cannot place value on such transient things as jobs, relationships, or social standing because if they should no longer exist, that can make the beginning of a significant downward spiral and personal crisis. Certainly, we expect to experience a loss — but personal worth, ideally, stands independent of circumstances and is strongly related to the resilience necessary to bounce back from personal crisis.

What I'm driving at is the need to distinguish things outside myself (relationships, possessions, work, etc.) as valuable with respect to comfort — in some cases, survival, others for my ability to thrive, but they don't denote my personal value as a human being. I understand this value is required to come from within — sometimes, that appears shaky ground. Just the same, if I were to rely on others to provide this reassurance, human fickleness and capriciousness would determine my value.

The fact that (at least, at present) I could have the relative security to spend time on this pursuit, gave rise to gratitude and humility. It hadn't become abundantly clear to me at that point what direction I would go with my life. I sincerely hoped the soul searching would lead to the discovery of a renewed purpose and fulfillment. Meanwhile, I had an awareness that not a great deal of anything permanent comprised that which acted as a buffer between my life of comfort and ease and becoming homeless. I had endeavoured to embrace simplicity in my life, but even still, I had considerably more than would fit in a shopping cart. I make this statement not to flaunt my wealth, but rather, to continue to ask myself how much is necessary?

As stated earlier, while in Europe, living out of a backpack, I got by well without everything that I'd left behind in my apartment. Somewhere lay the balance point, and I probably wouldn't get all the answers today. On those rare occasions when I did wander through a mall, I became overwhelmed by all the stuff. Year after year the shelves stood full. An item gets sold and replaced. The original item gets taken home, used or worn for a while, and then thrown in the garbage or, perhaps, finds its way to a second-hand store or garage sale, where it gets sold again.

I remained in it. Had participated in it to varying degrees, but no longer saw the point of it. (I don't suppose I ever did, but I got so busy participating that it didn't occur to me to question whether it had any point.) Frankly, I don't see how it's sustainable.

What might the archaeologists of the future conclude about our societies when they unearth landfills that occupy acres of land? "They produced, they consumed, and they discarded."? Sites excavated now from civilizations of the past seem to reveal relatively few items—a few tools, maybe weapons, domestic items, and jewellery (in the case of people of status). I might conclude that the absence of stuff might indicate that they spent more time living. If even one home of someone from the twenty-first century got discovered hundreds of years after becoming buried by a cataclysmic earthquake, then those working on the site might think that either there must have been dozens of people living there to warrant all that stuff, or the few people that lived there must have been so busy using it all. Little would they know that the truth came down to the occupants of the house spending all their time working to afford to buy the stuff, but had little time or energy left ever to use it. Or, once the novelty wore off, they went looking for the next distraction, and it all just sat on the shelf.

Back to matters at hand—I knew what was required and what my part was. The labyrinth needed sweeping, and I'd come here to do it and would do so, in the rain.

The air temperature felt warmer today, due to the cloud cover. Rain continued to fall, but only lightly. I set about sweeping the labyrinth surface and noticed that the leaves and path surface had a shiny appearance as though dipped in a lacquer finish. Due to being wet, the leaves also stuck to the pathway, requiring extra effort to clear. I became aware of some of the people walking through the churchyard—a few had become familiar (in as much as I recognized them), as they came through regularly.

Did my commitment to what I did in any way touch or, perhaps, inspire them? Not necessarily to do the same thing (though, of course, they could). Those that saw me each morning might think this my job—that I got paid to do it—and could grow surprised to learn that I just showed up of my volition. Then again, they might think me nuts! It might prove more impactful if people knew this discipline as entirely voluntary; however, the point wasn't to take it on for personal recognition. I saw myself as a one-man sociology / anthropology / spirituality "crash test dummy" and researcher. And hoped to find purpose and fulfillment through my self-inquiry, as well as inspiring others to do the same — to follow their path. I wouldn't presume I had all the answers but did know I wasn't the only one that had felt stuck in their life. For certain, value lay in continuing to look inward for my answers.

Those that witnessed the walking, the Qi Gong, or the meditation, day after day, might feel encouraged to undertake something that their hearts called them to do, whatever that might be — an art class, singing, more exercise, or anything that honoured the sacred within themselves. Perhaps I could serve simply in the capacity of, "if this guy can show up every morning and do this, then I could do (fill in the blank)." How beautiful that would feel.

The rain stopped before long, and I realized that I wanted to make a contribution to something that mattered — beginning with me.

Day 15 Questions
(Simplicity)

01) Have you every considered simplifying your life?

02) Where might you start?

03) Do you have a sense of what might define enough for you?

04) Have you heard of the idea of voluntary simplicity?

05) Have you considered "being and becoming" rather than just "having"?

06) Could less be more?

07) What might you have more time and energy for if you simplified in some areas of your life?

08) What if poverty (beyond just defining financial status) also described an inner consciousness?

09) Could simplicity be a means to realizing greater inner wealth?

10) What effect would consumption based more on genuine need have on day-to-day living?

11) Does simplicity have to be about scarcity?

12) Do you have difficulty saying no—resulting in over commitment?

13) Have you considered the time spent communicating (answering/reading emails, calls/text messaging, or watching TV)? Could you limit it, or even in some cases, eliminate it?

14) Do you spend any time alone (solitude) in quiet time?

15) Do you find yourself frequently eating on the go?

16) Could you feel okay with a smaller home? Smaller car? One less car?

17) Is your chief concern, there are not enough hours in the day?

18) Do you feel guilty doing nothing?

19) Do you frequently feel exhausted?

20) While driving, do you apply makeup, shave, talk on the phone, and/or eat breakfast?

Sample Answer

Question 8—What if poverty (beyond just defining financial status) also described an inner consciousness?

Question 13—Have you considered the time spent communicating (answering/reading emails, calls/text messaging, or watching TV)? Could you limit it, or even in some cases, eliminate it?

I suppose, on paper, at this stage of my life, that monetarily, I'm at an all-time low. Four years ago when my former wife and I parted ways, I worked full-time. Between the bank and us, we "owned" two properties (a 2500 sq. ft. townhouse, which we lived in, and a house with upper and lower suites, as a revenue property). Of course, either one of us could have assumed full ownership of either property—as it turned out, no one had any interest. At the time, I worked in a relatively new job that I had grave reservations about. So, as I considered the prospect of living on my own again, I didn't want huge mortgage payments or the complications of being a landlord to create the need to remain in that job (or require me to continue to need that income as a minimum just to stay afloat). So, we decided to sell it all and split the assets. This allowed me to make a decent down-payment on a small one-bedroom condo, which lowered my monthly overhead considerably. After giving that employer the benefit of the doubt, it turned out my gut-instinct was correct, and I resigned. That would have become far more complicated if I had kept the larger properties, and the likely outcome that I might have felt obliged to stay with the unsatisfactory work situation.

The neighbourhood where I live has a grocery store, pharmacy, coffee shops, and restaurants (within a five-to-ten-minute walk). The downtown business district takes a twenty-minute walk from home, and also a variety of other amenities stand within walking distance. I haven't eliminated the need for a car (or, I continue to choose to have one) but have managed to cut back on its use by quite a lot. I enjoy walking (well, I never really didn't enjoy it—I just often thought I didn't have time). It gives great exercise, feels relaxing, and I meet different people en route, and see things I don't notice while driving.

I don't suggest that anyone follow exactly what I do or tries to make someone wrong because they drive—just that some creativity and an attitude of what you can gain by simplifying goes a long way. Rather than doing it with the idea that I'm making a sacrifice, which proves more apt to breed resentment. While I no longer have the real estate portfolio I once did (and whatever that represented for my future), I gained considerable peace of mind, ease, and spaciousness to focus my attentions elsewhere (no yard maintenance, phone calls from tenants, etc.). Again, I don't say that these things are wrong. My life seemed up for some serious evaluation, and I wanted to simplify things so that I would have the ability to do that. As this made for an ongoing story, I couldn't say that, come retirement time, these choices wouldn't have impacted me. However, I couldn't keep living the way I had, and had no more guarantee that financial planning would remain intact come retirement or that I wouldn't have met an early demise had I stayed the previous course.

It was actually while visiting my former brother-in-law, long before the aforementioned scenario, that I felt inspired to give up cable (ah ...! What? No TV?) They had just a little bookshelf-size monitor and (at that time, a VCR) to rent and watch movies. For so long, I had felt frustrated with the cost of the cable service in relation to the quality of programming. Of course, I couldn't blame them for the fact that I could plunk myself down to watch "one show" and remain there hours later, sometimes not even switching the channel. Nor for the way the channel packages got bundled and marketed along with the constant saturation of commercials (which, again, I paid to receive). All this, collectively, became an irritant. Just the same, I sat, I watched, the bill came, I paid it, and on it went. Certainly, it gives a great example of an unconscious habit and repeating pattern (one of many—but that is another story). It seemed as though I'd become spell-bound, and then to go to this household with no cable, it gave the proverbial wake-up call (*hey, I don't actually have to continue this!*).

The additional time this opened up (and, of course, money), I utilized voraciously to begin reading personal growth books and attending seminars/workshops—what changes that invoked. It is neither necessary to give up TV nor take up reading; these offer just some examples of the changes that I brought about in my life. To simplify, it sometimes looks like giving up something I might have previously thought absolutely necessary (or unchangeable). It came down to doing less of something I didn't feel so keen about to make more time for what I really wanted to do.

As for other electronic gadgets, I do have a cell phone but use it sparingly. It's a cutting-edge iPhone at the beginning of my contract (which has been over for nearly a year). Of course, that means by industry standards that mine is now a dinosaur. I bought into the hype when the time came to replace my previous phone (which, frankly, I felt prepared to hang onto, but when I went to the outlet to see about a new battery, they laughed at me, indicating batteries were no longer available for my antiquated technology). So, I justify a Mac phone to maintain compatibility with my Mac computer, which I suppose is true as far as that goes, but largely, I don't care.

As I said, this current phone now approaches four years old— multiple new generations have come out (while I know precious little about the operation of the original). It's not that I couldn't learn more about them—I just don't enjoy the time spent doing so, relative to what I get out of it for having learned the particular function.

After a call to my service provider, I dumped the data package and other extraneous features and cut my bill in half. I have a computer to browse the net, email, etc. If I want to watch a movie, I want to do so on a screen bigger than a baseball card. For now, I can make a call or send a text—good enough. Oh, I know the day will come when this phone no longer holds a charge, and then I'll have a decision to make. But enticements such as, "this bad boy is where it's at, over one hundred thousand apps written for this!" don't sway me. My point is that I barely want the programs it comes with. And if the day comes when I need to tune my sitar or download images from the Hubble Space Station while searching for a coffee shop in Venezuela, I'll give them a call.

Day 16
(Connection)

Though I had an awareness of the number of consecutive days I had shown up for my practice, the number didn't seem the single most significant factor, if indeed it mattered at all. It added up to greater than halfway to the original commitment of thirty days, but neither of those numbers reflected the newly established vision. I suspected that this, for the most part, came down to no more than my mind trying to categorize, give meaning, and establish the arrival at some sort of landmark, rather than just acknowledging my journey and appreciating the scenery and discoveries along the route.

They say it takes twenty-one days to establish a habit, though I don't feel sure that I am looking to carry on with this entire practice as an ongoing habit. Aspects of it, I intend to carry forward. As well, I would hope to gain insights during the process that will serve to inform my life henceforth. As for quantifying events now, while it can be said that time and continuity will lend to refinement and deepening the practice, there is something to be said for quality versus quantity.

In that regard, the days I had completed didn't much matter, and neither did the days that lay ahead (I hadn't even shown up for them yet). That left today — this day, which while it gives a continuance of previous days of practice and represents a stepping-stone to a vision overall, in many ways it stands alone. All that I was and could bring forth, in a measurable manner, I applied to today.

If any habit could get carried forward, I saw the ongoing need for me to recognize and honour the sacred. It could not, nor should it, get ignored, in self or others. Though the paths may differ, they end up placed upon the heart of each — I cannot presume that someone on a path that differs from mine is going the wrong way. It is not until I place the focus on what unites us, as seemingly different members of humanity, that the illusion of separation falls away — where only love remains. Not always easy — it seems the "norm" is to focus on the perceived differences coupled with a lack of understanding, even ignorance and fear around the differences that can give rise to a greater degree of divisiveness.

The power of conformity proves insidious and pervasive. A conscious intention to seek and acknowledge the universal needs that define the humanity of someone that might appear different on the surface can offer a useful way to bridge the gap. Even endeavouring to adopt such a practice goes contrary to the societal status quo.

I recognized the challenges as I worked on improving my communication skills — I recognized the limits of the mindsets that I'd adopted over my lifetime — "either this or that," and, "right or wrong." I mentioned "bridges" earlier, and this polarized variety of thinking is more conducive for building walls, and not the least bit effective for connecting with others.

It's not about trying to point the finger at anyone in particular that I learned to communicate (or not communicate) this way — it had now become about seeing what didn't work and looking to evolve beyond the limits of old ideas. Gandhi said, "We must be the change we wish to see in the world." — When I considered this for myself, I thought of a point of view that had long influenced my behaviour. The principle I would have told you I upheld was inclusion. The unfortunate way I went about that was that, sometimes overtly, often covertly, I acted out intolerance of those I perceived to practice exclusion.

As I became more conscious of my wounds (fears) around abandonment/rejection, I recognized that perceived slights or criticism (even disagreements) would trigger this abandonment story and elicit defensiveness on my part or what amounted to prejudice toward the person or groups of people by whom I felt alienated. So, in effect, the stand I took in life was to behave with intolerance and exclusion of those I felt were intolerant and practiced exclusion. As I examined my life and attitudes, it seemed that precious few could join the ranks of my "inclusive" club — in fact, I pretty much made for its only member. No one else could get beyond the screening criteria and, frankly, I had equal (or greater) contempt for myself. And though for many years I attempted, unconsciously, to expel myself, I felt grateful today that I had proven unsuccessful and, through various means, had been afforded the opportunity to begin to wake up. I hoped that, subsequently, I would live long enough to truly stand and represent what I held sacred and, in doing so, would have a positive impact on the world within my sphere of influence. I had become clearer that I wanted to invest my energies in what I wanted in life and the world (not pitting myself against what I didn't want).

As I have mentioned, part of the daily practice involved a seated meditation after completing the walking of the labyrinth and Qi Gong exercises. I'd brought along a gardener's kneeling pad to sit on and set myself up under a large oak tree. A part of this portion of the practice entailed a walk toward humility (which I understand as the ability to see and accept the truth of who I was — not who I believed I was). In relation to other people, I proved no better than and no less than, but it went further than that. I believed in the interconnectedness of all life on the planet, and so I needed to consider myself right-sized in relation. This also applied with respect to the universe and the creative intelligence present throughout.

The oak tree figures prominently in the ancient spiritual paths of the Celts/Druids and felt significant to me due to my Irish ancestry. I believe that nature itself holds wisdom and teachings relevant to my life. We are, at our essence, one. To receive these lessons, I must present as teachable. I don't believe that humans are meant to dominate over nature — in fact, I believe the opposite to be true: We are interdependent.

So, my preparation for the day's meditation was to ask of my "hosts" to share with me their inherent wisdom. I also held myself in reverence to the spirits of the First Nations peoples, as the land I sat upon used to be their traditional home, and I only visiting. I gave thanks and asked permission to be there.

That particular tree had a formidable presence — apparently, the roots reached as deeply into the earth as the branches reached skyward. Hundreds of years elapse as one of this size evolves from the acorn that

176

once held this massive being as mere potential. Though all branches reach skyward, no two do so with anything that resembles conformity. Each seemingly twisting and contorting along its span as though some multiple barriers to its growth presented—however, to no avail, as it simply made a slight adjustment on its path and continued to fulfill its preordained intention to develop. Deeply grounded and rooted here on Earth. At the same time, the branches form the intricately woven antennas that reach toward the heavens, constantly collecting life energy and wisdom.

A closer look at the bark that enveloped its form revealed the deeply contoured complexion carved by time itself, each a testimonial of dues paid to acquire the wisdom of the ages. This tree's life began long before I decided to sit myself at its base, and it may conceivably live long beyond the time I leave this Earth. It had been a presence on this land throughout the various transitions that had occurred—silently witnessing all that transpired in its midst—a demonstration of life itself. Yet it remained the man-made edifices that house or become the recipients of any sort of reverence. The mighty oak, which had survived for all these years (though protected by endangered species legislation), could get felled at any time by the fickle whimsy of humans—if they decided, for instance, its canopy blocked sunlight from entering the sanctuary through the stained-glass window. Under the auspices of progress, the protection status could get overridden with a story that the tree had become diseased. At which point the ancient timekeeper would prove no match for the city-sanctioned, chainsaw wielding expert.

Truly, even the pseudo-awareness that there exists on the planet endangered species (comprised of a small percentage of the overall animal kingdom) proves misleading. The practices and attitudes of the modern world, which have at their roots power, control, and greed, might more accurately place all life on the endangered list.

I could see no end to self-proclaimed expertise cited as justification for such practices, such as scientific consultation presented to bolster various decisions. Widespread access to the Internet makes more information available to more people than ever before. Yet there is often lacking, in these decisions, anything like wisdom. Certainly, greater minds than mine have addressed technological development forwarded in the name of progress, but that lacks anything in the way of conscience. That it has been said before does not, in any way, diminish its truth or relevance. It is not just an old idea now out-dated. To ignore the wisdom is to invite the inevitability of the consequences. I believe that to pick up a newspaper or watch the news on television quickly bares witness to this.

I also considered this from the perspective of one who has gone from a life lived completely unconsciously. I don't refer to moral conscience. Many of the choices I had made proved misguided. Rather, I mean actions performed with an absence of forethought to consequence to others, my surroundings, and ultimately, to myself. I am clear as to the impact this has had and, though the only person I have any power to change is myself, by merely considering this unconsciousness, multiplied to represent a varying sized collective consciousness such as could be found in a community, region, or country, the widespread implications become apparent. Again, it is not my purpose to point at others—each must make their assessment. It seems a full-time job becoming accountable for myself and determining in what way I can show up in the world in a way that is far less self-centred.

As I sat, I felt grateful for all the teachers that had come into my life—in my case, I felt unsure that it was entirely due to "when the student is ready the teacher will appear." It might be more like, "I've got a great deal to learn." I saw no point in lamenting over why not before now, and just embraced that the time had come now.

Day 16 Questions
(Connection)

01) What is your current level of connection to yourself? (Physical, mental, emotional, and spiritual.)

02) Do you see your relationship to others as one of us-and-them or we? (Neighbours? Community? Nationally? Internationally?)

03) What about the relationship of humans with nature? (Plants, trees, animals, air, and water.)

04) What are you doing well that fosters your feeling of connection?

05) What could help you feel more connected? (To self and others.)

06) Have you ever tried any form of meditation?

07) Can you see beyond differences to a place of connection? (Do you feel willing?)

08) Why does exclusion exist? Is it necessary?

09) How do you feel if you believe you have been excluded?

10) Have you ever considered the disconnection from self that might occur when following the crowd? Does it matter?

11) How do qualities like empathy and compassion come into play in your life?

12) Do you know what it is to listen deeply?

13) How does it feel to be heard — truly heard?

14) Do you spend any time discerning/listening to the call of your heart?

15) If you found yourself in the habit of putting others first, what would it take to give your needs some priority?

16) Have you ever considered how, in upholding your beliefs/needs, you may create disconnection with someone else?

17) Are the motivations of divide and conquer, continual competition, and consumption working? For whom?

18) Is there a better way to coexist?

19) What do you think about the idea that if you hurt another, you hurt yourself as well?

20) Does anyone win in the true sense if someone else or a large group of others loses?

Sample Answer

Question 1—What is your current level of connection to yourself? (Physical, mental, emotional, and spiritual.)

I guess, like everything else, this idea of connection could be seen on a continuum. I can think of a time, for example, many years ago now when I had gone for the first time to a practitioner of some form of massage. This would be at a time in my life that I thought I would achieve nirvana exclusively through the physical. I went to the gym and ran, and consumed all sorts of nutritional supplements in search of the magazine-cover physique (which I ended up successful at attaining). Ironically, the need for the massage came, in part, from muscle strain from exercising. So, there I lay on the massage table, and the woman picked up my leg by my foot and said, "It's okay; I've got it."

I replied, "I know that. I'm aware that you're holding my leg."

She said, "Yes, but I want you to give it to me—relax your leg; you're trying to help me."

At this point, I grew confused and, maybe, ever so slightly annoyed, and answered, "I am relaxed. Go ahead and do your thing."

"No, actually, you're not. Just let go and relax."

The likelihood of my relaxing had become increasingly unlikely as my irritation rose (not due to anything against this individual, more from a complete lack of understanding of what she wanted). I said, "What do you mean, let go? It's my leg. It's attached to me."

"Just let it go limp—give me the full weight of your leg; I can handle it."

I don't think it came down to a case of not believing her (though I'm sure I could have, unconsciously, assessed her, upon first meeting, as being of fairly small stature and therefore not too strong—if there were any question of that, she certainly laid that to rest soon after beginning the massage). It would seem that even when I tried to give her my leg, she continued to tell me that I hadn't.

In hindsight, this pointed out my complete lack of awareness with respect to my body (as evidenced by me thinking my leg relaxed, and she telling me that I held my leg up). The other thing at stake was trust. I wouldn't have spoken of my experience at the time, indicating that I didn't trust her and, certainly, would have never told her that, but trust definitely made for an issue. If I were to unpack this matter somewhat, my physiology presented with many of the qualities that comprised my thoughts and beliefs: Resistance, immobility, rigidity, and fear. The list goes on. The more I study holistic models of our being, the more I realize this stands to reason, as there is no separation between these various aspects (contrary to perspectives that would suggest physical manifestation of symptoms begin and end in the physiology). I don't look to discredit any particular school of thought but simply share my experience and what my journey led me to view as being possible while exploring life's mysteries and seeking the truth.

As I examine my life through this more comprehensive lens, a far different picture emerges.

Therefore, physical symptoms can have a connection with, and point to, corresponding energies in my beliefs, which in turn, has an effect on emotional responses and, of course, entails a spiritual component as well. The inclination of medical science and its practitioners in the Western world seems to be to compartmentalize the human being within the physical realm. Then the approach becomes to target the symptoms (which represent only the tip of the iceberg). Left unattended are the underlying causes and effects, which comprise the considerable mass of the iceberg, and which remains unseen below the surface.

Without the same comprehensive analogy, I can assure you that my knowing of the emotional and spiritual aspects of my being had grown equally estranged. If one considers the implications of that, how would it be possible to enjoy anything like wellness or peace when I had been so completely oblivious to such a significant portion of myself?

This, of course, left the mental faculties. Here, I found my refuge. Without exaggeration, it was as though my consciousness lived only from the neck up (the body had a use for providing transportation for the head). To be clear, this refuge (mental construct) provided, for a necessary period, emotional safety. But there would come a time when the refuge, its walls built to withstand the most ardent attempts to penetrate it, would become a prison that denied access to such qualities as intimacy, connection, passion, vitality, love, and joy. Thus began the arduous prospect of dismantling the walls.

Day 17
(Self-Love)

Another day within which I considered the sacred—what would my life look like if everything I approached, I did with respect and reverence? In other words, not restricting the recognition of the sacred only for specific times and practices, but instead, to look upon everything as though no such things as ordinary tasks exist: No ordinary people—no ordinary moments. The idea excited me on one level while, at the same time, seeming somewhat daunting. I would have liked to think of myself as fairly consistently conscious, but the truth is, I couldn't, not in all moments. Still, the more I embraced change, then the more I might realise a vision of personal transformation in all areas of my life. Many circumstances had existed where I had remained for the sake of security or fear of change. I'd had plenty of experience of living my life seeing through the eyes of resignation and boredom. The thing is, as I considered that, not at all times did that situation seem appropriate. More accurately, I deluded myself through rationalization that the situation was acceptable. To remain in these circumstances, it became necessary that I check-out in some way—to abandon my truth to the point where I no longer knew what it was.

This took me back to the idea that the sacred came down to a personal choice and required a daily decision to continue to uphold it. I pondered the idea of my needs and ensuring they get met, as well as the personal responsibility necessary for this to occur.

This could make for a challenging path to walk, considering the cultural consensus toward self-sacrifice. How then, could I assure a balance between not becoming completely self-absorbed and not becoming so concerned for the needs of others that my needs get neglected detrimentally? How many people gave of themselves beyond their capacity?—Thus creating an ever-increasing personal deficit for the sake of keeping the job that allows them to eke out their survival.

When those in economic think-tanks consider the ongoing sustainability of continued usage of non-renewable natural resources, do they consider how sustainable those in the workforce will continue to be? Who wins with all this self-sacrifice? All this dissatisfaction and burnout, at the very least, contributes to high employee absenteeism (either abuse of sick time or legitimate illness).

I worked in health care for many years as a Licensed Practical Nurse. Now, here is an environment where the accepted norm is self-sacrifice. A closer examination reveals that, nearly always, someone else's needs become more important than that of the frontline care-giver. Don't get me wrong, I recognize the need to provide a service and that the patients of any given facility wouldn't be there if they didn't require some level of care. However, the system is dependent upon, and places a great deal of pressure on, those working there who deliver the care. Where the workplace culture upholds a "patient comes first" philosophy, that places the care provider in an ever-increasing self-compromising position. Budgets get cut—staff gets cut—and, still, the workload remains. These constraints mean that fewer people try to do the same or more work. Overtime becomes an expectation. People get tired. They get coerced to work additional shifts.

Of course, each remains free to choose to say no; however, they then face getting labeled by management and coworkers as a non-team player. The day-to-day stress of this peer and systemic pressure has many succumb to choices that don't represent their best interest. At what point is the ability of the care provider compromised to ensure competent judgment and care? One cannot effectively care for another if running on empty themselves. Nor, frankly, can they accurately assess their ability to do so, as the faculties to make that assessment fall subject to the same exhaustion level, and therefore, they would be trying to determine their fitness to perform their job through senses dulled and compromised by the same fatigue they need to assess.

It is my view that the health field needs to become far more proactive and aware of the wellness and care directed at, and available for, those providing the care. Wellness must begin at the grassroots—with the frontline workers. Then, and only then, can it fan out from there and extend to the patients.

At the very least, this phenomenon proves costly to the employer—through employee sick time and reduced productivity. What of the cost to society overall? In what ways does this feed the mental/emotional breakdown that leads to violence, whether in the workplace or at home? I no longer talk specifically about health care but now include any place of employment. Again, I refer to the news where stories appear of disgruntled former employees returning to their workplace and killing or wounding others and then themselves. How many people are walking the line approaching breakdown? Of course, other extenuating realities could exist, and the cycle I speak of doesn't always lead to such catastrophic results, obviously. Still, what's to stop multiple people from reaching their wit's end all at once? Maybe violence would not be their choice.

At that point, I considered the previously unthought-of scenario in the U.S. whereby hundreds of people unable to continue with their mortgage payments simply walked away from their homes. If this were possible, what's to prevent hundreds of people from walking away from their jobs? The "I Hate Mondays" consciousness gets raised to a crescendo, and people—en mass—just keep right on walking, past the door of their workplace. The economic system seems to presume that people will continually consume and, within that, employers assume their employees will continue to show up to work. The employees themselves assume the job will remain there as long as they choose to hold it, and so they spend and consume accordingly. That's a great deal of assumptions at work. Large employers layoff hundreds, even thousands, of people all the time—done (seemingly) with impunity and lack of regard for each of the lives impacted. The scene is set, placing the employer in the driver's seat, due largely to the inequity present in the power dynamic—i.e. people's livelihood is at stake, and so there has to be a certain assurance that they will continue to show up. But, really, if people in other parts of the world will take to the streets by the thousands (risking their lives, in some cases) to protest various regimes, it could happen here, couldn't it? Or, have we become so addicted to big-screen TVs and cell phones that, without thought of dispute, we'd just endlessly join the ranks in the commute?

It seems to me, though I'm not a global economist (the understatement of the century—no one will ever come to me for financial guidance), that the world economy is a precarious house of cards. It seems quite likely that more people than not have become so busy in it that they don't realize its illusory nature or how quickly it could unravel, just like yanking that loose thread on the cuff of your sweater, and it becomes sleeveless.

Of course, what do I know? Many would say of my current situation, "If you would go out and get a job, you wouldn't have time to walk in circles around a labyrinth posing such inane questions." They could have it right, but then they'd be saying so, while in the next breath, uttering the all too familiar mantra, "I owe, I owe, so off to work I go." It could be said that this is walking in circles, too—but maybe just by me, the guy walking in the labyrinth.

Oh my God; I just realized, what if? No, couldn't be … had I grown disgruntled? Naah! Perhaps just moderately vexed. It had more to do with me wanting to be the change I wished to see in the world. This determining my path felt a little lonely sometimes. I mean, really, seventeen days of walking this labyrinth and no one has offered to join me. Many walked through the churchyard; they avoided eye contact, though (maybe they felt afraid that whatever I had, they didn't want to catch it). Who knew labyrinth walking and leprosy had something in common besides beginning with the same letter?

At least the Jedi Knight talked to me (at least, I thought it was him—back when he wielded his light-sabre-cum-leaf-blower, he wore a face shield and ear protectors, which made recognition challenging). He picked up around the grounds, so I felt pretty sure it was him. He wished me a good morning, and we engaged briefly about the weather (often, I'd considered such discussion trite and pointless). After the thunderous silence, interrupted only by my thoughts, his voice gave a welcome interlude.

I'd become no stranger to the challenge that presented at times to connect with others. What if this made the sum total of our conversation? Did all discourse have to be revolutionary or extraordinary to be worthwhile? No ordinary moments—no ordinary people. I had no idea what the impact of my speaking with this fellow might entail—and, let's face it, it's not without impact that he spoke to me. Just another ordinary miracle—two people with what seemed disparately different objectives reached across the void. The result? If I'm not mistaken, I think connection just happened there.

Maybe next time, I might revolutionize my human evolution and introduce myself.

Day 17 Questions
(Self-Love)

01) What do you think about the idea of self-love?

02) Do you love yourself?

03) Is it okay to love yourself?

04) In what ways do you go about loving yourself?

05) What prevents you from getting the love you need?

06) What is the relationship between love and personal responsibility?

07) Do you believe yourself worthy of love?

08) Are there behaviours of yours that might be seen as non-loving?

09) Can love occur in solitude?

10) How easy (or difficult) is it for you to ask for what you need?

11) When you hear no, or a rejection occurs, who does the rejecting?

12) How open are you to giving and receiving positive reflections?

13) How important is the approval of others?

14) Observe your self-talk—how do you speak to yourself?

15) Do you honour commitments to self?

16) Would you welcome a friend in your life that treats you the way you treat yourself?

17) Can you see that saying yes to self can be saying no to another?

18) What importance do you assign to your needs? What about your needs in light of becoming aware of the needs of another?

19) Do you feel responsible for meeting the needs of someone else?

20) Can (and will you) celebrate your successes? How able are you to let go of your failures? (What does failure mean to you?)

Sample Answer

Question 3 — Is it okay to love yourself?

Question 7 — Do you believe yourself worthy of love?

Question 8 — Are there behaviours of yours that might be seen as non-loving?

Question 14 — Observe your self-talk — how do you speak to yourself?

For me, it has proven useful to become familiar with what self-love means. It is not at all about becoming completely self-absorbed, conceited, or — in psychological terms — narcissistic. Rather, it is about knowing myself deeply and accepting all that I come to know — complete with faults and imperfections. It lies in having the ability to be true to myself, developing a healthy respect for myself, and coming to know and value my needs, and then taking responsibility in getting them met.

Considering self-love from this perspective, I determine that not only is it okay, but for me, it is highly desirable. Has it always been true for me? Yes. The need for it has always had a presence. And, no, I haven't always behaved lovingly toward myself. Therefore, both my awareness of when and in what ways I have come up short and learned to live differently have expanded over time.

Where worthiness for love is concerned, I have to say that I spent considerable time in circles of influence and environments where the discussion never came up. Had someone asked me, I would have likely responded with a yes (more from the standpoint that I wouldn't have openly suggested that I deserved not to be loved or to be treated poorly). So, yes, of course I'm worthy. The evidence in my life, however, would collectively point to quite a different conclusion. I knew nothing of healthy boundaries — lived as though love and approval sourced from outside myself. My sense of self had become such that it ebbed and flowed with the approval and disapproval of others. Absent was an ability to stay congruent or consistent, as, foundationally, my sense of self, I'd built upon quicksand rather than firm bedrock. Trust me; it feels so difficult to remain true to myself when I have a lack of certainty about who myself is, combined with a constant want for the approval of others.

This underlying low self-esteem (which, for me, operated unconsciously) became the defining element in my life. Unquestionably, it provided an aspect of my addiction. It formed part of the inner pain that I attempted to numb. Of course, initially coming to recognize that dysfunctional pattern created a backlash of pain and further erosion of self-esteem. It also shaped my confidence with respect to my ability to seek higher education, and became a factor in the work I chose, relationships I formed, and how I allowed myself to be treated. For years, I felt convinced that this all took place outside myself — it just happened to me, and I had nothing to do with these realities. I'd turned into the consummate victim.

To come to know myself in this regard has proven a lengthy process and, even within the process, I would fall into self-condemnation for what I learned about myself. Gratefully, as the process continues, I have learned and developed the capacity to return to a place of self-acceptance. I have a willingness to embrace compassion and empathy for myself as I move forward. I have found self-exploration painful at times. A gentle approach is the key. If I continually get down on myself for what I discover, it just increases the pain; not an effective strategy to motivate myself for change. It remains of great importance, therefore, to stay vigilant with respect to my self-talk. It might seem self-evident that *trashing myself is not okay* (I wouldn't let someone do that to a friend of mine), but I've had to learn to befriend myself and at least lighten up (ideally, eliminate) on limiting beliefs and destructive self-criticism.

As I hope I have conveyed here, it makes for a process, and one not necessarily linear in nature. I have become aware, for example, that though I still have work to do, I have made considerable progress evidenced by that fact that I am willing to disclose (in writing, no less) these aspects of my journey. A time existed in which I would not share of myself at all (from what I would have considered constituted a negative light), as surely, it would lead to rejection. Now, I feel confident that I can handle the rejection. I ask, and the answer comes back as no. Sometimes, the door I knock on remains locked. Sometimes, the door opens, only to slam shut again.

However, if seen from another perspective, I look to develop the courage to ask while holding no expectation that the answer will come back as a yes. If what seems at stake is an ongoing need of mine, then it's up to me to creatively arrive at another way to meet it. Up for healing is any continued mistaken belief that getting a "no" offers a direct reflection of my value/worth.

I have grown far more comfortable with my humanity, and even find my foibles humorous at times.

Day 18
(Choices)

It would appear that my reference to the Noah story, made earlier, regarding switching the timeframe of this morning practice from thirty to forty days was about to get made more real for me — the rains had arrived.

Didn't I wish that I could wax romantically about how the gentle drizzle caressed my cheeks as though a great cosmic atomizer spritzed me with an invigorating mist. Not so — this was frickin' rain pelting down with such ferocity it hit the ground and bounced back up. Not at all unusual for this time of year; in fact, dare I say, overdue. Good thing I remained alone, for if I made that comment aloud in a cross-section of locals, they might crucify me. Now, where had the "Jedi" gone? We shouldn't miss the opportunity to discuss this weather system. Maybe tomorrow?

Though not much in the way of fallen leaves to sweep, it took considerable extra effort to clear what was there because they had grown so soaked and stuck to the labyrinth surface. I became aware of the feeling of frustration coming up. This would make a good time to look for and let go of any perfectionist influences. In all seriousness, I just needed to see the pathway and had no need to make the surface spotless. Sure, it looked nice when all bare and clean, but according to what? I didn't discount the satisfaction of a job well done, but I'd made a distinction between that and the tyrant I discovered that resided within me that set a standard that no one (including me) could live up to.

This made for the perfect time to make the distinction for myself with regard to excellence versus perfectionism. I recognized that my desire to be seen as perfect or doing well had not been motivated by valuing excellence or competence or even the satisfaction of putting forward my best effort. It had stemmed from feeling flawed myself and hoping that my accomplishment and, perhaps, the accompanying accolades would, somehow, compensate for that. Of course, they didn't, and any satisfaction proved short-lived as the underlying dissatisfaction I felt quickly invalidated any compliment.

So, the question became, had I established the standard of excellence as a part of honouring the sacred? (With regard to the practice itself.) Did it make any difference? If the standard reflected my inherent need for accomplishment or quality/competence, then I honoured my sacred needs (which I would endeavour to honour in all areas of my life, not just in this instance). Conversely, if I held myself to the same standard, but the underlying motivation remained that I would berate myself with self-criticism if I found it not perfect, then the sacred within me would not get served. It would then become more like my getting enslaved to the emotions generated from a belief system that no longer served me.

The sacredness of the practice got lost for me at that point, as I also held my stand that I created no suffering in its observance. It may well involve discipline to uphold and adhere and, at times, a conscious choice to show up (versus some other distraction that seemed more attractive in a given moment). I say choice rather than sacrifice as, with the latter, I felt unsure whether it carried the energy of an empowered free will. More like martyrdom — i.e. "look what I'm giving up to follow this practice or commitment to myself." Without question, following my path may seem lonely (which, I suppose, depends on what one makes aloneness mean). It could reflect the way I related to myself, and if I felt okay with my company and the pursuit I'd engaged in, I could find perfect contentment in being alone while doing it. If I felt some sadness in conjunction with aloneness, I might need to check in with myself. Perhaps the feeling stemmed from a lack of connection to self, or maybe the time had come to connect with someone else. It hadn't, necessarily, got anything to do with the activity itself. Abandonment of my path to serve the feeling in my experience wouldn't prove effective in bringing about long-term fulfillment. Actually, it would bring about more pain.

I realized that sometimes I created a busyness to avoid the feeling. It looks good on the surface, with all kinds of productivity going on, but truth be told, was misdirected. This had become well accepted cultural strategy, as someone seen as busy often gets credited with being successful and ambitious. Again, it comes down to underlying energy — did my passion and enthusiasm drive me? Or did it have more to do with the fact that if I stopped for even a short while, I would get faced with myself? Then, I would need to recognize that this went on and decide whether this avoidance served my greater good.

I had dressed for the weather, so felt warm to begin with, but the steady assault of rain soon soaked through my clothing. While doing the Qi Gong exercises, I could hear the rainfall around me, which is (or should I say, could be) a soothing sound — after all, relaxation CDs exist with rainfall recorded. Here, I had the real thing. I felt mildly irritated due to the wetness, and so the calming effect of the rainfall got lost on me. Instead, I looked forward to the hot tea in my car that I'd brought to drink once I had finished. Oops, there went the moment. I determined that this would not turn into an instant-gratification experience, and that it might have untold benefit in the bigger picture. However, right then, it just seemed really wet.

I went to sit under a big cedar tree to meditate (rather than the usual oak tree), hoping the boughs would provide more shelter from the rain — which worked to some degree. Still, I found it wet and muddy below the tree. I decided the attributes of flexibility and reasonableness worth considering within this exploration. To get soaked to the skin and then get sick would seem contrary to the sacred in the form of self-care. Perhaps an equal danger existed to a sacred practice when dogmatic adherence replaced the in-the-moment guidance of intuitive input.

Translation — an abridged meditation and I'd get out of there!

Day 18 Questions
(Choices)

01) What part do your choices play in your day-to-day experience of life?

02) Do you believe that your choices can change your experience?

03) Do you believe you can choose the experience you have?

04) Do you have any choice?

05) Can you see doing nothing as making a choice?

06) Is doing nothing a valid choice?

07) Can you think of examples of choices shifting within an on-going commitment?

08) What determines for you when it's time to choose the end of a commitment?

09) Is it any less a commitment if the parameters get expanded through choice so that the terms of the original commitment have now changed?

10) Can you make a distinction between the circumstances you find yourself in and what you think about it?

11) Would declaring a conscious choice with regard to a given circumstance have any impact on how you relate to your circumstance? (I.e. "This situation feels challenging and not entirely to my liking, but I choose to remain here see where this is going," versus, "I don't like this and there is nothing I can do and I am stuck right here.")

12) Do you think you are obliged to stick with a choice once you have made it, or could you choose again?

13) What does choosing response over reaction mean to you?

14) Can you see a correlation between personal freedom and saying, "I choose"?

15) What happens if you acknowledge that you always have and will make choices?

Consider the outcomes of the different choices you make. Can you take responsibility for those choices? (Whether it goes right or wrong.)

Sample Answer

Question: 1—What part do your choices play in your day-to-day experience of life?

Question 2—Do you believe that your choices can change your experience?

Question 3—Do you believe you can choose the experience you have?

The important distinction I am learning to make is that I might not have created a particular circumstance or event in my life but, certainly, create the story I tell about it. So, for example, if I continually evaluate my life through the lens of what is missing, I can lose sight entirely of what is actually present in my life. I can decide I no longer want a particular circumstance in my life without necessarily making it bad or wrong that I currently find myself in these circumstances.

It may be a process to arrive at that perspective but, certainly, it will remain bad and wrong if I continue to see it as such. I don't suggest that certain feelings might not be present, either directly from the circumstance or, perhaps, repressed feelings that rise as a result of the current situation being similar to the original event. So, I can have feelings generally associated as negative (either by myself or others), which could make it more challenging to allow and express them, or I can just let them be. Often, I might find myself in a stew of sorts, which includes denial, unconsciousness—perhaps a gradual recognition of feelings—and a choice to express them, resulting in further clarity. I don't claim fluency with these practices or that they go cleanly in a linear manner with no need to ever look back. But there is, undoubtedly, some relief available to me through an attitude adjustment and a willingness to change my mind. At times, I fully realize that many people in the world would feel happy to be in my circumstance — while at other times, I can think I am so hard done by. I might want the situation to change, but much as anything, I need to see it differently, which could transform the situation entirely, or at least, it lessens my suffering while I go about planning and implementing the necessary changes.

Day 19
(Peace)

It pleased me to see, upon awakening this morning, that the deluge had subsided. It had dawned a bright and clear morning. (What a difference a day makes.) I still bathed in the afterglow of yesterday (the date, November 11, 2011 — 11/11/11). The day known here in Canada as "Remembrance Day," which honours the veterans (and civilians — perhaps the latter, in my personal acknowledgement) that died in various wars — far too many wars, in my mind. It saddens me, the tragic loss of lives. Perhaps I haven't reached a consciousness whereby I have the willingness to relinquish my survival. I wonder if everyone on those battlefields felt clear why they were there — if even the reasons they were told they were there are true. Of course, many of these situations have long and complicated histories. There has been, and continues to be, oppressive regimes operating in the world.

How, then, does the attempt at violent eradication resolve the problem? My concern is that, in doing so, there is so much collateral damage (the term conceived to represent those who had wanted no part of this insanity; however, they ended up in the wrong place at the right time and, consequently, lost their lives). How does that not create in the mind of the survivors a vengeance consciousness? I suppose it remains equally possible that they might be more profoundly convinced by the pain of their loss that the atrocities of war must not get repeated and, thereby, become a cause for peace. Does it have to repeatedly unfold this way? Clearly, parts of my story make it obvious that I haven't always had much in the way of a reverence for life (mine or anyone else's), and I do recognize the depth of conviction that these men and women embraced and laid their lives on the line to uphold. Maybe this gives an example of the need to allow oneself to become fully consumed by something bigger than oneself — perhaps, this doesn't always result in loss of life but, rather, becomes the defining catalyst for that life, instead of just self-preservation.

I have to acknowledge that my life, when deeply examined, could be said to have been more about my survival, and what I wanted, than to serve a greater cause. As you know, I spent many years working in health care as a nurse and, though there certainly was a service component inherent in that work, and I supported many people, I didn't feel called to the work. Therefore, my personal dissatisfaction meant, increasingly, that I had more difficulty hiding my frustration — particularly with co-workers. In hindsight, it might not have mattered what I did — I had a need to find peace, and it would have to come from the inside out.

I don't accept that violence offers the only way to resolve differences and conflict. What if, to begin with, differences got embraced? What if they gave rise to curiosity and inquiry rather than fear and contempt? I believe that continuing to develop and stockpile new technology for the purpose of warfare continues to hold as a reality the next war. If I walk around carrying a knife or gun (which I can't do legally in Canada anyway), then what does that say about the level of my fear? Wouldn't those in my

206

community see it as preferable that I deal with the fear? If I feel that scared, what would it take before I thought the use of one of those weapons had become warranted?

What of the need for the safety of everyone else? Would my neighbourhood become safer because I carried my knife? How long before word got out? And then the neighbours thought, "He's got a knife — I'd better get a bigger knife—maybe a bat. Let's see him get close enough to me to use that knife when I start swinging my 'Louisville Slugger!' Better still, we'll organize a group in the neighbourhood and will all carry bats—maybe a couple of machetes." This does not give cause for concern, though, because these machete-wielding blokes are the "good guys" and intent on upholding freedom and peace in the neighbourhood. I can see the scenario:

"We saw that Rob character the other day — he shaves his head and has two earrings (in the left ear — don't know what that means, but it can't be good)." And, "He took out his knife in broad daylight (well, ya, it was a Swiss Army knife, but this is Canada) — what was he doing?" And, "Well, he had the scissors out and was trimming his fingernails but, obviously, that was just a diversion, he was listening to some old song called 'Imagine' — I think he's delusional. I mean, really? Imagine? Let's get real!! Did I mention he's left-handed? He was sitting near the playground. What if all the kids started to think they could use their left hand? First, we got to keep an eye on that guy — stick to him like stink on a skunk, and then we go upstream and sever his supply line. That's right, the 'Swiss.' From now on, those in the Neighbourhood Libertarians will no longer purchase or consume that cheese (it's full of holes, you know — would you eat an

207

apple that's full of holes? I rest my case). This is not only a neighbourhood threat but also a direct threat to the economy and sovereignty of Canada. Are you with us or against us?"

I have to admit that, in the grander scheme of things (i.e. the forwarding of human evolution), I can't say that all the wars and lives lost weren't necessary to create a shift in consciousness. It just seems that violence results in more violence—attack brings on retaliation. So, I work at holding a vision of peace.

Even having done my regular morning meditation, I sat again at 11:11 a.m. and lit a candle and meditated, holding in my mind and heart a feeling of gratitude for and honouring the lives lost. Also that they did not die in vain—that peace would become the way of the future.

The current date also had great significance with respect to consciousness and paradigm shifts—many different perspectives exist, and likely, no one knows for sure what the outcome might be. For all I know, maybe the inspiration to take on this morning practice of mine had gotten brought about through these shifting energies. If nothing else, if hundreds of thousands of people, on this day, came together collectively in circles or individually, and focused on such higher ways of being such as love, forgiveness, connection, and healing, it would have to be better than everyone thinking, "Dog eat dog."

That evening, I attended a Bhakti night, which began with a multiple-course vegetarian East Indian meal (prepared in a devotional way). The rest of the evening, a Kirtan was held (call and response chanting), for an evening of heart-centred devotion to

God (Great Spirit, etc.). They put no insistence on any particular belief system.

Meanwhile, back in the here and now, it had come time to sweep the labyrinth. I noticed that though there had been a great many leaves fall since yesterday, there seemed relatively few on the labyrinth surface. They lay all around the perimeter as though some force had repelled them from the inner core of the labyrinth and pushed them to the outside. Maybe the "Jedi" had come here already — still possible even though early. Not important, however; I just noticed.

As well as the leaves, I noticed a pair of squirrels (that I had seen other days here), one grey, one black. I don't know if they were partners — I had observed them chasing one another, so maybe they were rivals or could be running off somewhere together. Anyway, today, they stood together on the trunk of the oak tree I meditate under. As I stopped my work to watch them, they scrambled up the tree — round and round the tree trunk as though ascending a spiral staircase (there's that spiral shape again). It reminded me of the concept of Ying and Yang (particularly because of their dark and light colouring), though I couldn't feel clear whether they collaborated or competed. No doubt, some form of harmony will get achieved eventually — though I wouldn't witness it, as they ran down from the tree and disappeared across the churchyard.

I resumed my sweeping. A car pulled up on the street adjacent to the church grounds — the stereo in the car played loudly. I could hear the song playing — Louis Armstrong singing, "What a Wonderful World." The song, and my surroundings, touched my heart, and my eyes welled with tears. At that moment, I became embraced in "Wonderful." The car remained only for the duration of that one song, and then left. Random? Coincidence? Maybe, unless it wasn't. The beautiful interlude struck me. A short window in time where an alignment of unrelated occurrences connected and then ended just as suddenly, leaving me wondering if that had just happened.

Further to that, how many beautiful moments do I miss on any given day because I get so ensconced in the catacombs of my mind that I become unaware of what unfolds right under my nose? I felt grateful that day for the driver of the car who provided my movie with such a fitting soundtrack and, of course, thanks as well to the dancing squirrels. I could have grown annoyed at the noise instead, and might well have done so had a different song played. This brings us back to the choice we make between suffering or peace, and the stories we make up about events.

Day 19 Questions
(Peace)

01) Is peace possible?

02) Does peace matter?

03) Is there a difference between personal inner peace and keeping the peace?

04) Does avoiding conflict lead to the creation of peace?

05) What is your comfort level with conflict?

06) What is the difference between conflict resolution and avoiding conflict?

07) What strategies do you use to create peace in your world?

08) Does being peaceful mean abandoning your truth?

09) What might peace mean beyond just the absence of war?

10) Have you considered the different forms of violence? (Physical, emotional, and intellectual.)

11) What does "peace being an inside job" mean to you?

12) If conflict is inevitable, does that mean there can be no peace?

13) How might the way you interact with others rob them of their peace?

14) Consider retaliation and reaction versus reconciliation and restoration.

15) Many countries have a war department; why, do you suppose, they have no department of peace?

16) Can connection be established and maintained in the presence of conflict?

17) If you subscribe to a win (or profit) at all cost paradigm, what are the associated costs that you deem acceptable?

18) Do you know what it costs to win or profit?

19) Do you have any idea what your consumption costs communities in other parts of the world?

20) Have you ever considered how what gets venerated in one culture as the means to security proves completely destabilizing to another community?

Sample Answer

Question 3 — Is there a difference between personal inner peace and keeping the peace?

For a significant period of my life, I would have used such descriptors as "easy-going," and, "open-minded," and, "flexible" to describe myself (it seems laughable now, looking back on it—my assessment simply didn't represent the reality). I thought myself so easy to get along with—pretty much a walking/talking model of peace. The truth was, I had a great deal of difficulty saying no, which meant I ran around trying to be everything to everybody. Later in life, I discovered that I operated from a variety of "peace at all cost" ways of being—the cost being my peace. I deeply resented these people and their insatiable demands. It proved beyond me, at the time, to recognize that all they'd done was ask—I had the choice to say yes or no. I'd trained them to know that if they asked, I'd say "YES." So, of course, they asked. A great deal of time and energy on their part could be saved; rather than going through a number of people with their request, just find me! Of course, I had something in it for me (I got rewarded with such accolades as "reliable" and, "I always know I can count on you," and, "You're an angel," etc.). Now, there's nothing wrong with being helpful and of service—certainly nothing wrong with people expressing their sincere appreciation; however, this is not what went on.

A sincere intention to be of service didn't motivate me. I lacked the self-esteem and confidence to say no, and the compliments, etc., gave me a temporary sense of well-being and value. Because, so frequently, I had no sincerity on my part, I believed that I was not respected and that I got taken advantage of and, consequently, seethed with anger. The truth was, I didn't respect myself. By relying on people outside myself for my sense of worth, while harbouring a fear of not being liked and not speaking my truth, it was I that abandoned myself. (This all went on under the radar — therefore, I blamed everyone else.)

Another thing: I avoided conflict — to me, conflict remained synonymous with confrontation, and that meant someone would get hurt (most likely me). I simply didn't have the tools and skills to either recognize these various dynamics or communicate effectively in the face of inevitable conflict. (It seems obvious to me, now, that conflict must present — everyone has their unique experience and perspective.) The only way we can agree all the time is through dishonesty. Which, as I outlined through my experience, breeds resentments and fails to earn true respect, as no one respects a "yes man," and least of all the man himself (precisely where the respect needs to come from).

Of course, swing the pendulum all the way over to the other side, and it presents an issue as well. As I learned to speak up for myself and be what I thought more assertive, it turned out that I actually became more aggressive. (Not particularly reasonable either; in hindsight, my new mantra became, "say no to life." Not that I went around saying that, but I might as well have). Whatever the question, the answer more often than not became, "NO!" Though I learned to work the application of the word into a myriad of different circumstances, I still didn't have much in the way of communication skills (and many of the underlying fears, etc., had yet to reveal themselves). So, in essence, I practiced disagreeing by behaving disagreeably. Not, I might add, an effective path to peace. (I mean, if you consider it as just a period of time in my life, then overall, it became part of the process of coming to a place of greater self-awareness and expanding skills. However, the period of time itself didn't become my "crowning glory").

So, I began to learn that peace truly did begin with me — that it was not okay to try and attain peace for myself through denying or robbing someone else of his or hers. The irony of it came in the seeing that doing so gave no source of lasting peace (I might have gotten some rather short-lived sense that I had "one-upped" someone, or that I'd "won"). Afterward, I would reflect on what had happened, and my illusory peace would unravel. I realized, eventually, that hurt brought to another also became a hurt I visited on myself (which doesn't mean that I always act gracefully — but overall, I have learned to tread lightly as I speak my truth — realizing it's equally, if not more important, to understand the truth of the other person as well).

Day 20
(Interconnected)

I arrived at the churchyard just shortly after 7:00 a.m. —the time change worked favourably with respect to arriving early, as it remained plenty light enough. It being Sunday, I would normally see the minister out for a walk before the service (the previous weeks I was a little later arriving, so I might not see him today). Last week, I noticed him smoking a cigarette as he walked. My mind flooded with thoughts such as, "Isn't he supposed to be the spiritual leader of this church? Can he provide said leadership while still indulging an addiction?" Having grappled with addictions during my lifetime, I knew that to connect with someone who had been there had great value. He made no attempt to hide the fact that he smoked, so presumably, his parishioners knew, and no one had found it necessary to invoke the diocese equivalent of voting him off the island.

Upon examining my thoughts more deeply as to their source, I realized that I'd constructed them from the fabric of assumptions formed in my childhood that ministers/priests, etc., were super humans and impeccably virtuous (or carried the message this was the code of conduct required while here on Earth and in the hereafter). My assumptions, formed through my innocence, dictated that they walked their talk. Somehow, I never felt I measured up in their presence—and, come to think of it, I don't remember any of them making any attempt to reassure me that my assumptions weren't the case.

Still, here was a fellow not afraid to be himself and without concern for what anyone else might take issue with (including the guy walking the labyrinth). Needless to say, plenty of people would consider the church he led (and all religions) a weakness. I would hazard a guess that if the subject of some local guy up at seven in the morning on a Sunday, walking in circles around the labyrinth, were to get raised with a cross-section of people, say for instance, in workplace coffee rooms etc., well, let's just say the commentary might well prove not all that complimentary. All this to say, the both of us, in our own way, are involved in walks of life not necessarily widely embraced. Still, the value, at least to the individual, does not get affirmed from outside myself. It would seem that I might need to prepare to stand alone at times upon a given chosen path.

Truly, I didn't judge him—I had smoked myself. Why, there was a time in my life that if I heard you could catch a buzz from drying and smoking dog droppings, I would have gone in pursuit of the neighbour's pet, looking to collect a specimen.

It did raise questions for me around spiritual paths and attaining peace and/or freedom from afflictions/addictions. In twelve-step rooms, followers credit a spiritual path as that which gains them liberty from their compulsion. Is something lacking in the church that all don't gain this same freedom? Of course not. Everyone in the recovery rooms gains and remains free of their compulsion. This doesn't even begin to address the significant number of people who consider themselves atheist or agnostic but who still, given the fervour with which they pursue their interests, could be said to observe a form of worship. Or, because they don't embrace the theology of man-made religions, a connection and relationship with the spiritual are not possible. Again, I considered what comprises the sacred — what one sees as an obsession, another sees or lives as their passion.

This morning, I had company walking the labyrinth. After my first time around, a woman arrived and stood at the entry point. Just about to wish her "good morning," I got the sense to hold off, whether in reverence to my walk or as an observance of her practice (or both). She remained silent. The wisdom of the guidance to stay quiet became clear while we both walked our respective paths through the labyrinth — separate yet together. I continued to walk past the entrance, at which point she began on her journey. I couldn't always see her, but felt her presence — the addition of another and her intention and energy made the walk more than it had seemed with me alone.

This made for the first time someone had joined me in the morning (and joined gave an apt description — certainly, I had no sense of intrusion). Occasionally, we would pass on parallel paths (or within the same path), and still not a word got spoken. On occasion, we exchanged a smile, or made a connection in the form of eye contact, but neither of us missed a step or diverted from our path. Like two planets orbiting the sun, in a universe of their own, as well as part of the greater whole. I had no idea of where she came from or where she was going and nothing of her story. The same would prove true for her — yet, despite this, we remained connected by the presence of something far greater than us individually or what either of us did. Surely that brings something sacred.

It intrigued me to consider the practice with respect to my fellow traveler. What path had led up to her now walking the labyrinth? Had she done this for long? If so, what insights had come during the journey? How had they impacted her life? How did it affect the way that she now showed up in the world? I had made reference in a previous journal entry that, perhaps, I'd gotten influenced by the energies of those that walked before me—now, I may walk with one of those very people. Did she feel any of the shared experience that I felt present to? I didn't feel that her being there detracted from my experience. Even though we were, likely, in our individual processes, there seemed something unique about the shared experience, beyond merely getting validated in the experience by the fact that someone else did it too.

It felt an honour to bear witness to someone else on their quest—without even knowing, specifically, the questions that she posed, or whether, on this day, she received an answer. I knew what it was to have questions that came from nowhere and, once revealed, refused to get dismissed. They would begin as an innocent curiosity about life, and then, as though fed by the very attention they elicited, they grew to a commanding presence, which not only questioned life but also became the path and vehicle by which life got shaped. To what end? Well, at this point, I would say for the purpose of formulating more questions. For either of us, it could be asked, is the walking of the labyrinth the answer to a previously posed question? Will life's riddles get solved in this fashion?

At one time in my life, I had thought I had all the answers, but then I got to a place where I thought I didn't know enough and needed more answers. Now, I seem to think what I may require is to learn how to ask a better question. Maybe, just maybe, a continual generation of higher-calibre questions and living into that inquiry is, in fact, the answer.

Day 20 Questions
(Interconnected)

01) How connected or not do you feel to yourself? (To your body, your emotions, and your heart.)

02) Do you feel connected to other people? (Family, co-workers, friends, and your community.)

03) What is your sense of connection to humanity overall?

04) Can you acknowledge a connection in the presence of diversity? (Ethnicity, religion, politics, socio-economic status, cultural, age, and gender.)

05) What about connection to nature (the planet, life)?

06) Do you feel yourself to be a completely separate entity?

07) When alone, do you feel peace and solitude or, perhaps, lonely and fearful?

08) How effective are you at honouring your needs and the needs of others?

09) Do you consider your needs equally with those of others? (Or at all?)

10) Do you consider needs beyond your own?

11) As one person, can you make a difference?

12) How do you feel when another acknowledges you favourably?

13) How do you feel when another acknowledges you negatively, or ignores you?

14) How do you think the effect you have on other beings affects the quality of your life?

15) Do you think in terms of "them and us" or "we"?

16) Is there any distinction between relating and being related?

17) Are you willing to listen beyond establishing being right and trying to understand?

18) How does your inner peace affect peace in your home? Your community? The World?

Sample Answer

Question 1 — How connected or not do you feel to yourself? (To your body, your emotions, and your heart.)

Question 2 — Do you feel connected to other people? (Family, co-workers, friends, and your community.)

Question 3 — What is your sense of connection to humanity overall?

In our Western world, much of what gets touted as normal has, as an effect, more disconnection than anything else. I feel no doubt that I have been influenced by this orientation to life. Therefore, I could be described as being one of the disenfranchised and disconnected. This most certainly applied with regard to me in relation to others; I perceived that a vast divide existed between others and me, which created a sense of profound isolation. So, then, in truth, the greatest disconnect existed between me and myself.

The conditioning and programming that I took on with regard to masculinity in combination with an unconscious repeating pattern of behaviour, to avoid my feelings, meant that I lived almost entirely in my head.

Not until I first entered into recovery from addictions did I begin, through various group experiences, to become educated about the existence of this emotional body. From there, my vocabulary would expand to include a language that allowed me some emotional awareness. I felt flabbergasted to realize that I had so many feelings on the emotional spectrum. It would take considerable time before I had any personal appreciation or experience beyond an intellectual understanding. I had gotten in the habit of repressing, numbing out entirely, or seeking to bring about an unfounded euphoria; therefore, early sobriety opened a doorway to reconnect, but it proved an incremental process to develop the willingness to face myself. Over many years, I made various reconnections. My natural curiosity and, likely, the prompting of my higher-self (some might say soul), had me seeking out various modalities that offered portals of access to various levels of my being.

In hindsight, I realize that when one becomes so completely disconnected from the emotional aspect of their humanity, it proves difficult (if not impossible) to have compassion/empathy for others. The problem comes from a complete lack of ability to relate, as it is like another language is getting spoken.

Nowadays, I would say of this matter of connection/disconnection where men are concerned, that far less do I believe that we are created differently. I would say it is more a case of to what degree boys get taught and conditioned to disconnect. And then the degree that each succumbs to the reinforcement of this conditioning, through culture and peers.

More recently, I have had the opportunity to be in groups of younger males, where it seems to me, they are already more emotionally present and conversant. This gives me a reason for hope. My foray came about from personal crisis and a need to address the profound dysfunction I lived. I would hope that more men would come to evolve and embrace this as a natural way of being without their survival being at stake.

Day 21
(Flexibility)

Three full weeks. The number of days it takes to establish a new habit. I feel unsure how true that is—I've done different things for far longer than twenty-one days and had them (allowed them) to fall by the wayside. Conversely, I have never tracked how long it took me to establish a behaviour or habit that I subsequently discovered no longer served me. Some of them didn't take that long before they became deeply entrenched.

I believe it worth acknowledging my success at upholding the practice (while just as important a part of the practice is keeping my feet on the ground). Far more important than the time spent (though, of course, it was required) are the discoveries made during the journey—the many ways I have come to know myself along the way. Some of which, as you may recall, didn't prove particularly helpful in the continuance of the practice. Valuable insights got brought to light. But, more important still, will be how I respond to this knowing. What I have come to realize so far, I could use toward further empowerment or, collectively, as an alibi to remain stuck.

It seemed an absolutely beautiful morning, which gave rise to a lightness of spirit and proved conducive to feeling in a celebratory frame of mind. I slept in this morning, and so I didn't arrive until almost nine. When I got into my car to go, I sat to consider the logistics of the morning. I had an appointment at 10:00 a.m. Would I have enough time? I also remembered that I would need to make a couple of phone calls to get more information to take to the meeting. I felt grateful to remember this (as I had not thought of it since a week previous when the appointment got booked), but it also gave rise to further concern for time constraints. I shut off the car, and the idea came to me make the phone call, get the appointment over with, and then go to the labyrinth later in the day. I'd almost bought into it when I realized, "You know, I recognize that voice." It offered a rational idea that made sense initially; however, I happened to know that, often, the "I'll do it later" strategy proves ineffective. Therefore, the time is now.

I spent the usual amount of time clearing and walking the labyrinth—the only thing I abbreviated this time was the sitting meditation. Being a little later in the morning, the warmth of the sun felt like a big loving hug. I chuckled to myself as I thought about the comment a gentleman walking through the churchyard had made as I finished my walk, "Don't get dizzy walking in circles around that thing." Do I have room for humour on this quest for the sacred? As far as I'm concerned, I do—in fact, it's mandatory. It has become my experience that the spiritual journey does require serious commitment, but it need not always form a sombre experience. Though not a hundred percent successful at living the following suggestion, it offers great value to the degree I can embrace it: "Don't take yourself too seriously."

When I got home, I realized that my appointment wasn't until 10:15, which meant that I had time to walk to the meeting and get more fresh air, exercise, and another round of those delicious full-body hugs from the sun.

Day 21 Questions
(Flexibility)

01) Can you allow room for flexibility in your commitments?

02) Does commitment mean rigid adherence?

03) Consider the example in nature of trees (rigid versus flexible) in the event of a storm.

04) Procrastination or inaction—dressed up as flexibility or spontaneity—how might that affect your commitments?

05) At times, the best way to breathe new life into a commitment is to shake it up some—consider a new approach or take a day off—can you give yourself that sort of leeway?

06) If you ask someone to do something, are you able to allow him or her to accomplish the request his or her way?

07) You may well say, "A change is as good as a rest," but do you believe it? In what ways are you able to live it?

08) As an "old dog," are you willing to learn any "new tricks?"

09) Do you suppose there is truth beyond what you believe?

10) What might the relationship be between what's possible and what you believe?

11) What if certain things you believed about particular aspects of your life weren't true—what else might be possible?

12) Are you willing to expand what you believe as true to see what's possible?

13) Have you ever considered that not possible might be more defined by the rigidity of your beliefs than by the truth?

14) Do you suppose there is any relationship between flexibility/rigidity of mind and body? Flexibility/rigidity and the creation of opportunity?

15) What might happen if you let go of some of your belief frameworks?

16) Plans and goals are useful—do you leave some room within for life to happen?

17) Does an initial failure signify the end of the project or the beginning of a new approach?

Sample Answer

Question 1—Can you allow room for flexibility in your commitments?

Question 2—Does commitment mean rigid adherence?

Question 3—Consider the example in nature of trees (rigid versus flexible) in the event of a storm.

I have to admit that I have often called upon an all or nothing approach (not altogether ineffective). I have accomplished various goals this way. However, I must say, over the longer term, it's maybe not the way to go (the clue getting conveyed in the nothing part of the phrase). It doesn't give an effective strategy for longer-term continuity/consistency. Perhaps, at times, a step back would prove more productive. It can allow for fresh energy and perspective. The key being that some sort of action would resume.

So, when I speak of flexibility, I don't (generally) talk about stopping altogether. Yes, value lays in knowing when enough is enough or when to walk away temporarily. I don't suggest that flexibility is synonymous with quitting (though it could be). If I find that I'm beating my head against the wall with a particular pursuit, and that it no longer served me to do so, then perhaps some flexibility in mindset or beliefs would allow for letting go. Of course, only the individual can make that call—I know for sure that I have continued down a particular path, and it could be said in hindsight that it no longer served me.

However, in some respect, it did. The continuance made part of a process whereby I became ready to let go. It's worth considering in these cases, "Is my persistence an element of my necessary continued application toward a particular goal? Or is there any other underlying motivation not in my best interest at all?"

The "my way or the highway" thinking has, at times, made achievement more difficult for me than it might have otherwise been. Sure, I felt satisfaction in accomplishing something for myself, but that didn't mean that I couldn't benefit from the guidance of someone with experience. It can save much time and energy and unnecessary frustration.

The analogy of the trees and flexibility during a storm makes for a powerful metaphor and teaching. The rigid tree that doesn't sway with the wind of the storm can suffer extensive damage, with limbs getting torn asunder or even the trunk of the tree breaking or becoming uprooted. Those more flexible trees sway with the wind, bending and offering less resistance and, consequently, remain undamaged by the storm.

I think of the different goals I've had with respect to physical fitness, for example. A beneficial intention to improve my wellness, unless if, in the dogmatic pursuit of my goals, I injured myself because the schedule called for another workout, and though my body hadn't fully recovered, I pushed it through. Or I came down with or recovered from a virus and, rather than rest and get over it entirely—fixation on the goal (improved wellness)—I drove myself to resume and prolonged the illness. I would have, in these cases, likely benefited from flexibility in my approach.

So, perhaps the focus remains on the goal, and I need to utilize creativity in how I go about reaching that goal. It is no less a commitment—the strategy need not become carved in stone.

Day 22
(Focus)

Up early once again—this morning, I found no question or hesitancy apparent in my mind. I got dressed quickly and then read from the daily readings of a couple of inspirational books. Without even giving it any thought, I next looked at some readings that come via email— followed by the notion, *"Much time can be lost on the computer—get moving!"*

While the computer can make a useful tool for my writing, connecting with others, and researching, the true value of any of that is only if, in the moment, any of those pursuits meet my objective or intentions. Otherwise, the computer can become a means to avoid something, which might well be calling for my attention. It happens to be a convenient dodge, given that I do my writing on this same tool. The problem arises if I sit down to do write and succumb to the allure to just check my email quickly; then, after reading this and clicking on that link, my plan to write gets left marooned on the rocks, like the mariners in the ancient myths, led to their demise by the alluring song of the sirens. To be clear and honest, I am both "mariner" and "siren"—nothing or nobody can lure me where I don't already want to go.

I don't know that the myth or scenario I describe reflects much in the way of personal responsibility—let's face it, I don't know about anybody else's email, but really, there is not much in my inbox that is alluring—even a note from a close friend will prove every bit as heart-warming, after I do what I have set out to do. I mean, after all, if I weren't home to access the computer, I wouldn't even know that email had come in until later. How did people used to manage when they lived thousands of miles apart—separated by weeks or months of travel and likely the same time to receive a letter? I guess that the rest of their life didn't go on hold while they held vigil at their mailbox or the post office.

It's possible to take on any activity and have it become a diversion from something I want to avoid—suddenly, cleaning the bathroom becomes this pressing priority (of course, it needs doing; but, right at that moment, I had planned on sitting down to write). It's so easy to shift the focus and energy; I can even justify it at the end of the day by pointing out how busy I was. However, busy doing what? Even if, eventually, what got done needed to get done, did what I set out to do get done? Busy does not mean productive, and it certainly doesn't mean focused. Just because, at the end of the day, I feel fatigued, it doesn't give automatic cause to celebrate my effort. If spun just so and along with a little self-deception, I can create a story to prove how busy I was.

What if I expended the same energy on setting and working toward personal goals? Some have said that it's human nature to choose the path of least resistance. If this holds true, then to choose a more challenging path presents a problem, given that I am human. It seems to imply that I must find something beyond my human limitations to travel the more challenging path and, unquestionably, applies if I intend to create my own path.

At any rate, I took heed of the potential pitfall I teetered on the edge of and got on my way. I had climbed into in my car when I realized that I had forgotten my gloves—would that make or break my practice, though? No. Sure, the gloves would prove useful at this time of year (i.e. on this clear, sunny, and frosty morning). Still, this one time, I could go without the gloves to avoid going back upstairs and deciding to water the plants or do the dishes and delaying myself further. It would also prove useful to practice some mindfulness and organization and having what I need for the morning ready to go at the door. A useful practice to consider is to ask, given my objective, will the activity I'm considering move me closer to, or further from, said objective?

The sight of the frost-covered churchyard looked dazzling, and the morning sun illuminated it as though blanketed in diamond dust through the night. There, frozen (pun intended) in time, was a moment of beauty and awe, leaving me to wonder, "Because I don't have more moments like this, is that reflective of minimal beautiful moments existing or a call to become more present to the beauty constantly available?" I suspect the latter.

I began my walk. On each step around the labyrinth, I attempted to feel my foot connect to the earth, in turn seeking to connect to myself within and to all that surrounded me. I felt in the tenderness of my heart the yearning to connect. Also, I discovered anger present—memories of times that I'd felt excluded or got ridiculed when particularly vulnerable. Below those thoughts, there came more hurt. I continued to generate a willingness to let go of the hurts and resentment. I acknowledged my

236

defenses could and did keep me from a sense of belonging and connection. I invited the spirit of forgiveness with a wish to unburden my heart and dismantle the defensive behaviour. Ideally, to heal the wounds behind the creation of the armour in the first place, which stood between the knowing and experiencing of the presence of love. The process had involved uncovering and stepping into considerable pain—I understood there was no way but through.

Love for self involves first facing myself, including all the demons and skeletons. I never believed in the "Hallmark" portrayal of love. I now practiced and worked at believing that something within me had a knowing; that I could stand in love and all that it demanded. First and foremost, facing the truth about myself. In the presence of truth, healing and growth become possible. That doesn't necessarily mean comfortable, warm, or fuzzy. Love, then, represents a force that lies behind bringing about the highest good. As far as I can tell, my part is to let go of any preconceived notion of what that looks like. Perhaps the pain exists, in part, created from my resistance to what is. Or my insisting on holding onto that which is not true.

My suffering, then, came from my resistance to how love would have me show up in the world. Of course, this is precisely what the Buddha said. He also suggested that his followers not take his word for anything—that they consider his teaching in their day-to-day life and see if his words rang true. I can't say I'm a card-carrying Buddhist; however, I can say that it would seem Buddha was onto something. I had conditioned myself to defend. I now walked through my fear, practicing trust, and faith, opening to receive and give love without expectation, one step at a time.

Day 22 Questions
(Focus)

01) What challenges do you face with staying focused?

02) What successful strategies have worked for you to maintain your focus?

03) If busyness creeps in to take you away from your intended goal, how might you see to the other aspects of your life and still meet your objectives?

04) Do you have the support in your life to allow you to stay on task?

05) Can you ask for the support you need?

06) Can you (will you) disappoint others at times to stay the course you laid for yourself?

07) What priority do you assign your goals/needs?

08) Are you punctual and reliable (accountable) to others?

09) Can you see the need for the same accountability to yourself?

10) Have you considered that allowing distractions to dominate your attention could be a form of self-sabotage?

11) Do you have an awareness of how many different tasks can be on your plate and handled effectively?

12) Do you have any difficulty saying no? (With over-commitment?)

13) Have you considered a meditation practice?

14) If you have poured yourself into what you are doing, can you recognize the need to step away occasionally? (Reenergize and refocus.)

15) Do you recognize the difference between focus and driving yourself relentlessly?

16) Prioritizing, organization, and balance are some of the ways to negotiate the demands of your life—give some thought to how you might consciously apply these tools in your life.

17) Do you ever check in and determine whether your present choice forwards your intention?

18) Once you make a choice, more attractive options will often present—how will you remain focused?

19) Do you have the ability to refocus (i.e. you have allowed distraction to become the priority and need to regroup)? What do you have in the way of focus resilience?

20) How about the ability to remain focused in the face of the doubt of others?

Sample Answer

Question 1—What challenges do you face with staying focused?

Question 2—What successful strategies have worked for you to maintain your focus?

Question 3—If busyness creeps in to take you away from your intended goal, how might you see to the other aspects of your life and still meet your objectives?

As already described in this chapter, at times, other tasks can seem pressing priorities and then get used as a means to avoid doing what I originally set out to do. This can happen, for example, when I've planned to do some writing, or maybe there's an uncomfortable conversation I want to avoid. In either of these examples, when examined more closely, I discover a fear present. A vulnerability that I attempt to avoid. In the case of writing, I have the idea that I will sit in front of the blank page and nothing will present. It may also prove true that I need to, at least, stay aware that other needs of mine also call for attention. If I don't feel at ease with my company, or feel the need to connect with someone, then perhaps, I need to set an intention to do that and not just let the unmet need pick at me. It also remains possible that writing into what I feel, might give enough to bring my attention to the distraction, allowing my being able to carry on with my original intention. This is where I learn to prioritize and allow time for the various aspects of my life.

It can be effective to make an appointment with myself to, for example, do some writing, and then I honour that just as I would an agreement made with anyone else. The point is to set the time aside, keep the appointment, and plan to do other tasks, leisure activities, etc., around the scheduled event. I can take note of the other activities and tasks that come to mind. It may well be that they do need attention. A good chance exists, however, that it doesn't need to happen just at the time I had planned to write, or make the call to have the conversation.

If, during the time I intended to write, I come up blank, then I can at that time make a new time to resume, and then attend to getting a bit of fresh air and exercise or connect with a friend or even do the chores. Chances are, the break will create the clearing to continue and will certainly address the other aspects of my life, but not at the cost of my intention.

I have had plenty of successes at remaining focused and seeing various commitments through to fruition. I have also come to recognize my penchant for procrastination, over-commitment (which amounts to either doing numerous things in a mediocre manner, or not being effective at any of them and giving up, feeling overwhelmed. A strategy I have used for this has been to take on less so that I can enjoy the success and satisfaction of completion.

Another trap I have set for myself—a spin on procrastination—is something akin to perpetual window shopping. This gives the illusion that I am moving something forward—there is, after all, energy expenditure, but when all gets said and done, there might prove more smoke than fire. It doesn't have an affinity with making distinct choices and taking affirmative action. It is a choice—the choice to waffle and sit on the fence. Despite the rationalization of due diligence, I can and have allowed inertia to set in rather than making a start. Fear of criticism and failure (looking bad) lay behind these behaviours and, ironically, bring about the very thing I fear—no action will invariably bring about failure to produce (or make a change) or develop a raw talent. I am learning to embrace the vulnerability of uncertainty and failure, etc., determining that, for me, it is better to attempt and fail than not to attempt at all (albeit sometimes the truth of that seems marginal at best).

Day 23
(Humility)

Perhaps this exploration I had undertaken was, in itself, part of a process, and as such, not only did it make an evolution of the practice itself, but also along with its evolution, came my personal development. Such a morning, a morning of contradictions. It started out with peaceful readings, meant for reflection, and to inspire hope and plant the seed of change. All semblances of that soon got lost.

I speak of myself and that which I'm going through as a period of transformation—in part because it feels difficult to find adequate descriptors to offer explanation as to where I'm at. Now, I don't refer to departure from reality—I know, geographically, where I am, time and date, etc. Rather, I refer to my spiritual journey and the realities held within. I can't say I've reached an identifiable place on the path or whether I've grown nearer or farther from clarity.

I struggled for the willingness to write about today, however. I'd committed myself to this process and that my journaling would reflect my authentic experience; therefore, my concern for image management must take a backseat to the truth of the process. I wouldn't say that it represents the truth, just that I would not take creative license with my story. The journey itself occurred to me as vastly more important than how I looked at the end of the day. Though I did wish to bring the best possible version of myself into the world, the man I saw in the mirror at times seemed a far cry from self-mastery.

After completing my morning reading (and before going to the labyrinth), I decided to follow up with the cell phone company (having had a conversation the previous night which hadn't resolved the issue) with regard to my bill being considerably higher than I thought it should be. I had hoped to avoid the "we are experiencing a higher volume of calls than usual; however, your call is important to us ..." recorded song and dance by calling early. In that regard, I proved successful and got right through to someone. However, the conversation that ensued felt extremely emotionally charged (I became furious at times). I feel sure it seemed no picnic for the customer relations agent either. Whether this would have gone any differently after my morning practice, I had no idea. I guess I struggle with being someone with a morning practice and, just the same, a person who completely lost his temper.

I didn't expect that this current practice in and of itself would change my life. The point was that I'd done extensive personal work prior to this, and still came the emotionality. What lay at play here? Sure, money issues could prove a trigger for me — perhaps, too, this included a latent rage against the machine, but my God, it felt like I fought for my life at some points. Of course, I'd heard about the various "Occupy" protests around the world. Grassroots movements of people had unified and voiced opposition to the power granted to, and wielded by, the corporations. Hence, a relative few benefited at the cost of the majority. Did I take my personal struggle with, and intention, to stand more fully in

245

my power and allow it to get blown out of proportion? Perhaps this guy represented a lifetime of situations where I'd allowed myself to get victimized, and the situation uncorked the collective rage? I can tell you, I discovered considerable force bottled up there. I feel certain that channelling these energies appropriately could move mountains—and equally sure that this was not the time or place. All this anger and frustration that I held toward myself, I'd unleashed on the poor representative just doing his job.

As I'd suspected, I had gotten overcharged due to a technical error involving the designation of a couple of phone numbers as "free anytime" calls. I had called these numbers (long distance) frequently and talked at length on the free premise, which consequently racked up quite the bill. Of course, their records showed that I'd made calls—I remained adamant that I'd made no unusual calls. In fact, I said, I rarely used the phone outside of the free call times. They, of course, saw differently—"you frequently make calls of significant length," was their assertion. And then it dawned on me, "Wait a minute—what are the numbers you show for these calls?—Bingo, those were supposed to have been free."

"But you haven't designated them as part of your 'favourite five.'"

"I sure as hell did—using the online options right on the phone. I can assure you, I wouldn't have talked to this person at such length if I thought it would cost me for every minute I stayed on the line. This person was up island—some of those conversations involved the two of us trying to find peaceful resolution and, at times, became heated and not particularly enjoyable. No way would I have entered into these lengthy interactions had I known the meter was running. It would have been cheaper to drive up there and have the conversation in person!"

Well, you get the idea—in essence, both the phone representative and myself operated from our respective perspectives; however, a third truth escaped both of us for awhile. I have to say that this guy sounded like Gandhi on the other end of the phone. We did, eventually, find the truth, which was to his credit; he held his centre beautifully under considerable heat and attack. The man could have just hung up, and I feel pretty sure I would have if the tables got turned. Then I would have still gotten left with this balance owing and made an enemy of the guy who could and did help me sort it out. For all I knew, my account might have ended up flagged there as "hostile client." Or, maybe, if that happened to be one of those "this call will be recorded to assure quality customer service," and they actually recorded it, it might get used as a training audio to demonstrate both an example of a raging client and the use of exemplary communication skills in the diffusion of hostility. Not exactly how I had hoped to get immortalized.

I had not always been good at standing my ground (in fact, I'd not always known upon what ground I stood). Still, I must acknowledge that while I waged war with Corporate America and, likely, the spectres of my past, I felt fully prepared to make this guy collateral damage. This would be the same guy that rode out the fury of my assault and offered me

247

solutions, which I deflected in my zeal to be right. Ultimately, he had the power to credit me the amount of the overage; cutting my balance by more than half. He could have just said f−k you, Charlie, you have a balance due−balk at that and your account will get bounced to the collections department. Some humanity existed in this bureaucratic hell−not that I did anything to finesse it into play.

I apologized for losing my cool and acknowledged his grace and skill at weathering the storm and thanked him for helping me straighten out this matter. In return, I received understanding, connection, and respect at the closing of the call. I don't have any more regard for corporations as a whole, but I can see at least one person in their ranks that strived to put a human face on the landscape. So, then, maybe more than just one exists.

It seemed my healing journey had often involved facing my internal pain. When considering the previously mentioned interaction, I became aware that it didn't give me the right to become a pain. I had become more aware of the presence of anger (feelings that had gotten long repressed over various circumstances in my life). I don't suggest that I wanted to go around angry all the time. I must become more skilled at the healthy expression of this and other feelings−become aware of what goes on beneath those feelings and address those needs. The energy of anger itself seemed to contain significant power−power that, if mindfully directed and channelled, could get put to positive use.

The pitfall that I identified for myself was the notion that a good spiritual person doesn't get angry.

If I subscribed to that idea, I could then stuff my feelings, but now in the name of spirituality. What good would that serve? I wouldn't say that I should run around using my anger indiscriminately as a weapon, or as a means to manipulate and try to get my way. Still, it had its purposes—a bit like the warning lights on the dashboard of a car. They come on to indicate an underlying issue (you can ignore them, even disconnect them, but the issue will continue, and likely will become more problematic).

So, no, flat-lining through life doesn't give an indication of spiritual wellness. God knows, I'm no saint. Having said that, maybe the saints would not have turned out that easy to live with either. Any that I know anything about certainly didn't make their mark in life being doormats, and they left no doubt as to where they stood.

I had been told that I was right on schedule. I suppose I could trust that no changes had been issued to the schedule. My impatience and frustration would, for certain, do nothing to advance my development. Perhaps a greater degree of patience, as well as tolerance, empathy, and compassion for self was called for. This, then, offered my opportunity to continue to develop these qualities.

Though later than usual, I still went to the labyrinth. Without question, in the past, an interaction or situation that involved this much emotional intensity would have, in my mind, given just cause to take me right out. Did this make me a hypocrite? I didn't know—I just showed up where I'd said I'd be, the day I'd said I'd be there, despite stormy weather en route. I'd say that I remained a work in progress.

The wind blew while I swept. To the casual observer, this would look like the leaves returning to the labyrinth surface as quickly (or quicker) than I swept them off. This could become an exercise in further frustration but, instead, I chuckled as I put the broom down and just changed over to walking. I then pondered, how frequently did I try and assert endless energy upon a person or situation I remained powerless to control?

Day 23 Questions
(Humility)

01) Are you aware of the difference between humility and humiliation?

02) What does the idea of seeing yourself as right-sized mean to you?

03) Can you see that thinking yourself greater than or less than others lacks in humility?

04) Humility is frequently misrepresented—consider the strength of character required to carry oneself humbly.

05) Why do you suppose attributes such as aggression, control, and domination get equated with strength?

06) What about false humility? Speaking of your abilities in a self-deprecating way to get the approval of others.

07) Can you remain equally grounded with either compliments or criticism?

08) What does the idea that pride comes before the fall suggest to you?

09) Can you see the correlation between lack of humility and separation/disconnection/isolation?

10) Consider the difference between humility and beliefs/behaviours of insecurity/inadequacy as well as the difference between arrogance and greatness.

11) Can pain or challenge in your life teach humility?

12) Do you believe that anyone can become your teacher?

13) Are you quick to admit when you make a mistake?

14) No man is an island—reflect on what that might mean to you.

15) Humility, from the Latin word "humilitas" (noun), from the adjective "humilis" (adj.), meaning humble—also "grounded" "from the earth" "low", from the term "humus" (earth). How might one live in alignment with these ideas?

Sample Answer

Question 1—Are you aware of the difference between humility and humiliation?

Question 2—What does the idea of seeing yourself as right-sized mean to you?

Question 3—Can you see that thinking yourself greater than or less than others lacks in humility?

Here is a topic that I feel to address I must tread lightly—to suggest I know nothing of it would cross the line into false humility. To claim any particular mastery could be likened to trying to pour the contents of a glass of water into my hand, squeeze it, and then claim that I still carry the entire volume of water in my palm.

At one point, I couldn't have distinguished humility from humiliation. For the sake of this discussion, I now define humiliation as profound embarrassment (maybe even shame), which might involve the participation of someone else (but not always), characterized by a deep personal sense of being flawed or a mistake (versus making a mistake). Humility is more about a de-emphasis on self-importance. Therefore, it lacks in humility for me to think of myself as greater than or less than others.

Certainly, some of my life's more embarrassing moments—though, perhaps, collectively they have made me more teachable—at the time of their commission, I had no intention on my part to lower my pride. If anything, I got too wrapped up in myself, which would have played a significant factor in their occurrence.

I suspect that I may still serve on an apprenticeship where humility is concerned; perhaps for the remainder of my life. Even during periods that I identified as active spiritual development, I have come to discover arrogance, judgment, and pride rather than a modicum of humility. For example, it's one thing to admit my errors and short-comings and to take full responsibility. But to believe, act, and speak as though so much more superior to others because I judge they have not been as thorough as me (in their self-appraisals) proves both ignorant and arrogant. To presume that I know what they need to do to advance spiritually is to say, at the least, misguided. At that point, I have once again taken the lens of assessment from myself and directed it outward. It is not taking what I learn about myself and allowing it to humble me. Perhaps that I can recognize this now, indicates that a gradual shift in my perspective may have occurred. I wouldn't presume to say that I have my pride down for the count.

Somewhere in the mix, there must exist a healthy sense of worth (a balanced need for appreciation), but not to incessantly believe it necessary to get validated through constant recognition and special treatment. My path is just that, my path. If I identify the need to do some particular work on myself, it doesn't mean that everyone else needs to do it too. Ideally, any improvement I achieve for myself would allow me to better show up in service to others. There is no humility (nor does it serve any greater good) if the energy I expend on spiritual development only serves my ego. In fact, to carry myself in this way has created further separation for me. I don't know that pain makes a necessary portal to humility. Certainly, it has been present for me. It does not serve to beat people over the head with what I think I know (first of all, this knowledge might turn out as only a temporary perspective), and if I have assimilated it to a place where I can act from wisdom, I would realize that an act of humility might look more like me holding space for someone and listening deeply, rather than telling them what I think I know.

The experience of my emotional/spiritual pain can feel humbling in as much as it gives me insight into the pain of others—it can become an equalizer in this respect. Pain finds its way into the lives of everyone—its assault is not personal (though the experience is). Compassion requires an end to comparison and judgment—to hold your pain as though it were mine (to have empathy) calls upon me to know what it is to have pain and realize that the superficialities of human existence seem to set us apart. When I look upon you more deeply, I see myself.

Day 24
(Autonomy)

The morning began early; I awoke a 4:30 a.m., and my body felt nowhere near ready to embrace activity. Though I stayed in bed, I didn't get back to sleep, so I got up at six. I had agreed to pick up a couple of friends and take them over to a third friend's house, where they would gather to go to a four-day spiritual workshop/retreat. As it happened, I did this easily and still honoured my morning commitment. I had sat in sacred circles with those three in the past (in fact, I had just opted out of one they had for 11/11/11 in favour of just going with my flow). It felt good to see them all and be present to love for my friends and, that despite this connection, there remained a need to honour and keep sacred our individual paths. It seemed fun to share in their energy—a mix of excitement and anticipation, as there was no telling where a journey of that sort would lead. It reminded me of the excitement I'd felt when I'd begun my new practice. I felt a mixture of joy to be part of the first leg of their adventure and a little sadness that I wasn't going along. Having said that, I carried them in my heart during my morning practice, so truly, there was no separation.

The work they would do would form part of a path they all followed, and in which they all had varying degrees of training. This same path had provided the framework for the ceremonies I had taken part in. This identified my personal exploration and deepening connection as I looked to establish more for myself what my path was to be. This didn't mean that I found anything wrong with the path they followed. It remained no less sacred, and I would always address and participate in it as such.

I looked to establish my spiritual autonomy, to embrace a practice that resonated with my heart. At the least, I would stand as my own spiritual leader—various teachers would arise, but the acid test of any given practice, at any given moment, came down to the power of discernment from within. As such, when developed, it could become that which delineated an innately sovereign guidance and connection. This, I defined as sacred and divine in nature.

I felt the pull on my heart as we drove off in separate directions—I had suggested to one of the women to leave anything she didn't need up there, and would do the same with lingering vestiges of one of my old stories, "I don't belong; I'm not part of; I'm disconnected." None of which held any truth—I felt increasingly aware of my connection to all that is. I actively nurtured my awareness and connection to self. I looked within and to "God" as the source of all love. I worked at identifying and releasing the blocks within me to this love.

So, off to the retreat went my friends. I blessed them on their journey, in love. Then I carried on to my walk, also in the spirit of love. One step at a time, a new way of relating to God, to self, and to those in my life—Love without End.

Day 24 Questions
(Autonomy)

01) What challenges do you encounter with walking your individual path?

02) How important is the opinion/approval of others? (In determining your path.)

03) Can people really be "like-minded" and remain authentic?

04) How likely are you to speak a discordant idea in a group?

05) How do you maintain your "sense of self" in a group?

06) Does belonging to a group with a particular focus mean always agreeing with the group?

07) If you are part of a group that agrees on a certain matter—how willing are you to hear the perspective of someone with a different viewpoint? (Really hear it—not just gathering talking points to "prove them wrong.")

08) Consider for yourself the meaning of independence, interdependence, and autonomy.

09) Does autonomy mean to you "going it alone"?

10) Can you collaborate and still remain autonomous?

11) Societal/cultural pressure to conform can be significant—how do you deal with it?

12) Have you considered what might be going on for you when walk the other way from your values and beliefs?

13) How do you manage with respect to balancing community/connection and gracefully holding your space in the face of disagreement/disapproval?

14) Are you able to make a distinction between solitude and isolation? (Self-confident and obstinate? Alone and lonely?)

Sample Answer

Question 1—What challenges do you encounter with walking your individual path?

Question 2—How important is the opinion/approval of others? (In determining your path.)

I have to admit that, having come from what I would identify as a fairly profound lack of self-confidence and identity, reorientation to the idea of autonomy has seemed, and continues, to feel deeply challenging for me. However, having said that, I gather that self-determination forms a natural part of human development—I speculate based on my experience, which varies in difficulty depending on the foundational sense of self that we start with.

To begin with, I don't live and operate out of a vacuum, so of course, popular consensus and marketing, as well as universal human needs such as connection, love, acceptance, inclusion, to be seen and understood, and closeness all influence me. The challenge for me comes when I place the approval of others (which I can mistake for the meeting of these various needs) as more important than honesty, integrity, and authenticity. The irony of this is that if I attain the approval through this abandonment of my truth, it doesn't represent love, acceptance, or connection, as I have misrepresented myself to get it (so, in effect, I act in a non-loving, non-accepting, and disconnected way toward myself). Therefore, you don't love or accept me—you love or accept the presentation of myself that meets with your approval. Naturally, this could get withdrawn at any time—quite possibly the moment I drop the façade. So, an important distinction has become an awareness of personal responsibility with respect to the meeting of my needs.

This is where my reference to foundation becomes relevant. Perhaps, when you read this, you might think, "Well, of course, who would compromise who they are for the approval of someone else?" It remains up to the reader to determine if and when that occurs in his or her life and if it creates problems for them. I don't suppose that any absolutes exist where it comes to right or wrong; for example, in an employee/employer dynamic, a challenge can present due to the power imbalance. If one chooses to keep this job, even though they may find some of their job description disagreeable, a tension gets created. Given the need for the income, this can produce a significant values dissonance.

To walk confidently, well-grounded in self, I must have a clear sense of who that is and consistently show up as such. This, for me, has presented an ongoing challenge. Of course, it shifts and changes with age and experience. However, this is not a given. The personal growth work that I have taken on reveals that merely getting older didn't assure me of no issues; unconscious beliefs and longstanding behaviour patterns eroded my sense of self and impacted how I showed up in the world. So, I find myself conflicted with respect to autonomy, which I value highly, and what I have allowed (created) in my life.

The ongoing challenge becomes how to continue to pursue this autonomy without sabotaging myself. I have identified examples in my life of resisting opportunities that might well prove in my best interest, utilizing reflexive defensiveness and calling it autonomy.

I have begun to realize that this living authentically demands deep soul-searching and a willingness to court vulnerability. Certainly not my strong-suit, given I have crafted my personality over a lifetime to defend against the need to be vulnerable. At times, it seems like the greatest of injustices to discover that vulnerability makes the path to growth, healing, and joy (and the list goes on). Trust me; if another way existed, I'd be all over it. I have come to realize that this is my path (or that whatever package defines my path, it will include embracing vulnerability — *read, begrudgingly practicing*). Having said that, I don't spend my every waking hour running around making myself vulnerable. It seems the shell of my defenses has gotten penetrated — gratefully, I discover that it doesn't mean that I'm stripped naked and defenseless from that point forward. I happen to believe that divine intelligence oversees the process (though, at times, I have my doubts) and always requires my willingness, my free-will choice, to participate. As such, I liken it to exercise. I don't go to the gym all day every day — my muscles need to rest and rebuild after the stress of working out. And I believe the same to hold true for emotional/spiritual growth.

Through this path of growth and healing, I have come to know myself better. This, in turn, makes it more clear who and what I bring to such things as my vocational direction. Equally weighted on this ongoing walk toward clarity are the successes and failures. Of course, some of the answers produce another series of questions or the deepening of a previous question. I might ask a question you have answered already, or that you have no interest in posing for yourself. As a sovereign, autonomous traveler here on planet Earth, that is your innate right.

Day 25
(Honesty)

Though I arrived early to the churchyard this morning, I didn't get there early enough to arrive before the labyrinth had gotten cleared already. In fact, a great deal of clearing had gotten done throughout the grounds. Someone had blown all the leaves in the adjacent parking into rows along the roadside, likely in preparation for the city crews to remove them. Now, a crescent-shaped row of leaves framed one-half of the labyrinth, running parallel to its perimeter, piled uniformly and frozen in place by the sub-zero temperatures overnight.

The sweeping and clearing would prove quick today. Even so, I didn't feel like sweeping. And, right now, I don't feel like writing that I didn't feel like sweeping. So far, I had swept and written that I'd swept, but the whole thing feels so irritating right now. *Nobody makes me do this — so why do I feel angry about doing it? Does anything I feel have anything to do with what I'm doing?* Confusion, sadness, loneliness: I had felt inspired and enthusiastic; where did that go? What was the point? Where was this leading? Whose idea was this anyway?

Don't hamsters run in wheels? When was the last time anyone heard of a hamster becoming enlightened from running in a wheel? Meanwhile, I walked in circles then wrote about walking in circles and, for variation, I wrote about not wanting to walk but doing it anyway, and then I wrote about not wanting to write about not wanting to walk. I don't need to go to the fringe to find the lunatic. I think I've found him and, frankly, I believe he feels pissed off that he has now gotten exposed.

A master of subterfuge is he. Oh, sure, you'll catch a glimpse of him from time-to-time, spouting off. He likes a good rant and, like the wolf in sheep's clothing, niceness and congeniality can become the cloaks behind which he dons the armour of righteousness and indignation. Frequently, he turns his sword upon himself, which is of little consequence upon the world around him, except on those occasions when the rage turned inward gets projected outward toward, for example, a cell phone customer service agent—then, not so benign. What kind of bitter irony was this? I walked and meditated, seeking peace and, instead, I found a boiling cauldron of rage.

What played out there? What was the guidance? Had I now limped to the sidelines where the coach (God) puts an arm around my shoulder and tells me to walk it off? I have read that the dervishes dance (whirl) to achieve an ecstatic state and greater God realization. Of course, dogs chase their tails. For the same reason? Or different? Is it a coincidence that dog is God spelled backward? Canines are masterful at living in the moment—which is where I'm told God exists.

So, I walked in circles around the labyrinth—whom or what, then, was the true mystic, the Sufi adherent, man's best friend, or yours truly? Around and around and around I went and where I'd stop nobody knew.

Was this not supposed to make for some form of spiritual journey? How then to explain the presence of this anger? Many would have me believe that spiritual people don't get angry. I wouldn't suggest that it's desirable for me to walk around angry all the time; however, if an element of this earth walk (which, at the moment included this #$%@ labyrinth walk) was about coming to love and forgive myself, then I submitted that it would include my anger (and what it is that I have done or not done).

Might this indicate some colossal failure? Examination of the anger revealed layers of pain below. The anger, though often responsible for reinforcing a sense of disconnection and separation, had frequently become the default feeling—seldom did it lead to a satisfying outcome—but it certainly felt less vulnerable than acknowledging and expressing pain. The old expression from around the 12-step rooms came to mind, "You're only as sick as your secrets." This told me that I must remain honest about how I felt and the ways I repeatedly thought, believed, and acted (which, at the end of the day, could result in my getting angry with myself). During times of limited awareness and honesty, I had directed this anger at others—trying to make them responsible. It served no useful purpose to discover my anger, pain, and limiting beliefs, and then get further angry at myself over what I had found. Just the same, I had done that.

The anger proved misplaced and self-defeating. Were this someone else, then frequently, I could hold the perspective that they did the best they could with what they knew at the time. If they had a willingness to change, then it served no useful purpose to continue to beat themselves up for past choices and behaviours. Chalk it up to a lesson learned and move on. Am I any less deserving of compassion, understanding, patience, and empathy? The truth is that I often have treated myself (in thought, choices, and action) as though the answer were no. This, in itself, brings a realization that could have a profound effect on my life ongoing if I practiced it more regularly.

So, perhaps the walking in circles here had borne some fruit—that of self-recognition (granted, I'd rather not have these qualities, but that is where the honesty comes in). Continued denial would perpetuate far more destructive and repetitive circular patterns. So, it came down to a choice between the short-term pain of this recognition and the more chronic pain of living my life the product of my limited beliefs.

Day 25 Questions
(Honesty)

01) What does it mean to you to be honest?

02) Have you considered the difference between transactional honesty (cash-register honesty) and emotional/self honesty?

03) Have you considered the distinction (and impact) between "honesty is the best policy" and the lies you tell within social agreements?

04) Where does the line exist between guarding another's emotional wellbeing and where the truth might be the true act of kindness?

05) Do you engage in self-reflection?

06) What is your capacity to be honest (as well as non-judgmental) with yourself?

07) Have you considered the relationship between being honest with one's self and such things as self-trust, self-respect, and self-confidence?

08) "To Thine Own Self Be True" — What does that mean to you?

09) Can you think of an example in your life where the short-term pain of truth felt preferable to the longer-term suffering created through denial?

10) What prevents you from more honest self-expression?

11) What might increased honesty bring about in your life? (What sort of changes — positive/negative?)

12) Is it possible to be honest all the time?

13) What's at risk with being honest?

14) What is the pay-off for not speaking your truth?

15) What are the costs (to self or otherwise) of remaining silent?

16) There is a Yiddish Proverb, "A half truth is a whole lie." Consider for yourself the ramifications of that.

17) How well do you know yourself (i.e. strengths/weaknesses)?

18) Do you, generally, feel free to be yourself? Under what circumstances may you answer or behave contrary to how you think/feel/believe?

Sample Answer

Question 6—What is your capacity to be honest (as well as non-judgmental) with yourself?

I can honestly say that I have experienced considerable expansion in my capacity to be honest with myself over the latter half of my life (not that the timeframe matters—for me, more important is that it has occurred). How does this process begin? For me, it began by becoming willing to look at myself (willingness can come about in any number of different ways and at different times). For example, reckoning with addictions, this set off an ongoing process of self-exploration. On this occasion, willingness looked a lot like necessity. Later in my life, a marriage ended, and I also found myself further searching for meaning and purpose in my life, vocation, etc. I grew tired of the same-old-same-old and had, finally, come to a perspective that called upon me to see my responsibility in its creation. Such self-honesty and accountability brings a mixed blessing (from my experience), which is why I included in the question the ability to be non-judgmental while assessing myself.

That didn't always prove the case for me, which resulted in the escalation of my suffering at times. First, I would experience the pain of recognition that I, indeed, had a part to play in these various aspects of my life. Previously, I had identified the cause as outside myself (as well as looked there for the resolution). Second, I would judge myself and become self-critical about what I discovered. As I consider this now, I recognize the mindset and mistaken belief system that insists on my getting punished for my misdeeds and that I applied unconsciously to myself. Such an attitude didn't bring about the impetus to effect positive change. The need to alter remained a constant; however, the motivation to do so, I've found more effective as an act of love rather than admonishment.

I don't feel inspired to change when I receive the negative reflection or criticism of others, and therefore, I don't believe it any more effective coming from myself.

Day 26
(Boundaries)

An old saying goes, "Early to bed and early to rise makes you healthy, wealthy, and wise." If that is the necessary protocol, then that covetous trio of attributes might well still elude me. I got the early-to-rise part (well, perhaps not by farmhand or bakers' standards). I rose before 6:00 a.m. Where I had deviated from the program was that I remained awake at 2:30 a.m.—having just got back to bed for the second time at two. I had gone to bed considerably earlier the first time but couldn't get to sleep. So, I got up and meditated for a half hour, and then ended up on an Internet chat line with a friend in Maui. So, at the most, I got three-and-a-half-hours sleep, and as I write this, it is now 3:00 p.m. the next afternoon, and surprisingly, I don't feel the least bit tired. I say surprising because, despite the sleep deprivation, I still got up and did my full morning practice. I finished in time to get to the polling stations just after they opened to cast my vote before the line-ups formed. I then went home briefly, enjoyed a brisk twenty-minute walk to attend a morning study group, went to lunch with the group afterward, and then took a twenty-five-minute walk home.

On the way home, I got a great deal on a hat at a yard sale. Given I have chosen to part with all my hair; the value of a good hat come summer time can't be underestimated! The same woman had had a table out over the last two weekends. Both times, I offered her three dollars for a Tai Chi DVD she had for sale. I felt only moderately interested in the DVD (though I would like to learn Tai Chi). I had more interest in getting it for what I felt prepared to pay, and remained willing to walk away otherwise. I might have learned something of value from the video (though I believe the benefit of attending a class in person would prove far more effective). The exercise had more to do with upholding my intention and trusting that if I were meant to have it, then it would be available to me at the price I offered. I didn't want the desire or impulse to compromise the intention. This, to some, might seem a ridiculous game with no inherent value; however, if I can't hold to my path in a simple situation like this, what chance would I have in holding my ground when the stakes got higher? Meanwhile, I will stay open to how a Tai Chi practice might present.

It seems interesting to feel so energized on so little sleep (I had thought I felt a subtle shift in energy as the days of the practice rolled on, and I think my meal portion size has decreased too). I don't know I can attribute this to the practice specifically (however, I haven't done anything differently in my life to account for these changes). If this increased energy persisted, it would lend itself well to an enhanced ability to get things done. Of course, a clear direction to direct the energy would come in useful too.

As I walked the labyrinth, I heard a car door shut, and without breaking my concentration, I got the sense I was to have company. Sure enough, a woman who had come to walk joined me. I can't feel sure if it was the same woman from last week. On both occasions, we individuals wore hooded jackets with the hood up. Though I did make eye contact with my fellow seeker last week, my recollection of her face proved incomplete. If it was the same person, she had a different energy about her today—no smile in passing, and she walked the path in a non-yielding way (so, even though there is room for two to pass one another, her stride and positioning on the path seemed to indicate that she had no interest in sharing it). Of course, she could have been deep in her thoughts and unaware of this. Perhaps she had come in an attempt to clear her mind, move through some emotion, and let it go. Clearly, I had something to let go of—I needed to get back to my reflection and let go of my story about what she was up to.

I had finished in the labyrinth, and so made my way back out just as she began. Soon, I sat under the oak tree for my meditation. If it had been her intention to walk alone in the labyrinth, she would now have it to herself. She left after one time around and drove off quickly in her car. I held space in my meditation that both she and I come to the means to enjoy peace and resolve turmoil.

I reflected on those times when I become upset and the effect that must have on the peace of those around me, or with whom I interact. With having just been in the presence of someone I perceived as upset, my feelings gave me insight into how it might feel for others. Of course, she might not have felt upset at all. It could be that that was completely the fabrication of my mind; in which case, my feelings were more about my idea/belief that I had been around someone upset. It didn't confirm this as true. While considering this, it allowed me to examine any fear I might have of being present to someone experiencing strong emotion and fear of potential confrontation. I then posited the question, "How well can I hold my centre and stay present in an emotional storm?" In truth, it has gone both ways. I have remained calm and detached, and I have taken it personally, become emotionally triggered, and lost it. So, it is safe to say, I can continue to grow in this regard.

Good awareness to have when considering my interaction with others — what is present for me? What is mine? I'm more likely to relate in peace if I know what belongs to me. I can then become less likely to project my stuff onto the other person. Once I realize empathy for self, then I can extend it to the other person.

I noticed at the base of the tree, where I leave the tobacco offerings, that all was not as I had left it. The tobacco had gotten taken clean away — none to be seen. There had also been numerous feathers scattered around on the grass near the tree (as though a bird had been in a fight or, perhaps, an encounter with a cat). Anyway, I had taken four large feathers and placed them in an arrangement to represent the "four directions" of the medicine wheel — I suppose, it could have been seen as a cross as well.

It had all gone too — the scattered feathers had not been cleaned up, just the ones I had arranged (along with the tobacco) — they could have blown away. Or, maybe, someone who observed me there each day and saw what I left behind had decided that I performed unholy acts and removed them. I noticed the significantly different internal response I got as I considered these different possibilities. It interested me to note that I had no way of knowing what was true, and still, I could observe a reaction to my differing stories of what might have happened. The bottom line comes down to my knowing in my heart the energy and intent of my observances. I happened to notice that the almonds I had placed there for the resident squirrels remained there—maybe the "cleaner" had an allergy to nuts!

Day 26 Questions
(Boundaries)

01) Have you considered for yourself what your physical, emotional, mental, and spiritual limits are?

02) Consider circumstances, past or present, that result in feeling uncomfortable or resentful—ask yourself what causes this? (Resentment can result from a perception of being taken advantage of.) Is, then, the request or expectation of another at or beyond what you feel comfortable with?)

03) Upholding the boundary in the previous example is a personal responsibility—what might prevent you from going ahead and doing that?

04) Fear, guilt, and self-doubt can become barriers—how do you relate to these emotions, and how do they impact your personal relationships?

05) Self-awareness figures significantly with respect to boundaries; therefore, that is largely what this book is about—are you prepared to give yourself the opportunity to better "Know Thyself"?

06) What am I doing (or allowing)? What is the other person doing? (What is the impact on me?) What is mine? What is theirs?

07) What (if anything) can I do about this situation?

08) What do I have any power over?

09) In family dynamics, and subsequently, in your present life, are you inclined toward a caretaking role? Do you often feel as though you are always giving yourself to someone else?

10) Has ignoring your needs become habitual?

11) How might you move toward a more healthy balance of give and take?

12) If you are living or working in an environment where there is an implicit expectation that everyone goes above and beyond, it may prove challenging to take care of your needs (though certainly a good place to become aware of them—while you're there). How might you begin to shift the balance? (Keeping in mind this might be a gradual process and not necessarily an overnight transition.)

13) How would it be to look at putting yourself first? (Consider if your cup is full you are better able to be there for others in your life.)

14) Would you consider eliciting various forms of support—maybe a friend to role play or act as a sounding board—coaching, counselling, or communication training (i.e. nonviolent communications)?

Sample Answer

I believe my experience will touch on aspects of many of these questions and, maybe, some points not specifically covered.

It can become quite an undertaking to identify the need to build and/or refine these skills — worthwhile, though. My life experience in this regard is like many other areas of my life; I can reflect on being at the extremes, and now practice living upon the middle road. Occasions have arisen where I have allowed myself to become the proverbial doormat. At other times, my newfound attempts at assertiveness ended up far more aggressive in nature than assertive, and therefore, not unlike the behaviour I wanted to address in someone else. Neither is "I submit" the basis for healthy relating.

Another consideration is that, initially, it may prove necessary to become fairly firm with my stand on a particular matter (it so often depends on where the other person is coming from). If it is an ongoing relationship, the possibility exists that room remains available for ongoing discussion and negotiation. Of course, given this is about upholding my needs, which is my responsibility, I can make these choices.

Something else I encountered was that if the people in my life were used to me showing up a particular way, and then I decide to pursue personal growth, not all of them would embrace the changes with open arms. Some relationships had gotten based on the status quo, so these changes could prove challenging for everyone involved. Some relationships are dynamic enough to flow with the changes of those within—some, it appeared to me, were not. I had people in my life apparently content with my being rather malleable, and they offered resistance to my changes; others honoured my request without even batting an eye (much to my amazement). The surprise was not that they seemed receptive to what I asked, but felt just such a wonder to me at what became possible in my life when I spoke up.

Another progression came from learning that there is being honest and honouring my needs and that there is also much merit in developing the capacity for open connection (that still strives to honour the needs of both parties) and isn't about right/wrong or win/lose. You might see these boundaries as more permeable. It's more about my trying to maintain a flow and understanding than keeping others out.

I must emphasize the idea of practice with the idea of steady growth and improvement over time. It is good to recognize that part of the process will, on occasion, look like an interaction that is a throwback to old ways, which doesn't come off smoothly (or gracefully). These ways of being require support (from and for myself), as well as practice with others, who are mindful of these ways, and ongoing work to reinforce the tools. It also requires courage (which, for me, seems absent on some occasions), but it will get summoned again when the time comes to look at where I fell short, and then step up and try again.

Day 27
(Self-discovery/Respect)

Without the slightest hesitation or resistance, I got out of bed and prepared to get to the labyrinth. Today, I recognized not just the individual components of my morning practice, but also the self-care that the combination of activities represented. Now, I couldn't say with any assurance that everyone would benefit from this same practice (they might—all aspects are known to have proven benefits). For any of it to become of benefit to anyone else, they would need to believe it true for them, or at least, have the willingness to believe it's possible that some or all of it could become of value to them. Then they would need to sustain that long enough to see for themselves. None of these activities necessarily yield immediate results, so a fair trial would be necessary.

Given the Western world conditioning to immediate gratification (i.e. fast food, instant credit, and 30-second sound-bites, etc.), this can lend to an appeal deficit.

It becomes a marketing issue to some extent, in as much as it's not a quick-fix solution—not as easy to demonstrate; hence the widespread appeal of alternative strategies that offer more immediate results. (Which I can't claim to be exempt from.) I share my experience and acknowledge while steeped in the same cultural milieu that I now scrutinize with respect to the impact on my life.

To some, marketing and spiritual practice might seem at odds with respect to compatibility. I think of it at its bare essence, as raising awareness. Of course, beyond that, innumerable strategies exist, as well as underlying ethics and purposes. But marketing could involve educating someone about the existence of something they had no previous knowledge of. (Without any intent to influence their willingness to try it.) Although, again, in the Western world where most everyone seems stressed out about time and, therefore, looks for a shortcut, I won't say, "do what I did"; however, I think it only fair to let the uninitiated know that they would need to invest some time and patience. Also, I wouldn't insist that anyone take on activities that specifically form part of any spiritual practice. I do suggest that what you do to look after yourself can be deemed and become your spiritual practice. Or, if you like, something you know to be good for you. Not because someone tells you that you should, and not even because you tell yourself, "I should," but because you know within yourself that when you do, you feel amazing and miss it when you don't.

It becomes a different mindset, and progress can seem glacial by comparison—all I can say is that it is a worthwhile undertaking for me; perhaps, the single most important decision that I have made in my life. Twenty-five (plus) years and counting have gone into that journey. The events that spanned this time prove too many to detail; however, there's every likelihood that I would not have had these years of living had I not begun this journey.

It is not necessary to reach such a critical crossroad to embark on the spiritual path—though it offers a darn good motivator. Truly, the fact that the individual stands to benefit for themselves need be the only motivator. Upon commencing an examination of self, eventually, I became able to muster enough concern for myself to take on a journey of growth, healing, and expansion. In my opinion that would constitute exactly the reason to begin, because each person is worth the effort. Again, I can't make the determination for someone else as to whether they should start, but if curious or feeling even the least bit inclined, then I would wholeheartedly say to give it a shot.

If you do consider it or have thoughts about it, then my experience tells me that this is what you could think of as the spirit within, nudging you to make some changes. The teacher (life) tells me I can pay attention to the nudge. Or the attention-getting can intensify to become more like a two-by-four between the eyes. I should also emphasize that the nudge always precedes the more abrupt awakening. I don't make a case for a punishing universe or a cruel world, but I do suggest that the laws of cause and effect can provide a gentle demonstration that all is not well, and that, perhaps, a subtle course correction might restore harmony. Continued neglect can bring on the need for a more complete deconstruction and spiritual renovation. The fact that I can describe the latter might give you a clue as to which route I chose.

In my case, I would have to say it became necessary because here I am, and it took what it took — not for a minute do I suggest it compulsory for everyone to do it the hard way. Sure, no matter what, it will take some effort. Still, sooner than later may lessen the complications.

I can say I have benefited immensely from the practice. Yes, uncomfortable feelings have come up —

and even still, I've noticed a beautiful connection to myself. Here, I don't speak of the unfettered pursuit of self-indulgent, hedonistic pleasure, but rather, refer to the spiritual uplifting made possible as a result of the nurturing of myself. I feel far abler to extend myself to others from this cup-full place, rather than try to give from an empty tank.

Here it is—I matter, and therefore, I need to show up and treat myself like I matter to me. No one can do that for me. Sure, plenty of people might treat me well out of love, care, and concern, and even courtesy, but I can't sit back and wait and expect this to be so, hoping someone will recognize my unmet needs and rush over to meet them.

I am indeed the one I've been waiting for. That begs the question, *"Where have I been? What took me so long getting here? Now that I'm here, will I stay? Is there more of me yet to show up? If so, is there any better time than now for this debut to take place?"*

It seems to me that it matters not what I observe as sacred—it is that I search my heart and determine what that is. Then, with love and attention, I sweep the floor and polish the altar of the sacred temple that is myself. Not for self-aggrandizement. No, the light that shines from the soul, and is honoured and embraced with love, will serve as a beacon which directs others to the love within themselves.

Where do all these questions and observances come from? I recall, a number of days ago, considering those that have walked this labyrinth before me; after all, it has been here for eleven years. What about the people that have prayed and continue to pray within the walls of the cathedral? What of the indigenous peoples that walked these lands for centuries before I was born? Which brings to mind the multiple generations in my ancestral lineage—what might they call forth from or through me? There is the collective wisdom and intelligence of life itself represented in the trees and leaves and the animals, the sky, and the earth. Why, there is even life itself, growing between the bricks of the labyrinth in the form of moss and grass. Life will not get contained; it will find expression and advance upon the natural path of its evolution. So, then, if it can be held as true that I am in communication, communing and in connection, with all of this and more, perhaps it all collectively conspires to first suggest then coax and, finally, demand that evolution be allowed its due course. As such, the life within each of us seeks a unique expression of this evolution. It's not that I want more from life—life wants more from me. As such, I'm entitled to a great deal more respect, and it needs to begin toward me and from me.

Day 27 Questions
(Self-discovery/Respect)

01) Are you willing to look at yourself and withhold self-judgment, criticism, and condemnation?

02) At a social gathering, what sort of conversations (people) do you find yourself drawn to?

03) Are you more inclined to seek like-minded people or opposites? Why?

04) What are the qualities that you find the most attractive? Less attractive? Repulsive?

05) Can you see any of these same qualities in yourself? How do they operate in your life?

06) What are the key elements in friendships/relationships that define your closest connections?

07) What elements do you possess that make you a good friend to another?

08) What would you most like to change about yourself? (I.e. more open, authentic, initiate more conversations, or listen more deeply.)

09) How do you define love?

10) What do you believe about love? (I.e. easy, frightening, here today, gone tomorrow, present only in fairy tales, underlying fabric of the universe, or present always, in all ways.)

11) How did you form these beliefs? Do they remain true for you today? Why or why not?

12) What do you fear most in life?

13) What would it mean to you if your deepest fear were realized?

14) In what ways do you limit your life while avoiding your worst fear?

15) When do you feel the most joyful? What are you doing during those times?

16) Do you believe in God? (In any way/shape/form.)

17) If not "God," what operates the universe? The world? Us within it? Why do you believe that?

18) If "God" exists for you — what qualities do you believe God to have? What has led to you believing that?

19) What is your current relationship with God/Creator? Is this the relationship you seek? How might it be different? Is there room for expansion of your current beliefs?

20) What beliefs around money did you inherit from your family (i.e. hard to come by, scarce, it's easy to make, having it/not having it defines me, I'll never have enough, give it away, etc.)?

21) What does money mean to me? (Security, power, freedom, ease, struggle, hardship.)

22) Generally, is the matter of money a source of peace or anxiety for you? Why?

23) Without monetizing yourself, do you consider yourself worthy of a life of abundance?

24) Can you allow yourself a bigger dream? If yes, what is it? If no, why not?

25) What are your greatest strengths/accomplishments?

26) What did it take to achieve them?

27) What do you desire most for yourself right now? Why? What needs to happen to move toward realizing this desire?

28) Consider the following list of words:

Love	Success	Honesty	Happiness
Soul	Inner peace	Acceptance	Intention
Commitment	Responsibility	Self-love	Truth
Fear	Reality	Judgment	Failure
Guilt	Shame	Joy	Fulfillment
Authenticity	Purpose	Anger	Frustration
Inspiration	Enthusiasm	Procrastination	Self-sabotage
Forgiveness	Spirituality	Gratitude	Presence

-Define these words for yourself for clarity.

-Expand upon the list for yourself.

Sample Answer

Question 1 — Are you willing to look at yourself and withhold self-judgment, criticism, and condemnation?

If you have engaged in some variety of self-exploration already, then no further explanation is necessary. For those who have not, I think the single most valuable thing I could suggest is that this exploration be done in the spirit of discovery without judgment and with the idea of embarking on an expansive personal adventure. Self-criticism and judgment became a pitfall for me. I can tell you that it is not helpful; however, if you discover, you tend to go there, then that is something you have discovered about yourself. Over time, with further willingness to discover what lay behind my self-criticism, more became known. It proves easier to move forward in the spirit of love and acceptance than not. It didn't turn out at all helpful for me to become further critical and judgmental about my discovery of being critical and judgmental. This might seem self-evident (particularly when seen clearly in print), but alas, I went there anyway. It made, for me, the difference between understanding intellectually that it was self-defeating while at the same time remaining unaware that I, nonetheless, did it even while understanding the futility.

In hindsight, I would offer that the sooner you can employ understanding, compassion, and empathy for yourself, as you look at yourself, then the better. If you're like me, then invariably, you will uncover things that do not please you. Keep in mind, first of all, that you formed these beliefs and ways of being for a reason (one that served you at one point in time). There had to have been an event or circumstance that had you conclude that this strategy was necessary — so, perhaps, have some compassion for what you experienced at that time. Maybe further understanding and compassion is warranted when you consider that these patterns that shaped various aspects of your life were, for the most part, previously unconscious.

Now, courageously, you look in the shadows of yourself and bring the dark to the light; therefore, I encourage as much love and understanding as you can muster for yourself (not to mention respect and kudos for "boldly going" where many simply refuse to go).

Day 28
(Freedom)

I don't know that I had any profound insights to share from today's practice (of course, who am I to say what someone else might find profound?). Nonetheless, I remained out there doing it—I felt good about that. Where today was concerned, I could say I felt good for no particular reason. I could turn that around to read that I have no reason to feel good—interesting; though I could see it as saying the same thing, it is likely that I could interpret both statements to mean something different. Does language merely describe experience? What is the actual effect that it can have on shaping experience?

Now, if I measured my life circumstances by some of the widely held models of success, well, suffice to say, I'd lack in some of the requisite criteria. But, what if, let's say, I never achieved those benchmarks? I don't know that that will be the case, but it seems worth considering. Would that mean that I have no cause to feel good in the absence of these missing measures of success?

I have read enough stories of individuals who endured horrendous situations in their lifetime. They had lost (or had taken from them) everything of material value and had little or none of the creature comforts that I, for one, take for granted on occasion. In some cases, they felt uncertain day-to-day whether their life would continue. Yet they resolved to hold fast to the one thing that no one could take away— their free choice to view their circumstances as they saw fit. They may have been incarcerated but remained free in their mind.

I am free, now, to make choices regarding my life. What a gift. Unquestionably, I will need to make some decisions and put something into action. But even now, that has begun, and I choose to express it through writing. I dare to call myself a writer—do I need to win a Pulitzer Prize or have something on the bestseller list first? I say no. Still, only as recently as, say, four years ago, this would not have been possible (well, in a sense, I suppose it always remained possible, but I would have said, "I can't do that because ..." and rendered it impossible).

I consider, now, that I have always been free; however, in effect, I incarcerated myself in a cell the size of the limitations I placed upon myself. Many have begun to fall away. More still reveal themselves through this very process. As I've said, I couldn't have written of this journey not so very long ago. It is equally true that I could not have taken on the practices I currently do in such a public place because of self-consciousness around being seen and judged and fear of criticism. I have experienced some relative growth in these areas. Now, my objective has never been to have this become a public display— regardless, it so happens that my chosen activities do take place in plain view of those who pass by at the time I undertake them. It feels great to have the relative freedom from my fears. Here, I don't talk about showing off in the sense of "look at me, I'm the spiritual guy in the churchyard," but more about my wanting to exercise my freedom to shape my life and not have it entirely defined by my fears and limiting beliefs.

Today, I enjoyed being me. I had not always had the ability to say that. On the surface, I might have managed to feign light-heartedness, but likely would only kid myself with that assessment. Unfortunately, the people around me often wore the oozing discontent of my unfulfilled soul. See, I became a prisoner of my thoughts and beliefs, but I didn't want to stay in solitary confinement, and so (I'm afraid) I took hostages (misery loves company), though certainly, the opposite didn't ring true — the company doesn't love misery. Contrast this to the present day, when I feel absolutely delighted to stand in my own company — this is not to say that I have become high on myself, but rather to say, emphatically, that I'm not trying to take myself out either.

It seems a bit like the Dickens' story "A Christmas Carol" — the transformation that Ebenezer Scrooge underwent, though I got spared the visitation of the nocturnal ambassadors of the spirit world. Certainly, I found no shortage of spirits in my former life (of the grain alcohol variety), and maybe that had some bearing on it.

Believe me; my head has not swelled, nor do I have it buried in the sand. Without a doubt, I have not arrived and don't presume that I can rest on my laurels. I haven't seen the last of the challenges in my life, and have experienced many during these past twenty-eight days, and feel sure there will be more to come. Given that I feel called to play a bigger game, which will involve further growing and stretching (there is no graduation from this university), it doesn't mean that I cannot appreciate and celebrate the changes and successes realized. In fact, that would be "enjoying the journey." If I were to wait for the anticipated arrival to give thanks and feel joy, then the arrival point would become merely the viewpoint for the next goal, and joy would get withheld indefinitely. Though following the heart will not eliminate the need to face challenges, and in fact, the path will include them inherently, I believe that the rewards of doing so strengthen the spirit and make me a more formidable presence better able to weather life's storms.

Day 28 Questions
(Freedom)

01) What does it mean to you to have freedom (or be free)?

02) Do you believe in an ever-present freedom to choose? (I.e. attitude, thoughts, beliefs, and responses.)

03) How might your life look different if you could gain freedom from some of your fears?

04) Can you grant yourself the freedom to fail?

05) Consider: you are never free of consequences but always free to choose.

06) How willing do you feel at allowing others the freedom to be themselves?

07) What is your relationship with the need to be right?

08) The Truth is said to set one free—how do you apply this in your life?

09) In what ways might you be a prisoner of the bondage of self?

10) Can your interior reality operate free and independent, or at least, can you see it as separate from external circumstances?

11) Who determines your beliefs?

12) How important to you is the opinion of others?

13) Do feelings/beliefs determine perception of reality, or does reality determine feelings/beliefs?

14) Can you allow yourself the freedom to choose again?

15) Are you really stuck where you are, or at this time, do you prefer not to deal with the consequences of change?

Sample Answer

Question 2—Do you believe in an ever-present freedom to choose? (I.e. attitude, thoughts, beliefs, and responses.)

For certain, I can attest to it appearing as though no freedom of choice existed when, unbeknownst to me, deeply entrenched attitudes of victim consciousness and resignation ran my life. There were those who tried to point some of this out to me (long before I grew ready to see it). Needless to say, I found it necessary to make them wrong (so, I exercised my freedom to choose to ignore this particular truth), which, of course, did keep me stuck in certain circumstances that I told myself (or, at least, acted as though) were carved in stone.

I remember talking to a mentor of mine at one point in time—I complained about the state of my life (which, incidentally, warranted little to complain about). He said to me, point blank, "If you are so unhappy about your life then *change it*."

"What do you mean?" I queried.

"Divorce your wife, quit your job, and move to another city. I guarantee that your life will be different."

The impact of the suggestion came immediately; my mind reeled while it conjured a multitude of reasons this couldn't happen.

The truth was, that though not absolutely necessary, any or all of it was possible. In good old hindsight, I had become quite invested (and identified with) the status quo. I, therefore, felt more concerned with the consequences of all those changes (which resulted in me creating the perception and story that I had no choice but to continue on the course I had charted). Freedom, however, existed throughout. I lacked the ability to recognize that I made the choice to uphold the current circumstances every day. I had the freedom to choose differently at any time. Without a doubt, there would be costs and consequences to deciding to bring about change but, at no time did I not have the freedom to do so.

Day 29
(Inner Treasures)

"Follow the Yellow Brick Road," said the guidance that Dorothy received in the classic story "The Wizard of Oz." After the epic journey through the mystical Oz, and once successfully overcoming the adversaries of fear and illusion, she and her travelling companions became the recipients of the objectives of their quest: Intelligence, Courage, Heart, and Home. All they desired, they found within each of them, and it had been there all along.

Perhaps the journey to reveal this truth was unnecessary (though it did make for a good story). In that light, perhaps, it was required to search outside the self first—walk that brick road, seek guidance from the masses, encounter witches and flying monkeys, get rendered unconscious (asleep) in the enchanted forest, and when, finally, the search proved fruitless and hopeless, an awakening occurred and the epiphany came: There's no place like home.

Now, I don't mean my mailing address when I talk of home—though, of course, there is the all-familiar expression "home is where the heart is." I am not familiar with the intention of whoever coined that phrase, but I have always thought it to refer to my love for my home or community. It can be experienced when traveling for a period of time and returning home to the familiarity of your hometown. What if it speaks more specifically about the heart of the individual, and to the degree that I become aware of and realize the call of my heart and answer this call, and get rewarded with the realization that I am home? Seen in this light, I could be at home wherever I might be. Another expression, "Be it ever so humble, there's no place like home," in a similar context, then, I could interpret as, "There is no home like that of a humble heart."

So, again, the idea that home is where the heart is signifies a coming home to Self—to the heart, to that place inextricably connected to all that is (some call it God).

What has any of this to do with walking the labyrinth? Well, it is a brick road—mind you, not yellow (however, the leaves that adorn it are). The journey begins on the outside and weaves its way round and about, eventually leading to the centre— home. The labyrinth, therefore, gives a metaphor (perhaps bestowed with mystical power) to lead one inward.

What of the "flying monkeys"? My mind takes concentration on every step, every breath, to keep it from jumping from thought to thought (from branch to branch and tree to tree) right along with those monkeys. It requires creativity (intelligence), courage, and heart to search myself, and it takes all of that and more to stay there and follow the inner guidance once there.

I see no need to believe in God to journey to the heart. However, I, for one, felt surprised at what I found once there. I recommend that before entering, you take off your shoes and tread lightly—this is a temple like no other that you will ever encounter. If ever there were a place to walk with and observe reverence, I would suggest that this is, indeed, that place. Plan to visit frequently once you arrive. Now that you have opened the door, ongoing honouring, nurturing, respect, and worship is required. Be advised; there is no turning back. To make this sacred connection begins a relationship like no other — worth the price of admission, but not for the faint of heart.

Day 29 Questions
(Inner Treasures)

01) Have you ever taken the time to honestly and comprehensively list your strengths?

02) What would your friends say they admire most about you?

03) Do you consider your inner attributes when identifying your assets?

04) Have you considered that what you admire in another, at the very least, exists as potential within you?

05) Who are your heroes?

06) What is it that you find so admirable about their lives? (Their accomplishments?)

07) Think of recent (or past) challenges in your life—what qualities, known and unknown, aided in getting you through?

08) Would you have known about some of these qualities without the challenging experiences?

09) What sort of things come easily (are natural) to you? (Leadership, team-player, creativity, speaking in front of groups, writing, systems, details, listening, healing, compassion, analyzing/problem-solving, conflict-resolution, or organizing.)

10) Are you willing to step outside your routine and explore new experiences?

11) Do you ever consider the inner qualities that you utilize or strengthen while doing a seemingly unrelated activity? (I.e. your regular exercise routine, taken on for physical wellness, develops discipline/commitment, patience, and perseverance, etc.).

12) Consider for yourself: Ingenuity, curiosity, love of learning, ability to teach, zest, courage, honesty, forgiveness, kindness, hope, humour, spirituality, awe, prudence, humility, humanity, and empathy. Do you share your gifts with the world?

13) Have you heard the saying, "Success is 10% inspiration and 90% perspiration"?

14) What if I told you there are no overnight successes?

15) Are you prepared to put in the focus and effort to develop your talent?

16) Consider—there is no one who lacks talent (inner gifts) and a unique way of expressing them, only a lack of willingness to recognize this and live accordingly. What does this mean to you?

Sample Answer

Question 1—Have you ever taken the time to honestly and comprehensively list your strengths?

Question 12—Consider for yourself: Ingenuity, curiosity, love of learning, ability to teach, zest, courage, honesty, forgiveness, kindness, hope, humour, spirituality, awe, prudence, humility, humanity, and empathy. Do you share your gifts with the world?

Question 15—Are you willing to put in the focus and effort to develop your talent?

I will grant you that there is, seemingly, endless emphasis on what we lack. The saddest thing about that is to discover how deeply I bought into the idea that I lacked in so many ways. So, for me, it became necessary to identify what these mistaken beliefs were within me; otherwise, no matter how well I did at anything, I could never see it as good enough (which gave a reflection of what I believed about myself). I'm not alone in this. However, this gives a reflection of myself (if the reader can relate along the way, then great, and if not, then that's okay too). Our culture bombards us constantly with advertising, which implies that contentment lies as near as the next purchase.

I can remember being in various group exercises that involved listing strengths—in fact, I recall the first time I participated in such a group. We had to list our own, then those of our fellow participants, and then give and receive these reflections and accolades. I struggled to come up with positive qualities for myself—it felt easier to identify them in others (though it remained uncomfortable for me to express these reflections directly to the person). It also became exceedingly difficult to receive the reflections of the other group members. I stood there (as required), but I felt like I would come right out of my skin and wanted to run. Much water under the bridge and many years (and much personal work) later, I am better able to acknowledge myself and let in the acceptance and reflections of others.

I don't blame society. I have come to see that, perhaps, this external emphasis on conformity and lack might make for the very catalyst that my inner-self (who I was born to be) pushes against to get realized and further developed.

I don't want to go through life never having realized my true gifts and taking the opportunity to share them. I have spent countless time lamenting over the gifts and talents of others (envious of their accomplishments and bemoaning their advantages). The fact remains, though, that they earned their accomplishments while I wasted time complaining. It became time lost that I could have spent discovering and developing my talents and passions. Even if they did have certain advantages, I stayed blind to the number of advantages I had and have. In other words, I got too busy complaining about the hand that life dealt me than picking up my cards and getting in the game. I have found that it is important to spend as much time as possible doing the things I love to do. I don't believe it any less work to develop my talents and share them in the world—but I can say something about a labour of love. Passion and inspiration will carry further when the going gets tough. Our gifts also include our dreams—the realization of which might touch innumerable other lives. Sure, we have personal gratification, but many more than me stand to benefit when I get myself on purpose and in alignment—in service.

Clearly, I don't speak of those who make a difference in the world already—they know their talents and passions and stop at nothing to do what they feel inspired to do.

This is for those who, perhaps (like me), have a litany of stories that stand in the way. I want to encourage everyone to look inside, discover your gifts (take that evening class, join the theatre group, publish your book, display your photography, take that trip, volunteer, make that speech, lead that cause, and follow your hearts), love what you find, and nurture it and share it. You will delight others with your gifts; we all have so much to offer. I feel infinitely grateful that I didn't leave my fruit to die on the vine. My journey leaves no doubt for me where acknowledging the inherent gifts and potential of every single human being is concerned. I want that realization for everyone. Get out there, please, and sing your song.

Day 30
(Discipline)

The thirtieth day is, as they say, in the record books. What a daunting undertaking this seemed back when I began. Thirty days was the original vision—I can't say, exactly, how I determined that number. I suspect that, at some level, I knew it would represent a commitment that would take something from me (while also benefiting me) to achieve it. It would require discipline. Further to that, an underlying belief in worthiness was required from within. This, then, became the catalyst through which I behaved both as someone worth committing to and, when challenged, to remember it as a commitment to self, first and foremost (whatever I commit to), rather than the activity itself.

As I worked at deepening the relationship with self, it became apparent that it must begin with developing the confidence that I could trust myself. It's not as though I lived a life completely without discipline—I had applied myself where the motivation proved sufficient and had proven successful at various endeavours. For example, achieving a black belt in martial arts, advanced scuba-diving certification, a college program that yielded me a Practical Nurse designation, and I trained for and completed a number of ten-kilometer runs. All took discipline, in their own right, to reach a level of proficiency.

Conversely, I found in many walks of life that the virtue of discipline is claimed as the principle getting upheld while many of which prove, instead, controlling and oppressive. I had an aversion to such frameworks and found them repugnant.

Having said that, it seems useful to make a distinction between discipline and the energies of control and oppression (as they aren't synonymous).

When I speak of discipline, I consider the presence of some sort of passion, interest, and (perhaps) a degree of natural talent (for a given pursuit). Then practice, persistence, continuity, determination, etc., become generally required to bring this vision (or goal) into realization or to develop a high level of proficiency.

I do not speak about discipline from a punitive standpoint (as in getting disciplined, as a form of retribution/punishment).

For me, I needed not only to consider what it would take for me to develop the continuity and consistency to succeed, but also what remained present that ran interference with that.

A new undertaking of any sort entails a learning curve, which requires practice (in the form of repetition). Impatience and lack of compassion for my learning process have, at times, hampered my success (or brought a beginning to an abrupt end). Perfectionism, which has at its roots shame and associated self-doubt and self-criticism, along with fear of failure and fear of looking bad (fear of humiliation), have become detrimental to my willingness to be a beginner.

What I came to know is that it proved necessary to apply discipline to the practice of an inner journey to acknowledge, understand, and release those tendencies to sabotage myself. The alternative was to continue to apply energy to activities and pursuits outside myself (only to eventually pull the rug out from underneath me).

Self-control became necessary—many forms of "self" had presented themselves on this journey and, as noted, many of them not conducive to my successfully realizing my goal. I needed to know that I would show up. I had an awareness that my not showing up for someone else might lead to disappointment for him or her—and if done frequently enough, trust would get undermined. Of course, circumstances arise where plans must change, but to abandon my commitment when I'd given my word damages my ability to trust myself. Therefore, promises to self remain every bit as important as promises to others. (In fact, more important.) Self-respect and the responsibility to meet my needs are at stake.

So, the practice I follow could be said to represent the sacred from a multi-layered perspective. It entails the various components of the practice—walking the labyrinth, Qi Gong, meditation, etc. To some, the activities themselves comprise aspects of the sacred. Independent of this is the fact that I committed myself to do these things and, therefore, at the very least, in relation to my commitment and myself, I had entered into a sacred covenant. It could just as easily involve any other activity (there need not be any so-called spiritual frame of reference at all). The point is the promise to self (and that part of self fed by the upholding of the promise) is sacred and should be treated as such.

I have developed the ability to treat that which I deem important as a priority because, in doing so, by extension, I give myself that same gift of recognition and worth.

I realized that a lot of me, myself, and I entered into these observations—did that then begin and end with self-indulgence? No, that was not my intention. I fully expected this path to lead to service. Though not clear at this point what form this might take, for definite, it has far more to do than serving my own nerve-endings. The last three years have seen almost everything I'd identified with come and go. This had become a complete makeover from the ground up. What worked and what didn't work? What mattered? I wanted for my life to become more than a mixed bag of unrealized potential. I wanted to show up as I had never shown up. That meant that that which had limited me in the past must get released. I couldn't allow it to define my present and future continually.

Love of others must begin with love for self, and that might well look like the ability to make choices that present personal challenges. It might mean saying no (when feeling pulled to say yes to something that seems preferable at the moment). It might be saying yes when fears say no, and then finding the courage to show up and follow through. Certainly, many things that happened for my highest good in the long-run may not have seemed so great at the time. Often, leading up to these situations, it occurred to me, "I don't feel like it!" At these times, I suggest that some form of discipline is desirable—in other words, choosing love won't always seem easy. Sometimes, an act of love feels exceedingly difficult.

I want to help others find within themselves more than they dreamed possible—but first, I must demonstrate this in my life. I can't just talk the talk — I must walk the walk. (Today, that looked like Day Thirty, walking the labyrinth.)

Day 30 Questions
(Discipline)

01) What does the quality of discipline represent to you?

02) Do you think that natural skill alone lies behind those you see as successful?

03) Do you see discipline as a path to rewards or something that limits you and requires sacrifice? (Examine your associations with discipline.)

04) Have you ever considered that you can derive freedom through discipline? (I.e. freedom from the consequences of lack of discipline.)

05) Even if no one is watching, do you ever really get away with anything?

06) What are the potential benefits of doing something even when you don't feel like it?

07) Can you frame the idea of discipline as an act of positive effort rather than one of denial?

08) As a strategy, have you considered the idea of scheduling times for yourself (i.e. morning meditation or a midday walk), and then treating these appointments as you would any other?

09) Are you aware that frequent, regular sessions usually prove more effective than one marathon session? (Even when training for a Marathon!)

10) How do you see yourself with respect to time management?

11) Do you have any awareness of your thoughts and feelings? (How these effect your commitments?)

12) Have you gotten into the habit of giving priority to your goals/commitments?

13) Does a setback of some sort signify, for you, the end of the commitment?

14) Can you let the satisfaction of meeting your goals be its own reward? (Avoid seeking the approval of others—which might both be denied and undermine your confidence.)

15) Do you try to take on too much too soon? (Potential overwhelm can lead to sabotage.)

16) As part of your goal-setting, imagine possible road-blocks (how will you deal with these should they present?)

17) Pay attention to your self-talk and what you tell others. If you are to be your own P.R. person (and you are), it might pay to watch what you say.

18) Do you have the willingness to start what you finish? If so, what do you gain? If not, then how does that impact you?

19) What is your awareness of the impact of your inner world on your outer world?

Sample Answer

Question 1—What does the quality of discipline represent to you?

Question 2—Do you think that natural skill alone lies behind those you see as successful?

Question 3—Do you see discipline as a path to rewards or something that limits you and requires sacrifice? (Examine your associations with discipline.)

Question 4—Have you ever considered that you can derive freedom through discipline? (I.e. freedom from the consequences of lack of discipline.)

Question 7—Can you frame the idea of discipline as an act of positive effort rather than one of denial?

I have to admit that when I thought about the idea of structure and discipline, it conjured the notion of repression, misery, and lack of options. It might prove of value to speak from the perspective of under-utilized discipline (and the results) as a means of demonstrating the advantages through contrast. For example, allowing distractions to creep in while working on a project can and has become detrimental to my peace of mind (if not overall success). Through procrastination and avoidance, I have put myself in the position to get near a pending deadline and, therefore, needing to cram in order to complete on time. This, for me, is no way to operate—it just creates unnecessary stress (as if there isn't already enough of that in the world). Chances are that my best work isn't as likely if I come under duress completing it.

It's amazing the sorts of things that can become alluring when I have an exam to study for or writing to do (which is truly remarkable, as I actually enjoy writing). Still, at times, the blank page can feel daunting. At such times, something inane, such as cleaning behind the refrigerator, might come to mind. Yes, a good thing to do from time-to-time; however, sometimes discipline can look like the need to prioritize.

Sometimes it becomes necessary to reframe an idea or belief. For example, if I discover when considering the idea of structure and discipline that I have decided it is limiting, repetitive, and boring, then imagine the difficulty I might have in putting in the time and energy necessary to complete a task that requires my ongoing attention. Likewise in developing a skill that requires significant practice to gain proficiency. So, while true, making a commitment can limit various other opportunities. Just the same, where the energy and focus get directed, that place yields the opportunity for increased familiarity, expertise, and depth of knowing. This would not be possible if addressed more superficially. Habitually jumping around can seem exciting as one continually courts the seduction of newness; however, in doing so, tasting the fruits that will ripen only with time, patience, and perseverance will remain endlessly elusive.

It never used to occur to me at all the time, dedication, and focused effort that individuals devoted to their craft (sport, musicianship, etc.). I became convinced that some were born with these talents and others weren't. Of course, now, I realize there are few, if any, overnight successes. Yes, of course, natural proclivities exist—gifts and talents—but, just the same, that raw ability requires consistent effort to reach full maturation. Otherwise, it may well remain a vast storehouse of unrealized potential—which I would suggest, from experience, carries a unique form of pain.

I would also suggest that other considerations that might fit well under the topic of discipline (at least, again, based on my experience) is to examine one's self rather than fall back on such notions as, "I don't have the discipline necessary," or, "I am not creative." It has proven useful for me to ask, "What am I good at?" And, "What am I interested in enough to devote some time and energy toward proficiency?"

"If it doesn't come easy, does that mean I cannot do it?"

"Am I willing to be a beginner (give up unrealistic notions of perfectionism) and do what it takes to pay the dues required upon the road of steady improvement?"

Invariably, the pursuit of almost anything can become a journey of self-discovery (if an intention to treat it as such gets maintained). Make no mistake, though, an intention to explore oneself requires a high degree of discipline—which, I'm happy to report, does (with diligence) offer considerable rewards.

Day 31
(Forgiveness)

It seems mind boggling to me that it's possible to spend so much time with a person and yet not know them that much at all. This rings particularly ironic when I consider that same statement in relationship to myself. There is no one that I have spent more time with than myself, and yet various self-exploration/self-development tools reveal far more to and about me that I had lived completely oblivious to—both negative and positive. I'd like to say that there exist equal parts of both, and maybe even that the positive outweighs the negative. I suspect a written inventory would still prove challenging (i.e. easier to itemize the negative than the positive attributes).

Self-love and inner peace, it would seem, are inextricably connected. For there to be self-love, there must exist self-acceptance. For self-acceptance, there must be self-awareness (in other words, to see myself as I am—not as I think I am). And I must come to accept all of me, warts and all. Along with this acceptance must come self-forgiveness and, while I'm at it, the list can get extended to include compassion, tolerance, patience, and empathy (for self) as aspects of overall wellness.

Why, again, all this talk of self? Because I want, as Gandhi stated, to "… be the change I wish to see in the world." I wish to see a world of love, connection, and peace. Therefore, I begin with me. I cannot become a part of peace in the world if love and peace don't exist in my heart. The love and peace that I generate within myself will flow outward naturally. Conversely, if I feel nothing but turmoil, I project that onto people around me.

The labyrinth offers a tool to explore the inner world. The practice itself feeds me on many levels, and therefore, becomes an aspect of my self-care. Those things that become known to me through the process, and that I come to realize no longer work in my life, I can see as areas of potential growth. I have no need to become self-critical or judgmental about awareness gained through a loving process. What is called for is more love. It, therefore, can be seen as a process whereby a connection gets made to the love within. Much of what I discovered on the journey, turned out to be those blocks that stood in the way of love flowing freely in and out. After identifying these blocks first, it led to a choice to release these blocks — somewhat like a plumber clearing the debris from a pipe to allow the water to once again flow.

All around me, I see the trees actively in the process of releasing their leaves — this in preparation for the next phase of their lifecycle. There isn't one big explosion, and then all the leaves go at once — it happens slowly, over time, on a schedule determined by life itself.

Nature knows when the time to let go has arrived, in preparation for the next phase of development. As part of this same web of life, would it not seem reasonable to believe that the same intelligence exists within our being? Even human intervention with the growth of plants, bushes, or trees demonstrates that, at times, it becomes necessary to prune old growth, which in turn, stimulates and makes way for renewal and lush new growth. As seen in the external world,

317

so it is in the internal world. That which no longer supports one to thrive, we can let go of to make way for all that previously lay in wait as potential to come more fully into being.

The season moves toward winter — perhaps more time for solitude and reflection — to recount the year past. What has worked? What areas of my life could benefit from a new approach? What do I do to look after myself — physically, mentally, spiritually/emotionally? It can be a time for visioning, a time of preparation, or laying the groundwork for things yet to come. Shorter daylight hours and long dark nights can offer a time to search the soul.

At this time of year, as the leaves and flowers dry up and drop off, the trees take on the appearance that nothing lives — that death shrouds all. If death is seen entirely as an ending, then it can add to the darkness — of course, there is the need to grieve, to acknowledge the pain of this loss as part of the soul's journey in human form. However, we can also see it as a precursor to change and part of the transition toward rebirth (transformation).

Though it appears as though nothing remains alive through the darkness of winter, life's energies continue quietly behind the scenes. So it is with these periods of incubation for personal/spiritual development; change is inevitable, and resistance will only make it more uncomfortable. Similarly, the period of time between letting go of the old and bringing something new into being can be experienced as uncomfortable, as it represents uncertainty. If at all possible, there need be no rush to fill the void. It gives an opportunity to create

318

something new from an infinite field of possibility. To hurry the process without first taking time for reflecting can result in simply recreating a set of circumstances identical to the previous scenario — nothing changes if nothing changes. It's not about just changing the externals. That would be as illustrated in the metaphor of "rearranging the deck chairs on the Titanic" — the ship will still go down.

Step-by-step, I let go, I trust the process, I trust myself. I'm willing to trust there are forces at play beyond my limited understanding, and therefore, what is left but to embrace the mystery?

Day 31 Questions
(Forgiveness)

01) What does it mean to you to forgive?

02) Can you differentiate between the person (including yourself) and the act?

03) Have you considered that the unwillingness to forgive binds you to the past?

04) Can you expect to get forgiven if you withhold forgiveness?

05) What do you gain by withholding forgiveness?

06) What are you afraid of losing by forgiving?

07) Are there unforgivable acts?

08) Examining your life, are there acts of omission or commission on your part, which you have not forgiven yourself for? If so, why not?

09) Have you considered it is yourself you set free with forgiveness?

10) You perceive you have been wronged (perhaps repeatedly), and given you were there, what is your part? (Not a suggestion of blame for the situation.) What might you be ignoring in your ongoing beliefs about yourself following this situation that may call for you to forgive yourself?

11) If justice is the required consequence of a wrongful act, does this consequence lead to peace? Does justice equal peace? If not, what might be missing?

12) Could harbouring grudges and resentment create more suffering for yourself than the target of your contempt?

13) If it's true that there is a widespread agreement in support of judgment and retaliation,

then what is the responsibility of the individual to becoming the change?

14) What part does self-righteousness play in justification for retribution?

15) Is it possible that seeking vengeance can only make a painful situation worse?

16) Have you ever considered the need to be right versus being happy?

17) If through getting wronged it leads to a completely different life trajectory (beyond anything you previously imagined for yourself), could gratitude be warranted?

18) If something "so wrong" becomes a blessing in disguise, what is there that requires forgiving?

Sample Answer

Question 3—Have you considered that the unwillingness to forgive binds you to the past?

Question 12—Could harbouring grudges and resentment create more suffering for yourself than the target of your contempt?

Question 13—If it's true that there is a widespread agreement in support of judgment and retaliation, then what is the responsibility of the individual to becoming the change?

Question 14—What part does self-righteousness play in justification for retribution?

Question 15—Is it possible that seeking vengeance can only make a painful situation worse?

Question 16—Have you ever considered the need to be right versus being happy?

No question, for much of my life, I had an operating system that ran behind the scenes with a preference for being right. Even when one day I got asked the question, "Would you rather be right or happy?" With little thought (if any), I responded with, "I'm happy when I'm right." With me thinking that I had handily parried that inquiry, my response then got met with, "If you're so happy, you might want to tell your face because it appears to be telling a different story!" And so began what would become a long succession of people in my life that not only saw through my various defense mechanisms but who also told me so. Admittedly, sometimes I wondered what compelled me to invite this into my life. It would take some time before I could recognize the gift of these people in my life.

What I learned about myself with respect to self-righteousness was that it made a convenient (and on some level effective) means for me to justify behaviour (and the beliefs that led to them), which when scrutinized, could be said to be at least as offensive as the acts I reacted to. Eventually, I saw that I rationalized some behaviour (that if we can agree social implies conducive to connection, and at least some concern for civility, then this behaviour was anti-social) that included a refusal to forgive. Now, forgiveness can be seen as a rather important component of spiritual wellness, but I would suggest it is effective as a social lubricant as well.

I had grudges and resentments that I could measure with calendars rather than clocks and, frankly, even with my considerable ability to intellectualize extensively, I found no peace in any of this.

I remember the first time I got introduced to the idea (suggestion) that I might consider praying for those I held in my treasured contempt—I laughed out loud. I thought the person had made a joke.

"What do you have to lose?" they asked.

Eventually, I came to realize that I certainly wasn't winning—sure, I have had a moment of feeling superior (through lashing out at someone and putting them in their place), but a backlash always came, which didn't feel any good. This, combined with my staying so focused on the unacceptable behaviour of the other party, meant that I ignored my culpability. In fact, their behaviour led to my behaviour (in the windmills of my mind). Not a path to peace; I can assure you. Seriously, how are my unacceptable actions any better than those against whom I retaliate? Why does their behaviour merit punishment while mine upholds some principle? (Real or imagined.)

Even becoming aware of the way my attitudes, beliefs, and behaviour had become self-defeating, I remained inclined to judge myself severely for what I learned about myself (so, at that time, I had no capacity to empathize or forgive myself). I also had a great deal of challenge in embracing the notion that praying for (and/or forgiving) was desirable. "What? Just let them off the hook?" I protested.

(Forgiveness is not about letting them off the hook — it is for yourself. You occupy the hook.)

"Huh, can you run that past me again?"

(Sure, the forgiveness is not for them, as granted by you, it is you that stands to benefit when you set yourself free, and besides, who appointed you the job of policing the world and deciding where forgiveness is merited?

(You are not upset for the reasons that you think — consider that the other in your life mirrors for you (either directly or indirectly) a behaviour or attitude that you yourself possess. Or the behaviour might point to a way of being or an expanded capacity that you could benefit from in your life, such as a willingness to forgive yourself. To the degree that you withhold this forgiveness of another, you deny it from yourself. No one denies the presence of your pain; however, in effect, refusing to forgive is choosing to remain in pain — to prolong the suffering. Indeed, it may prove necessary to let go of certain mindsets

324

in order to open the door to the possibility of forgiveness. Just the same, once that door gets opened, it becomes possible to gain freedom from the prison of your making. The suffering you experience is a creation and projection of your mind. Its cause is not real, though you experience it as such. Only love is real; therefore, forgiveness becomes a portal, of sorts, for a return to love (which makes the end of suffering), and in actuality, demonstrates that you had nothing to forgive in the first place.)

"Once again, herein lies a particular truth, the power of which I can only fully realize relative to my willingness to believe it as true. I have the freedom to believe as I wish. However, that freedom includes believing, or disbelieving, that which represents my higher good."

Day 32
(Heart-path)

Interestingly, walking in circles had offered me a new orientation. Now, some in my past might have said, "He was dizzy to begin with!" If they were to hear what I'd gotten up to here (exploring an inner journey through meditating while walking a labyrinth), then they might well grow more convinced than ever. But, you see, the thing is, it didn't matter. I explored my heart and looked to follow where it led. I endeavoured to find ground zero within myself (by which I mean to establish my own fundamental beliefs, values, dreams, and desires). As this made for a personal journey of discovery, external approval wasn't necessary or relevant.

The term "ground zero" is more commonly used to describe the detonation point of an explosion. Though, I didn't enter into this process with the intention of destroying anything. The image of a skyscraper (ready for demolishing) that implodes and crumbles in upon itself comes to mind as a visual, which reminds me of the many things that I identified with so strongly that virtually vanished overnight. I do not come from a place of self-pity (though, I have been there); it just gives a powerful representation of the sobering reality that the circumstances of our lives can change radically, and in what seems like the blink of an eye. This, therefore, is very much about, "Okay, so now what?" It also holds true that rebirth, regeneration, and new growth sometimes have as their precursors death, destruction, and what seems like complete annihilation.

I looked to determine what was inherently me—what mattered now, what no longer worked? From here, I sought to create. When I say new orientation, I mean perspective—on my life, not just that but also the world, God, spirituality, service, love, and peace. I don't look to recreate what I had already (I feel reasonably sure that won't happen because, as I consider the list just outlined, none of my life previous got created with conscious consideration around any of those elements, and so, even incorporating intention toward a few of them moving forward could yield a vastly different result).

When I considered these expansive perspectives, I could feel some freedom and spaciousness. To come out from under the oppressive limiting prison of my old beliefs, even when the reprieve came from just the tiniest ray of light shining through a crack in the walls, feels inspiring. To step into that light and live into the truth of expanded possibility; now, that feels exhilarating. Even still, I have remained unable/unwilling to accept the keys to the kingdom—apparently preferring to view it through the window, or experience it through short furloughs (though, inch-by-inch, they increase in length).

A question worth asking at this point might be, "How good would I be willing to allow things to get?" Instead of saying, "Well, this is okay; it doesn't hurt all the time—it could be worse, and many are worse off." (Don't get me wrong, it's never a bad thing to remember what I have to feel grateful for—but a life of resignation, I would suggest, makes a far cry from one of intentional fulfillment and joy.)

Survival is great (as far as it goes); in fact, it forms a baseline requirement (at least, with respect to the human journey); however, what would it be like to thrive?

What if I set my sights on greatness? Not necessarily fame or celebrity, but to discover my uniqueness and live that to the fullest. In my lifetime, I've never tried it. Mediocrity and half-measures had become my touchstones. What would I need to do to contribute to truly showing up? What would it feel like to exist in circumstances more enriching than draining? I recognize that periods of challenge will always exist (and I don't talk of Utopia or Pollyanna-thinking). I also know that part of what will create this reality for me is to track my attitude. Having said that, settling and/or growing resigned mean continuing to say yes to a situation that, if I paid attention to my heart, I would hear it screaming, ENOUGH!

I opened my eyes after completing the Qi Gong exercises (while standing in the centre of the labyrinth). It seemed still and quiet in the surrounding area (including my inner world). From around and behind the large oak tree scampered two, then a third, and finally, a fourth squirrel. I stood motionless, observing them as they went about their activity, unhampered by my presence. They moved sometimes quickly, and at other times, seemingly more methodically with curiosity. At one point, they moved within a few feet of where I stood—then, when startled by the clicking heels on the sidewalk of a woman passing by, they darted closer to the oak tree (I suppose, in case they determined the need to escape). It felt amazing to be present to what had

328

taken on the appearance of a choreographed dance. It gave one of those brief glimpses into something special (maybe even sacred) that ended almost as quickly as it had started—leaving the lingering question, "Did that just happen?"

I felt grateful to have occupied that spot at that moment. Perhaps, miracles do not always come of the Charlton Heston variety—i.e. the parting of the Red Sea. Maybe when one of the veils from within me lifts (or parts, if you will) so that I can experience the beauty unfolding in front of me, the bush itself makes for the miracle, and it doesn't need to get set on fire first.

Day 32 Questions
(Heart-path)

01) The head to the heart, though physically only separated by a short distance, can present a formidable journey when it comes to realizing your heart's desire. Consider your life thus far; where do you see yourself with regard to this journey?

02) What invokes your enthusiasm, passion, joy, and excitement?

03) How much time do you spend engaged in these pursuits?

04) Is it important to you to follow your heart?

05) If you don't realize the desires of your heart, what stands in the way?

06) Some degree of security is, of course, necessary. Do you have the willingness to shift the focus (if necessary) to realize more of your dreams?

07) Will you allow your dreams?

08) Do you believe dreams can come true?

09) Have you ever considered a connection between personal peace and the call of your heart?

10) Have you managed to attain a high-degree of success (career & lifestyle) but still find you have no lasting contentment?

11) What does your head tell you about dreaming or the pursuit of vocation that feels deeply satisfying to you?

12) When growing up, did those around you encourage you to seek your individual path? Did they encourage and support your personal interests?

13) How much do you value the expectations of family or society with regard to your life path?

14) What is your tolerance for risk?

15) The examination of your heart might well bring into question everything you believe about yourself (to find your truth) — what might be the first step for you? (Will you take it?)

16) Is it time you became more honest with yourself?

17) Is it time to stop pretending?

18) Take a look into your heart and ask yourself, what would you love to do more than anything else in the world?

19) What will it take to say yes to your heart (your dream)?

20) What are the potential costs of saying no or denying that your dreams are possible or even important?

Sample Answer

Question 15—The examination of your heart might well bring into question everything you believe about yourself (to find your truth)—what might be the first step for you? (Will you take it?)

Question 20—What are the potential costs of saying no or denying that your dreams are possible or even important?

If you'll pardon the pun, this journey is not for the weak of heart. And, having said that, the period that I delineate as my personal experience upon this path (though difficult to frame in exact linear terms) has proven the most exhilarating time of my entire life. Of course, given the complexities and mystery of life, this experience can't be told in a story that travels straight from point A to point B. It has turned out anything but an entirely smooth ride. It continues to unfold, and so I can't proclaim any popularly held happily-ever-after that might bolster someone else's decision to embark upon their journey. I have no pat formula with which to proceed (at least, not that I have discovered), and it might look any number of different ways during its pursuit and continuance.

A preliminary examination of your heart may lead to confusion, or even disbelief, as what you discover there might appear as completely out of your league or a complete hundred-and-eighty-degree departure from what you are currently doing (which, of course, if you're like me, may fast become the argument for impossible). My journey has demanded that I let go of everything I thought I knew about myself (to be clear—incrementally, not all at once). At times, this brought up regret and unresolved grief. To begin to follow my heart, I needed to start recognizing those things that I held true that would limit my ability to step toward further alignment. Elements of self-doubt (for example) were not just present in relation to a new vision—they had also operated throughout my entire life. So, the process of coming to see how significantly smaller a world of limitless possibility could be made, through the weave of my limiting beliefs, seemed disillusioning before it became anything like freedom or empowerment. It looks a bit like behaving as though I am pegged to a stake in the ground by a chain and ankle cuff—the chain will rotate, allowing a walk outward in any direction, though the limit remains the circular pattern determined by the length of the chain. The awakening takes the form of "suddenly" realizing that the chain had rusted and dissolved (years ago) while, in truth, it never existed, and even though I walked that same circle, I could have gone anywhere.

No question, my comfort zone got challenged constantly. Stability and security had gotten shaken significantly. Equally true, I had learned that my pre-existing resignation and embittered view of the world got, in part, fed by my compulsion to create absolute security (or the illusion of absolute). Will I retire, based on popularly held visions? Most likely not.

While conjuring the imagery of extremes (which does have some degree of truth), I renounced the familiar framework of predictability, routine, structure, logicality, rationally entrenched thinking, punctuality, etc. Of course, value exists in all these elements. My heart and soul, however, called for me to experience freedom, flexibility, spontaneity, creativity, intuition, healing, inspiration, passion, and love—all of which had remained largely (or entirely) missing from my life (or, rather, from my awareness). It seemed as though I stayed cut off from a huge portion of my being (which, I'll say for the sake of this discussion, was my heart).

What a full-body, multi-dimensional, absolutely delicious experience this has yielded. I have had an adventure (in fact, seldom does it cease), travel, discovery, mysticism, the pinnacles of love and passion, and the abyss of betrayal and abandonment (and everything in between). I wouldn't trade this experience for anything—I am fully engaged in my life. Which might seem an odd statement (where was I before?). My response would be that I had grown detached, disassociated, and despondent. What a joy to experience expanded presence and the ability to connect. If you are reading this, then you give witness to the power of this journey to make possibility from the previously impossible. Writing has made for one of the many gifts that have presented for me along the way. I don't know what will show up for anyone else—this is such a personal undertaking (including whether it gets undertaken). Certainly, you have no guarantees (of course, I have come to realize that neither were there any in my life previous, based in fear and highlighted by insecurity and resignation). Fear continues to present, but gone are despair and boredom. I have had many forms of support along the way, for which I remain deeply grateful.

I can't imagine regretting this profoundly life-changing choice (even though it's virtually impossible to speak in terms of absolutes)—I feel more certain that I couldn't have gone on the way I had. I see living, then, as like being the walking dead. I believe a journey such as this provides the opportunity for a far deeper satisfaction of life and the increasing ability to more fully participate in the world, and to see and contribute more consciously to daily miracles. That forms my experience thus far.

Day 33
(Crossroads)

One week from the forty-day commitment and it felt anything but a done deal on this morning. I had a mixed bag of feelings stirring within, which just happened to make the perfect blend of energies to awaken the dormant saboteur.

Already, I had determined I would have breakfast and then go to the churchyard, as I had a group study meeting in the neighbourhood nearby, so it made sense to arrange the schedule accordingly. Well, I slept in (not so late as to have missed the whole window of available time, but it did create a bit of a time crunch). As always, the saboteur made for the consummate opportunist (and, I might add, rather patient—just lying quietly in wait). Through the silence came the "voice" exclaiming, "Oh, what's the use? There's not enough time."

(What? Forty days, upholding a commitment, the sacred, following my heart, a book to get written (did I miss anything?), and, apparently, it all hangs in the balance.)

"Can't possibly get this done in the time available this morning; forget about it. Maybe later today."

(Jeez, this guy clearly has no regard for the sacred — and, frankly, not much for me either. Odd to consider, as it would seem it is I that generates this "idea.")

Hard to believe that all that has gone into bringing me to this moment could get forsaken in a matter of seconds—as such, I could see this as a crossroads of monumental proportions, and the cause I might sum up as a stew of emotions that you could label collectively, "*I don't feel like it.*"

Was this any way to view an activity that I had conceived as life-enriching and part of a path of self-exploration and development? And maybe even life changing? Could I allow such a flippant attitude to steer my life? Well, yes, indeed I could!

I have to say, this is not unfamiliar territory that I experienced here—of course, the scenario differed, but it also had an element of déjà vu about it.

Though not much for sports metaphors, one would seem to serve at this time. ... With twenty seconds left on the clock, I've got the ball deep in the opponents' end of the court, and a regular basket (two points) would only tie the game. Not enough time remains to move the ball close enough for the two-point shot anyway. From where I stand, three points would win the game. The cries from the crowd feel deafening—"For God's sake, shoot the damn ball!" Instead, I hand my opponent the ball and walk off the court to the showers, and the buzzer sounds—game over!

I've never been one to get enthralled with sports or entertainment celebrities (oh, I appreciate their talent and the dedication it took to develop their skills) and am not quick to hoist them to a pedestal. I suppose because, at some level, I know that none of these people can be the hero I look for in my life. In actuality, I need to suit up and show up in that capacity for myself. To be there in the clutch moments of my life and rise to the occasion.

(So, Hell no, the game's not over; get your butt out the door. You could adjust the practice to compensate. You

could arrive a little late to the group. Many possible options present themselves, but quitting isn't one of them.)

"Huh, don't know who's voice that is, but it sounds like a get-things-done fellow, who might just make an effective counterpart to the saboteur."

The lesson for the day was that, in the presence of emotional upheaval (by all means, acknowledge the feelings), you should not allow them to become the tail wagging the dog. So, you can acknowledge, feel, and release them. In this case, the process could occur while walking the labyrinth. I had nothing to gain by continually making myself the slave of my emotions; nor did it prove helpful to continue to generate self-defeating thoughts (which, ultimately, led to more negative emotions). To quit outright would offer another example of abandoning myself (not the first time this would have occurred) but no reason to continue to live out that pattern.

So, though I would not, necessarily, undertake today's walk embodying inner peace, it might well represent a victory of immeasurable magnitude. This could represent the beginning of a shift in how I went about doing things. And while walking through the blocks (resistance) might involve some discomfort short term, it may well become the path to a more consistent and lasting contentment. At this point, the book had still to get written, literally and metaphorically. Therefore, perhaps a life-changing decision had, indeed, gotten made; after all, continuing the walk made a necessary component in the book getting written.

Day 33 Questions
(Crossroads)

01) Think about various times you have been at the crossroads in your life. Journal about some of these experiences — consider the various factors that led to your choices.

02) If you found yourself at a similar crossroad, would you choose the same way again?

03) How easy (or challenging) do you find making decisions? What contributes to the ease (or difficulty) you experience?

04) Can you have all the information you need now to make a new beginning?

05) How much does the outcome of previous decisions effect your current decision-making process?

06) Do you use intuition or logical analysis (or a combination of both) when faced with making decisions?

07) Has over-analyzing left you at the dock when the boat sailed?

08) Are there any guarantees once a decision gets made? (Think, again, of your tolerance for risk.)

09) How much do you trust your ability to make decisions?

10) What do you believe for yourself about making a mistake? How might that influence your decision-making?

11) What if there were no wrong decisions?

12) Can your path get accurately determined by the views of others (or even your previous experience) when it comes to making a present-day choice?

13) Is logic the only reliable basis upon which to base your decision?

14) Consider the paths of various historic figures who thought outside the box; could they have brought into being what they had to offer the world if they had followed only what had collectively gotten held as true?

15) What does this say about strict adherence to logical/rational thought? How many ideas have you abandoned because they didn't make sense?

16) Even if it is accepted to be true that you can't go back, could you choose again to resurrect an abandoned vision?

17) Can you have both security and passion?

18) Will you choose again?

Sample Answer

Question 6—Do you use intuition or logical analysis (or a combination of both) when faced with making decisions?

Question 8—Are there any guarantees once a decision gets made? (Think, again, of your tolerance for risk.)

Question 10—What do you believe for yourself about making a mistake? How might that influence your decision-making?

Question 11—What if there were no wrong decisions?

I have often envied those that I hear telling of their life experience, "I always knew what I wanted to do." I can think of individuals that, even in elementary school, had certain interests, gifts, and talents and, sure enough, anecdotes or direct witnessing years later, revealed that they had taken those talents and, in some way, they became a major part of their adult life, career path, and contribution to the world. Baffling to me—as that has not been reflected in my life. This, of course, doesn't mean I haven't made decisions throughout my life—sometimes, I have decided not to decide (which still forms a decision). Often, I have allowed circumstances to determine my path rather than take a more proactive approach. There has existed a fear of failure, choosing what seemed to be the safer path.

I have discovered issues that affected my self-confidence (I choose now to share that, not as an excuse but the truth of my journey). Without a doubt, as my intention is to demonstrate the value of introspection and self-examination with respect to healing and beginning to live a life of increased expansion and possibility, a part of me remains that would rather present a flawless meteoric rise to success. However, that is not the truth—I have, therefore, decided to allow the transparent disclosure of my journey to tell it's unique story and, in doing so, I again choose to see that as a victory over (or through) the story itself. Do I have any guarantee it will work that way? None whatsoever.

I am guided only by my heart and desire to both write and to tell this story. I wouldn't have to go far to find any amount of reasons to become less than forthright in sharing my story. What with prevailing attitudes like, "Don't ever let them see you sweat," or, "For goodness sake, never expose your underbelly." I understand the fear underlying such beliefs (I have lived them myself). The point is, I am in the process of choosing differently. Am I now, then, fearless? Hardly, but I have committed to more consistently stepping up, despite fear. Let's face it; until someone else reads this, at this point, I only consider being courageous. If you're reading this now, you will know to be true that I followed through.

As for making the wrong choice, how would one determine that? For example, when in high school, a conversation with a guidance counsellor involved him querying, "What do you plan to do with your life?" The question left me completely overwhelmed.

I remember framing it at that time as, "I'm supposed to make a decision now that will determine the *rest of my life?!?!*" In essence, my choice was to dive headlong deeper into addiction. Not a stellar choice (as decisions go). I have immense gratitude that I survived. Just the same, this (as with any number of subsequent decisions since then) is all part of an ongoing story. Taken in isolation, there could be numerous assessments made of the decisions and the results. As part of an unfolding life saga—that's not over yet—how could I determine any of those decisions as good or bad? Where would I be now if I had said no to drugs, got a university education, put ten percent a year into RRSPs (Registered Retirement Savings Plans), married young, and had 2.5 children and a picket fence, etc.? I know all kinds of people that, more or less, did that and it didn't any more guarantee an outcome for them (and doesn't invalidate their choices either). Life plans of this sort can (and have) get wiped out by stock market crashes and company embezzlement of pension plans or bankruptcy.

Most probably, the wise thing to consider is that of saving for a rainy day, does that mean it will be there when the rain begins to fall? No. If, like me, that doesn't describe the current state of your life-plan (or that said plan was never really comprehensively considered), then a crossroad no less exists. Choices continue to be possible with respect to how I see the circumstances I'm in. It's only wrong if I view it from a fixed set of imposed standards. If I view myself as only being of any value based on my relative position in a consumption-based economy, whereby the annual salary and power to consume determines my

343

value as a person, then it could be said I have made a great many bad decisions.

I choose to see things differently. Even if I go on to become a resounding financial success, my values don't include ongoing unbridled consumption. That is my choice. Some of my contributions may well continue to take place outside the system of monetary exchange. Will I regret any of my past and present choices? Possibly, but it's just as possible that if I did everything right, I'd simply join the ranks of those that lamented on their deathbed that they wish they'd worked less, connected with friends and loved ones more, done more of what they loved to do, and pursued their dreams. I can't see how that would generate a great deal of regret, but hey, I could be wrong.

Day 34
(Creativity)

The morning weather didn't seem of an inspiring variety; it poured rain—even still, it didn't much present as a significant roadblock. I felt grateful to have the clothing to keep me warm and dry and decided I would do the labyrinth walk and Qi Gong and then come home to sit and meditate. I had very little to sweep on the labyrinth surface, so the walk commenced soon upon arriving. It felt good to allow, for both the observance of the practice itself and for creativity around negotiating the weather. Yes, the practice remained sacred, as it fed my spirit; it represented an aspect of my self-care. However, to sit on the soaking-wet ground in the pouring rain to meditate, I wouldn't see as in the best interests of my wellness; therefore, to be open to creativity (which, I believe, shows an aspect of the Divine) can broaden significantly what becomes possible. To adhere dogmatically to the routine would be a product of the mind, which judges this unbending approach as morally superior when, truly, it just creates unnecessary suffering. Without question, life involves pain, but suffering is another thing entirely and is, by no means, compulsory.

The supposition of some is that the suffering demonstrates the level of dedication present. Martyrdom (in my estimation) is not a required aspect of serving the sacred. I have found discipline and commitment are required, and a need to make a choice to uphold what you have set as the vision, and to prioritize (notice, I don't say sacrifice—at the end of the day, it might look the same; for example, something got set aside at the time to continue with the commitment. There is, though, not a sacrificial energy when doing so). I did not see this with eyes of deprivation, but looked at it as serving a higher good and performed it with joyous intent. It feels life enriching with no sacrifice.

So, even though I didn't feel an overwhelming enthusiasm to set out in the rain, I believe that the intent to continue on this heart-path of mine, coupled with openness, made possible the access to an out-of-the-box solution, allowing the intention (the practice) to get upheld. A win-win outcome.

I believe a rigid mindset or dogmatic belief system prevents access, during a given moment, to the spirit of living truth, which will not only be perfect for the present circumstances, it will also be perfect for me (or each individual) in that circumstance.

Dogma offers the same thing over and over again with an expectation (or promise) of different results — Albert Einstein said that this "… defines insanity." No one size exists that fits all answers. My path is not yours — yours is not mine. Certainly, we can mutually benefit from the insights gained from our respective paths. In sharing, we can gain an expanded view of the whole. Each has an independent connection to the source within. Therefore, the answers for each must come from within.

The walk around the labyrinth offered an exploration opportunity of this inner landscape. For definite, it didn't always feel like a "walk in the park" but, as I grew better acquainted with the various ways I had run from myself and recognized the self-defeating behaviours, unconscious for so long, something else became possible. Despite the challenges showing up each day, it occurred to me that it was a walk that led me home.

Day 34 Questions
(Creativity)

01) How do you express creativity in your life?

02) Do you consider only pursuits such as art, music, and dance as creativity?

03) What types of activity produce for you the sense that you have gotten lost in what you are doing? (When do you feel as though "in the flow"?)

04) Do you allow yourself time to daydream?

05) Recall those times when ideas, solutions to problems, etc., come to you as if from nowhere?

06) Can you allow yourself to try new things and new ways of being without becoming overly concerned with getting it right?

07) Consider that creativity is that which flows into your consciousness, those flashes of inspiration (that, perhaps, quickly get followed by a litany of reasons those are not good ideas).

08) Think of some of the ways you may shut down your creativity.

09) Did you get encouraged as a child to use your imagination?

10) Can you allow yourself some freedom to play?

11) Are you now in an environment that encourages innovation?

12) Do you have people in your life that can hold space for brainstorming and provide a safe environment free of negativity and criticism?

13) Can you give your critical mind some time off to allow creativity to flow?

14) Can you shake up routine at times to stir the imagination and explore possibility?

15) What is your relationship to playing by the rules?

16) Consider that you can utilize and express creativity in any area of your life.

17) Rather than dwelling on a problem, experiment with letting it go—stay open to answers that occur as outside your way of doing things.

18) Drive a new way home, walk instead of drive, and listen to a different radio station (or take a media break). Have a conversation or listen to someone that you completely disagree with (not with the idea of changing their mind, but try and gain understanding of their particular point of view).

19) Consider that even those well known for creativity and innovation have had countless failures, which far outnumber their accomplishments; the difference is that they continue to work at bringing their ideas into being and learning from the journey which, eventually, leads to a breakthrough (which often looks like overnight success to others).

20) Think about the implications of taking yourself, your ideas, your learning, and creativity lightly.

Sample Answer

Question 2 — Do you consider only pursuits such as art, music, and dance as creativity?

Question 6 — Can you allow yourself to try new things and new ways of being without becoming overly concerned with getting it right?

Question 8 — Think of some of the ways you may shut down your creativity.

Question 11 — Are you now in an environment that encourages innovation?

Admittedly, I once considered myself to be of the "I am not creative" camp. Much of this viewpoint, I could attribute to comparing my abilities (or perceived lack thereof) against pretty much everyone else I encountered. Most certainly, a self-defeating perspective, as it failed to discover, acknowledge, and develop the talents I did have while, at the same time, reinforcing the deep sense of defeat I felt, that I didn't have the talents I saw so clearly around me.

Ultimately, I chose life-paths that seemed safe and predictable, which clearly met needs at those times, but it also severely compromised the meeting of other needs (ones equally as important and that might well represent more of my authentic self). The work environments I chose did provide security, but they also held oppressive rigidity — comprised of routines and systems in place to create efficiency, but void of opportunity for imagination. Creative input got discouraged in favour of insistence on acquiescence to "how we do things" (whether effective or not). Add to that a hierarchy more interested in wielding its power than with collaboration; therefore, the collective power of a diverse human resource pool with a variety of talents and proclivities became homogenized into mindless drones. Eventually, I woke up to the fact that I was smothering in my life.

As I have said, I created some of these realities by my choices (and various needs got met at those times). The realization of my hand in creation seemed, at first, disillusioning but has since become a more empowering proposition. The point being, I have always had the ability to create — in hindsight, I haven't, however, proven particularly mindful about what I created. I don't know about anyone else, but consider this: Seldom have I, if ever, been short of an excuse, rationalization, or justification for why I can't do something or why I did do something else. What, if not creativity, generated all those stories? The issue is not lack of creativity; rather, it comes down to what did my creativity serve? (Oft times, it proved to be my fears.)

Self-confidence and willingness to explore the unknown go a long way to fostering creativity. A willingness to become a beginner, to not know, to make mistakes (said another way, to let go of perfectionism). Creativity invariably suffers if all kinds of expectations get placed on the process and outcome (especially in a brand new endeavour). Harsh criticism and judgment, for certain, become creativity-killers (in particular from oneself) — trust me; I know this intimately.

A big step in uncovering and resurrecting/redirecting creativity, for me, has been to become more open to the possible in my life. I spoke of oppressive environments; the story would be incomplete without mentioning the rigidity of my thinking and how limiting (oppressive) that can be. So, my experience showed that I don't necessarily need to abandon my existing life (move to the Mediterranean and become an artist) to express more creativity. Of course, I could if that was the calling. I can just as readily exercise creativity in imagining and living into changes — wherever I feel the need.

Day 35
(Release)

Today presented as a beautiful sunny morning with a clear blue sky—no question, I had far less resistance to heading out under those conditions. Which proves interesting to consider because the act of leaving remains the same either way. Simple, really; get dressed, open the door, and step through. What a colossal difference the state of mind can make to achieve such a simple act. Same requirement; however, the environment between my ears can offer everything from mild distraction to alibis, to resistance, to rebellion, and flat out refusal—which can complicate, considerably, walking out the door.

Within this train of thought lay the offer of expanded awareness as to the origins of conflict in my life. It occurred to me that the stage was set for these conflicts to happen, beginning with ignoring incongruence within myself. The resulting agitation experienced can lead to my seeking a target to assign responsibility for the disturbance I feel. More accurately, I have sought to restore equanimity—inner peace and balance at the expense of someone else. The problem with this strategy is that it ignores my original needs (which, unmet, created the agitation). If I target someone else or seek some external fix for the agitation, then the needs remain unmet, and inner peace cannot possibly get restored by attacking someone or something else.

It would seem there is no way to avoid conflict outside myself if I continue to remain conflicted within myself—unless I can become mindful of the agitation within me and determine what it is I need (the inclination can be to project my inner disturbances onto the world around me).

It also seems interesting to consider that this morning practice had presented to me as though something that would appeal to my heart—as though the idea came to me by way of my heart. As time passed and this experience unfolded, I realized that my heart led me, through my heart (meaning both being directed by it and also going on a pilgrimage of sorts to, and then within, the labyrinth-like passages of my heart). God only knows where that will lead.

Recently, I got introduced to the idea that, where pain is concerned, perhaps no one is at fault. The topic of pain seemed relevant, as I appeared to have encountered no shortage of it on this heart walk. I'm sure there is more to this human heart of mine than pain. In fact, I *know* there is. It just so happens that I spent so much of my life ignoring and repressing my feelings. No surprise, then, that my heart became a warehouse filled with hurts and disappointments and betrayal, neglects, and abandonment. My personality and who I am in the world, then, got shaped by an unconscious desire to keep the doors to this repository shut and avoiding additional suffering.

The stories did, at one time, have necessity; though now, had become a direct interference with a life of vibrancy and joy. To cling to them continues to perpetuate their legacy in the form of self-fulfilling prophecy.

Who would I then be without my story? I mentioned the ineffectiveness of the story in the present—that doesn't take away from the inherent familiarity and perverse comfort the story provides. To transcend the story (well, first it would need to get recognized — then a willingness to let it go follows), a leap would be required, to where, if only I knew — in general terms, into the unknown. Still, it is clear that leap I must.

A key element to becoming free from that which anchors me to the past is the act of forgiveness — with self heading-up the list.

I had taken a walk through pain to forgiveness — pain is, therefore, not present to continue to hold others responsible (nor myself). It becomes a teacher. What lessons have I learned through this pain? What qualities have I developed as a result of this suffering (recognition of both assets and liabilities)? If there were no one to blame is it possible that pain is a gift? I wouldn't readily invite more, but perhaps, I can become grateful for where it has taken me so far.

While I walked with that, I acknowledged that, as a member of the human race, I had a part to play in discovering my personal share of the collective pain of humanity and, more importantly, healing myself so I became less of a continual contributor to more suffering.

I may never know the pain of another, but I know what it feels like to hurt — I can, therefore, develop a deeper compassion for the suffering of others, knowing first-hand my own.

Day 35 Questions
(Release)

01) What are some of the long-term stories you tell yourself (and others)?

02) Have you considered what you get from continuing to tell these stories?

03) In what ways could these stories limit the possible in your life?

04) Have you considered yourself as the creator of the story? (Not necessarily the circumstances that occurred when the story originated, but the story itself.)

05) Are you willing to release any part of this story?

06) What would need to change to gain a new perspective?

07) Do you incorporate in your life any form of relaxation practices? (I.e. meditation, yoga, deep breathing, or an emotional freedom technique.)

08) Do you have the willingness to make space in your day that is entirely yours to spend as you please?

09) Do you have the willingness to become mindful of how much your day gets shaped by thinking, which includes such perspectives as, "I should," and, "I have to," and, "I have no choice," and "I'm obliged to,"?

10) What comes up for you when you consider the idea of being versus doing? Have you ever considered these distinctions in your life?

11) What impact does attitude have on your day-to-day experience?

12) Have you ever considered in what ways you become conflicted internally and how that might play into conflict in your external world?

13) Are you aware of the presence of tension, restriction, and rigidity? (Whether physical, emotional, or belief systems.)

14) What are your personal beliefs with respect to spirituality?

15) Have you ever allowed yourself to seek for yourself a spiritual answer?

16) Have you ever participated in any form of talking circle or support group?

17) Have you ever utilized the services of a counsellor, spiritual director, or therapist?

18) With respect to the previous questions, what would create for you a willingness to explore these avenues? What is the source of resistance to such exploration?

19) What is your relationship to pain? Were you taught to suffer in silence, or that emotional expression is irrational and a sign of weakness, or that emotional vulnerability leads to hurt or punishment, and finally, no pain no gain?

20) Is inner peace possible?

Sample Answer

Question 1—What are some of the long-term stories you tell yourself (and others)?

Question 2—Have you considered what you get from continuing to tell these stories?

Question 3—In what ways could these stories limit the possible in your life?

Question 4—Have you considered yourself as the creator of the story? (Not necessarily the circumstances that occurred when the story originated, but the story itself.)

What a can of worms this whole topic has become for me. It seems a bit like experiencing a long-term toothache and then having it stop. I had no full realization of how much pain was present until it had gone. I use this analogy because it aptly describes the coming to know of internal conflicts, limiting beliefs and attitudes, and experiencing the absence (or, at least, the increased awareness of their existence) and how that impacts my life once they lessen or no longer have an active influence.

It remains so much an ongoing process that I can't say just how entirely the suffering I have experienced was of my own creation. Certainly, I can attest to an occasional attitude adjustment as of great benefit. I can also now say that long-standing stories that featured me as a hapless victim (though I did not speak specifically in those terms) involved a far more active than passive participation on my part (even if I was actively being passive).

The truth is that, far enough back in my personal history, I had become someone who went through my life largely unaware of myself in it, or the impact I had on the world around me. I had no idea of the degree to which fear, for example, ran my life. I lived an unexamined life. I say that now, somewhat tongue in cheek, but it wasn't until I had enough of a state of chaos in my world that it both got my attention and opened a previously closed window, which allowed me to see that I made for the common denominator in my chaos. It didn't so much follow me, but I most certainly always had a presence when it broke out. I don't make light of the suffering I created for others, but I have gotten to a place where I see the comedy of errors in my experience. This, in itself, offers a profound example of healing and release.

I have a long-standing relationship with perfectionism and, therefore, it seemed near impossible for me to be seen making mistakes (let alone speaking or writing about it). This stemmed from deep-seated shame and a sense of inferiority and the mistaken belief that I was flawed as a human being (all unconscious but, nonetheless, a powerful underlying influence on my choices). And trying to uphold this air of perfection came from a misguided attempt to avoid the further pain of rejection and judgment (which, of course, proved impossible).

So, in my mind, being wrong came at way too high a cost. It all got tangled up in my emotional survival. I don't say that everyone will find this specific dynamic operating in their life, but you may find equally limiting frameworks of your own; the removal (or gradual dismantling) of which can have a widespread impact on your life.

I also don't insist that a spiritual approach is the only way to gain access to new ways of seeing and being. I have now experienced so many different modalities, and each has offered a valuable piece of the puzzle. Any can become a portal into a more comprehensive, conscious journey, as it doesn't matter which aspect of your being you focus on, they all connect with one another. Don't feel surprised if one path intersects with another. That has been my experience. I started, primarily, looking to improve my physical wellbeing. At the same time, I had embarked on a spiritual journey through the 12 steps of A.A. Even though, initially, it mostly happened as an intellectual pursuit, eventually, I found myself following the threads into a vast territory of emotional/spiritual exploration, which remained completely uncharted territory for me. In hindsight, at first, I had a great deal of resistance at various places along the way.

My point is that so much of what I thought about myself (and consequently life), I further thought as carved in stone and that has turned out untrue. To hold onto mindsets such as, "a leopard doesn't change its spots," will ensure that it becomes the truth (it is not the absolute truth but a relative one). My experience points to so much more as possible and, I suppose, that depends largely on how willing I become to examine and release (to make changes) much of what I previously held as true.

Knowing what has changed in my life, I believe definitely that this kind of profound change remains possible for anyone. So, if you've stopped dreaming, start. If you're already doing it, then dream bigger.

Day 36
(Harmony)

As I walked the labyrinth today, my participation in a Christmas choir performance came to mind. One of the songs involved a four-part harmony and, as it turned out, I sang the only tenor voice in the group. As we had rehearsed, and I learned my part, I became aware of the challenges of holding to my melodic line. I noticed how easy it was to get drawn into what the others sang around me. Now, if the objective were to sing in unison, it would sound fine, and all would join in on the same melody. However, the intention was to achieve the vocal tapestry of the blend of the four parts that created something greater than the individual parts. Which meant that each subgroup (and, in my case, me) must hold to their line to produce the harmony.

The point of this story shows what I recognized as I considered elements of the analogy in my life. All this introspection and self-discovery seemed great to a point, but only if what I uncovered then got brought forward into the world to make a difference in my life and the lives of others. There are parallels to the choir story. There can be a great deal of pressure (from within and without) to become like everyone else—in other words, to all sing the same melody. I believe what is intended is that each discovers their part, and then begin by living in harmony with that, and then continue to hold their individual melodic line (path) even when subject to the influence of the distinctly different lines of those around them. I think the key (pun intended) for me is that my line might sound dissonant (which doesn't mean it's wrong), and still, I seek to dance in relative harmony—there is no need to clobber those around me with my drumstick—rather, I continue to focus to my beat.

The choir of humanity got created with a wide range of diversity—did it make any sense that this diversity should get reduced to uniformity? I believe that the diverse voices combined would produce a divine harmony by utilizing and maximizing the power and strength of the diversity, not eliminating it. The tenors don't look at the sopranos and say, "Either you sing like us or get out." No, it remains critical that each knows their part and stands in it. No one part, however, has more importance than the whole.

Day 36 Questions
(Harmony)

01) How far should "each to their own" be allowed to go?

02) Is there a need to impose limitations on diversity?

03) Do you see the beauty of diversity, or see it as a threat?

04) Do you think that others should be more like us?

05) Is conformity necessary for harmony?

06) If you are conforming to the environment outside you, what effect does this have on your inner harmony?

07) Does your inner harmony matter?

08) When traveling, do you seek experiences unique to the area or do you look for a resort or chain franchise with "home cooking"?

09) "Globalization," what has its impact been around the world?

10) Are your unique gifts and talents getting realized and appreciated in your life?

11) Do you appreciate the unique gifts and talents of others?

12) How does an over emphasis on competition impact cooperation/collaboration?

13) What is being won if doing so comes at the expense of others?

14) Is it necessary to have someone lose? What of solutions that benefit everyone?

15) What challenges present to you when following your path?

16) Can you hold to your intention when others disagree with you?

17) Can you stay true to yourself with out behaving in a disagreeable manner toward others?

18) Do you look for a place where diversity can find harmony or focus entirely on the differences?

19) Was humanity created with so many differences only to become homogenized?

20) Do you need to give up your truth to harmonize with someone else?

Sample Answer

Question 16 — Can you hold to your intention when others disagree with you?

Question 17 — Can you stay true to yourself without behaving in a disagreeable manner toward others?

Question 20 — Do you need to give up your truth to harmonize with someone else?

Well, I can certainly attest to being aware of the challenges of being myself in a world that seems intent on defining what that would look like. Definitely, I don't stand alone in this, and neither is this something that I can address once and for all. After all, it involves a lifetime of discovering who I am and determining, at any given time, to which of my values I shall give priority focus and attention.

Many variables influence and impact the choices I make and how I present myself. For sure, how I feel about myself figures prominently in how I go about carrying myself in the world. There would also seem little value in comparing myself to others — being more like someone else cannot result in the inner harmony of which I speak. Which is not to say that, for example, if I desire a similar lifestyle as someone else, I couldn't attain that — I would, though, want to go about achieving it in alignment with who I am, and not necessarily try and follow their footsteps.

I do value inclusion, which might come as a result of feeling excluded and disconnected at previous times in my life. I have also had to examine my judgment and criticisms and discover that I behaved in an exclusionary manner in my attitudes toward various groups of people; for example, wealthy people and politicians. A closer look revealed that I felt envious of those with wealth. They had something I wanted, and I believed, at some level, it unattainable for me. I made them and money wrong and myself out as more virtuous for not having or wanting wealth. I might add that this line of thinking made me highly successful at repelling money (doubtful I'll ever hit the talk show circuit speaking on that subject). As for politicians, if I disagreed with their policies, well then, they were vilified: Pretty simply, my way or the highway. In truth, it had more to do with my feeling powerless to bring those sorts of things into my life and into the world that I value. I might add that I didn't do much about making this happen in even the smallest way—so, what better target for my angst (and not an imaginative one at that)? I made the political system my scapegoat.

So, I spoke of inclusion while I practiced exclusion. I harped on about principles, all the while exercising rationalizations and justifications that only served to reinforce my current actions and inactions.

Does this seem, in any way, a path to harmony?

The discovery of it has offered a vital part of coming to know more my authentic self, which I realize now, is a more assured path to harmony, provided I live it. As long as I continued to live from falsity, harmony would remain elusive; as I would continually stand out of alignment with myself.

I have come to discover the sacredness of my heart and path, through the walking of the labyrinth—the heart and journey of others are no less sacred. The challenge is to create the consciousness that can hold space for both. One that seeks understanding in the face of differences, and that neither surrenders my truth nor demands of others that they relinquish theirs.

I know this is possible. I have seen it work in my day-to-day relating. Perhaps this could be said to be on a world scale, benign and insignificant. I submit that in a life exemplified by disconnection and disharmony, the realization of inclusion, connection, and harmony makes for a profound shift. The ripple effect of this alone will have widespread implications and, therefore, has great significance.

I can assure you that the world continually changes as I change my view of myself and not just myself in it, but myself as part of it.

Day 37
(Expectations)

I believed I would begin my written account for the day near the end of the practice. Of course, in actuality, it wasn't the end of the practice on at least two counts. Presuming I awoke tomorrow, there would be further opportunity to continue the practice. Also, I had the rest of the day—the window of time that I might think of as the meditation break—where I could carry any sense of peace or connection into the day to follow (or not). Now, that distinguished the true spiritual training arena.

The cultivating of peace and compassion while alone under a tree comes not without its challenges; however, once I left the cushion and ventured into the world at large, life upped the ante and challenges abounded. To hold a vision of those virtues I wanted to live into being and continuing to return to that would draw me gradually more consistently toward the mark; however, I am human and don't always act with grace and ease.

As an aside—I chose to write the draft of this book by hand (which I rarely do, having succumbed to some degree to the age of electronics), and as I wrote this, my one and only pen ran out of ink. (I have been known to have multiple pens and a variety of other items on my person—to be prepared—for what? God only knows.) That little voice reminded me that had I insured another pen was available, the writing wouldn't have gotten disrupted. I then became aware that I sat in a teashop while writing (a retail outlet), and it occurred to me that a pen might not prove that difficult to acquire. I no sooner got provided with a pen when I proceeded to convince myself in a Zen-like manner that the mismatched ink colour didn't matter.

As I considered the flexibility I exercised, I amused myself further by remembering the old T.V. series "Kung Fu" with Master Po teaching his young protégé about the flexibility of the willow and how that allows it to bend in the wind without breaking. I got all prepared to hug myself over my assimilation of the teaching when I discovered it was a fine-point pen.

I'd never cared for fine-tip pens (it felt like I scratched the words into the paper). I glanced at the counter to see if there might be a medium-point pen—I stopped myself when I recognized that the universe (if you will) had provided me with an immediate answer to my dilemma—I was about to pass judgment on the form the answer had presented in rather than just feeling grateful and continuing to write.

This might seem a ridiculous example, but not if considered in the context of whether just a little or a lot, how frequently do I discount the solution because I don't like the answer? Having averted that creative process crisis and digressed considerably, let us return to the labyrinth.

It was through the Qi Gong practice that I experienced what I can only describe as a warm flow moving in and around my body. It brought along with it an overall feeling of being okay (well, more than okay—as I wrote this, several hours later, I felt ridiculously good—a descriptor that might beg the question, what is ridiculous about feeling good?). It might even occur as ridiculous to some that waving my arms in the air could produce such a sense of wellbeing. I can think of a time in my history when I would have thought that. Yet there I stood, experiencing just that. I am familiar with exercise-induced endorphins and the feel-good effect of runner's high—I doubt this activity lasted long enough or grew intense enough to duplicate that, and nor does the endorphin sensation last all day. Something's going on, folks, and before the starting gun gets fired to signal the beginning of the debate, I might add that I know this feeling came from the inside out.

Trust me; I could write a book on external fixes (in fact, I guess in part, I'm doing just that). There's little if anything at all with regard to that strategy (trying to make myself feel better on the inside with some form of external gratification) that I haven't tried (consciously or unconsciously), so when I say this is not what's going on here, you can take it as a highly informed statement.

Of course, there will be those that remain sceptical just the same—I bless you and your scepticism, for it cannot diminish my experience.

Upon completing in the circle, I took a seat below the oak tree to prepare for my meditation. I sat directly in alignment with the rising sun—so, I faced roughly east (orienteering is not one of my strengths). The brilliance of the sun's morning debut contrasted the skeletal forms, which appeared silhouetted—the many trees that now stood defrocked to face the coming winter.

Though the visual in itself looked stunning, the warmth of the sun captivated. I gave myself entirely to its embrace. I could feel the earth below me, supporting me. I swooned with gratitude to the intricacies of the dance that I had become involved in. The energy of the sun — life sustaining — without it our Mother Earth would become an inhospitable frozen environment not suitable for human habitation. The trees (and plant life) capture its energy for the process of photosynthesis — producing the life-sustaining oxygen that we breathe; the carbon dioxide we expel then gets taken up (again, by the trees) which cyclically ensures the atmosphere does not become toxic (well, at least from the waste of our physiological presence). What an incomprehensibly complex weave of interactions and interdependences. So seemingly robust and yet there exists, as well, a delicate balance — human existence is rather fragile and certainly finite (without getting into discussions on reincarnation, the afterlife, death versus another phase of life, etc.).

Life ought to be revered, respected, appreciated, and embraced — at times, so deeply lost in the dramas and traumas of my existence, I have grown completely oblivious to the awareness that it can all only occur because I have life — I am alive.

Now, I don't suggest the denial of the need to heal as part of ongoing growth and evolution, but at the same time, it is possible to acknowledge my feelings and needs with compassion and empathy while appreciating I am alive.

If I didn't know better, I'd swear I remained home, still wrapped in the warmth of my bedding, rather than sitting outside in a public space on November 30th. I felt in no hurry to rush off, despite a vague awareness of the intermittent voices of passers-by.

To cap off the experience, when I opened my eyes, one of the resident grey squirrels sat directly in front of me. It sat up and continued to watch me — I remained motionless. Slowly, it advanced closer until it reached about four feet away. I could feel its presence (a bit like the sensation that someone is watching — without the creepy energy about it). The creature had an air of curiosity about him (or her). I sat there, held fast by the privilege of the encounter and intrigued by the squirrel's intention to connect. I tried, slowly, to reach to my side to get one of the almonds I had left at the base of the tree — this proved too much for my furry friend, as its survival instincts kicked in, and it scurried off.

I felt a little disappointed in the result but, overall, humbled and blessed to witness one of life's moment-to-moment miracles.

Day 37 Questions
(Expectations)

01) Have you ever heard the expression that expectations can be pre-meditated resentment? What comes up for you as you consider this?

02) Have you considered a distinction between an intention and an expectation?

03) Consider that a goal is useful to set a target, but also, too rigidly attaching to the outcome could limit the ways toward which the goal gets attained.

04) Do you set attainable goals for yourself?

05) Are your expectations of yourself high enough? Do you stretch yourself, at times, to further reach expanding potentials?

06) How successful do you believe yourself to be in adhering to your expectations versus becoming overly concerned with those of others?

07) If you consider expectations a set up for disappointment, have you considered that you more expect to get disappointed than to realize your goal?

08) Consider the various times that an outcome far exceeded your expectations and may not have resembled at all your original vision.

09) Consider your worldview more reflects your beliefs about it than it forms your beliefs.

10) Are you conscious about the nature of your thoughts?

11) If your expectations of someone stays fixed, what is the likelihood that they can show up any differently in your eyes?

12) How able (willing) are you to being flexible in your approach?

13) Do you consider yourself able to go with the flow?

14) Do you get upset if things don't go your way?

15) Are you open to collaborative problem solving?

16) When resolving conflict, do you focus on mutual understanding and resolution or being right?

17) Can you think of a time when you grew so intent on a particular outcome that you missed a golden opportunity right in front of you?

18) How easy is it for you to speak contrary to the group in the face of group expectations?

19) How free do you feel of societal expectations when plotting your path?

Sample Answer

Question 1 — Have you ever heard the expression that expectations can be premeditated resentment? What comes up for you as you consider this?

Question 11 — If your expectations of someone stays fixed, what is the likelihood that they can show up any differently in your eyes?

Question 16 — When resolving conflict, do you focus on mutual understanding and resolution or being right?

Question 17 — Can you think of a time when you grew so intent on a particular outcome that you missed a golden opportunity right in front of you?

It has been quite an exploration unraveling and becoming more aware of how my expectations can affect me (for example, my inner peace). There exists a fine line between holding to my vision to bring something into being and doggedly holding onto my point of view even when it no longer serves (others, myself, or the situation). It truly can be a premeditated resentment if I expect people, places, and things to behave exactly the way I think they should. Even if I conduct myself a particular way in a given situation (and do so consistently), I must remain mindful of self-righteousness and recognize that my way of being is not the be all and end all. My behaviour isn't necessarily the gold standard (even at its most effective). It is still my way of negotiating life and relating. Unquestionably, it is an ever-evolving work in progress and has come about by trial and error during other periods in my life. Seen in that light, I could give others the opportunity to travel on their individual human journey and not judge how they walk it. Of course, if I become directly impacted, I can look after myself—but even if what I come up with is a request that someone behave differently, I have no reason to expect they will agree to do so (unless it serves them to do so too).

There is also, I've learned, a good chance that what I try to uphold for myself are various needs of my own. Deeper conversations with others can lead to greater understanding (for both), and even to the realization that we share common needs. Sometimes, ironically, it can be discovered that both attempt to honour similar needs and their respective ways of going about that happen to come into conflict. If both parties focus entirely on "my way," they might never come to realize that they have a common interest, which they could collaboratively seek to uphold. I have been that person. I suppose it made for a necessary stage of my development—I couldn't be any more conscious with my communication than what I had the skills and awareness to be at any given time. Still, it seems sad when I consider how many misunderstandings I could have avoided.

Another thing I have experienced regarding expectations is that I have not seen an opportunity (or, perhaps, an answered prayer) that was right under my nose because it showed up in a form that wasn't in keeping with my expectations. It is possible to render something invisible if I look at it while looking for something else.

What of people in my life with respect to expectations? Well, I can say that there were times when I felt so sure I knew all there was to know of certain people (before I had any awareness of the realities of projecting my stuff onto others). I felt convinced that I had their number, and they virtually couldn't show up any other way than how I decided they were. Talk about a limiting way of seeing others and my ability to be in relation to them. Where far more possibility could have existed, my viewpoint, attitudes, and expectations quickly reduced these possibilities.

Day 38
(Presence)

"The Long and Winding Road" sang the Beatles, and when I consider my life in that context, it has indeed been both a lengthy and winding road (and I'm not about to stop walking it yet—if I have anything to say about it). Most, if not everyone, wants to go to heaven (or some version of it)—considerably less would say that they're ready to go today (myself included).

My discussion in yesterday's musing included valuing and feeling grateful for my life, which turned out strangely prophetic. I received word later that same day that someone who had been part of a circle of people I had a connection with had passed away. Later the same day, another old friend emailed me to tell me her beloved Jack Russell had to be euthanized at sixteen years of age. All right, Universe, you've got my attention! I hear you knocking. Of course, I'm human, but rather than make sweeping statements about human nature, I will say that I often act as though time is endless (well, actually, it might be; however, my time within it, not so much). Plans or ideas that share the notion that, "Someday, maybe, or after I get this, that, or the other thing handled, then I'll do more of what I love to do," may lead to considerable disappointment or just never happen.

This being so, all the fuss about "the time is now," or, "Carpe Diem," becomes more meaningful. Sure, there's timing, due diligence, etc. These same considerations could also be cleverly disguised avoidance, procrastination, and the paralysis of analysis or, in one word, fear. I can and have put so much energy into playing it safe that there could be no realizing my heart's desire. What, do you suppose, is the likelihood of my ever being happy if I constantly ignore or deny my heart? I don't refer to becoming rich, famous, or any specific realized criteria other than aligning with myself.

Here's what I know—many have suffered the wrath of my discontent. Conversely, the more I get in touch with who I am and work toward bringing more of that into my life, into the world, then that brings about a beautiful, uplifting quality. Now, I can smile at the man in the mirror, and I can shave my neck rather than taking that space-age alloy, titanium five-blade razor (with aloe strip to ensure minimum friction and skin irritation) and slitting it ear to ear.

Before anyone accuses me of being detached from reality, I would respond that reality is relative and, exactly, who's reality am I expected to live my life by? I am not blowing smoke, trying to suggest that the instant you follow your heart, it's all "Raindrops on Roses and Whiskers on Kittens." But, consider challenges encountered on a path fuelled by passion versus the suffering experienced by showing up day after day, living a lie. Again, the heart-path is not synonymous with easy or guaranteed to be a resounding financial success—so much the better if it is. I don't happen to think it can be ignored, even if it's not a money-maker. I suppose it comes down to personal values.

I value integrity (not to say that makes me better than the next guy—I'm simply stating my value). I mean, it's important to me to become congruent with my inner guidance; it doesn't mean that I walk around without challenge or even that I stay in integrity all the time. However, it does help lessen the suffering. Unmet needs will remain unmet, regardless of how much energy I put into various pursuits if the focus doesn't include ways by which those needs will get met. The end result? More suffering. I acknowledge my responsibility for my hand in the creation of this suffering—I decide differently to create something else. Nothing to lose and everything to gain, and by that, I mean an expanded sense of self and what is possible. You see, just in adopting that change of attitude, then already, I am winning. This, to me, has nothing to do with "keeping up with the Joneses." I just declare them the winners, and now that's out of the way, energy can get focused on removing the limitations that will allow the best of what I have to offer to shine through.

Oh, ya! Now, that's worth getting out of bed for!!!

Day 38 Questions
(Presence)

01) "Nike" ads aside, what comes to mind when you consider the idea, "Just Do It!"?

02) Do you have a bucket list with numerous hopes and dreams that you will get to someday?

03) As you consider some of these dreams, what stands in the way of today (or sooner than later) being someday?

04) What would it take to make one of your dreams come true now?

05) Will there ever be another day like today?

06) Do you assume there will always be another chance to say or do what you want?

07) How present can you remain to someone else? Can you hear them deeply, or are you just waiting to speak your mind?

08) What is your capacity to enjoy the journey versus waiting for some preconceived condition(s) to define the destination and success or happiness?

09) How much do you allow an outcome contrary to your expectations to effect your perspective about your current circumstances?

10) What do you think about the idea of your future being defined by the qualities you invest right now?

11) Have you ever considered that the most important steps you take in your life are the ones that occur right now?

12) Have you ever practiced awareness techniques such as focusing on your breath or bringing your awareness to your body? (Scanning it

briefly, head-to-toe, and relaxing each area a few times a day.)

13) If you find yourself anxious/worried, have you considered the idea of examining your concerns to determine whether there is anything required of you (or that can be done about it) right now?

14) What do you think about the idea, "Life is what happens when you are busy making plans"?

15) What is your ability to bring acceptance to a given moment or circumstance? (This doesn't mean you can't want to make changes.) Can you get to a place of non-judgment and accept this is where it's at right now?

16) How much time do you suppose you spend wishing you were somewhere else or doing something else (or anything) rather than just appreciating the moment?

17) Can you spend anything in the way of quality time (with just yourself) without some form of distraction (television, computer, music, etc.)?

18) Are you able to spend any time at all experiencing your environment rather than thinking about it or something entirely different?

19) Where are you with respect to fear of the future and/or peaceful resolution of your past?

20) Has the grass ever really been greener elsewhere once you got there?

Sample Answer

Question 15—What is your ability to bring acceptance to a given moment or circumstance? (This doesn't mean you can't want to make changes.) Can you get to a place of non-judgment and accept this is where it's at right now?

Question 16—How much time do you suppose you spend wishing you were somewhere else or doing something else (or anything) rather than just appreciating the moment?

Question 17—Can you spend anything in the way of quality time (with just yourself) without some form of distraction (television, computer, music, etc.)?

Question 18—Are you able to spend any time at all experiencing your environment rather than thinking about it or something entirely different?

Certainly, there are times when I feel content in the moment. Not surprisingly, it is usually when engaged in something that I find meaningful, or that involves some of my passions and interests. It could be writing or walking out in nature—on these occasions, time seemingly becomes fluid, and I feel deeply connected to myself and my surroundings. I feel as though I am actively part of what goes on around me more than just passively (and impatiently) watching and waiting for time to pass (as though I am captive and enslaved rather than intrinsically connected). On these occasions, it feels more challenging to frame the situation positively and not to wish to be somewhere else.

Of course, wishing to be elsewhere doesn't do anything to change the reality, and neither do I bring the best of what I have to offer to the situation I'm currently involved in if my attention and focus stays on being elsewhere. Most certainly, my attitudes come into play with regard to my ability to remain present. The ongoing practice of self-awareness and communication of needs increases my knowing of what it is that gets triggered in me that can stand in the way of my being present to others, allowing for self-empathy and compassion. It also poses an ongoing opportunity for growth (authenticity and vulnerability) to convey this awareness. Frankly, for me, it sometimes feels intensely uncomfortable, but then, so is a perpetual longing to be connected (which means the ability to be present to what is going on within myself and a willingness to share that with someone else). It can be both extremely rewarding and terrifying—I don't consider myself the master of emotional intelligence, authenticity (vulnerability), or communication.

I do give myself the credit of recognizing my need to develop these tools (awareness) as a sign of progress. Having said that, my commitment to this practice frequently leaves me perceiving I'm in way over my head and wondering where is all that clarity, confidence, and assurance that I felt when reading someone else's experience with these ways of being, or while participating in a class or workshop? Naively, I think that having had some breakthroughs and victories in these circumstances, I can now step out into the world in my super-hero spandex as

"Vulnerability Man!" Needless to say, I get stopped cold in my tracks somewhere between seeing the signal flashed across the heavens and donning my tights.

In the moment, presence allows an opportunity for intimacy and connection that can prove quite rare in our fast-paced world that encourages superficiality and emotional stoicism, resulting in a chronic longing for connection (I know it to be true for me), which is relentlessly and ineffectively addressed through a myriad of strategies (all of which create further disconnection from self), and so goes the cycle. I have lived this orientation and obsession with externalization (at times, to extremes), and my experience of this could be likened to standing in a hole and looking for the bottom while continuing to dig.

An ongoing inquiry into my limiting beliefs and mistaken ideas can bring about a shift (sometimes life-changing). As it is, these very beliefs brought to bear upon the present moment can perpetuate the same-old-same-old or liberate. To fully appreciate the power and possibility at the present moment, I must become willing to engage in the unknown. All I can say with regard to my experience with that is that I am expanding my capacity to engage in change (learning to surrender more to the unknown), which said another way is exercising trust and faith.

It is through this lens that I see the various frameworks imposed by my mind that take what could be a broad field of possibilities and reduces it extensively. Increasingly, I become more aware of preconceived ideas, assumptions, or imposed expectations, which can then make it impossible to be fully present moment to moment.

I have come to realize that it is extremely difficult to take empowered action in the present if I remain consumed with fears about future outcomes or history repeating itself. (Which is highly likely to occur if I don't believe anything else is possible or perpetuate the same action or inaction.)

Certainly, I don't suggest that some sort of plan isn't of value in order to move toward a certain goal. However, waiting for the right time to begin something can lead to a lengthy delay or obstruction to commencing at all. There will never be enough information to plan for the unknown—start anyway! Don't let due diligence become procrastination. You are neither too young nor too old (start anyway). You have ample credibility—you don't need more education (start anyway). To make a beginning will teach you what you need to know. Yes, people exist with more education and experience (start anyway). Nobody else has lived your life, walked in your shoes, or has your unique gifts or perspective. Nobody can do it the way you'll do it—whatever it is.

Day 39
(Truth)

I suppose I should never presume; however, it would appear that I will complete this forty-day journey successfully (given this is the second-to-last day). Having said that, I don't know that to be entirely true—what would define success and what would give indicators that I am complete? To show up tomorrow will indicate that I have realized the vision of forty consecutive days of the morning practice. I am aware of a general increase in my feeling of wellbeing, but what of the effect of these forty days on my life ongoing?

This is not the first of my pursuits toward my spiritual exploration and quest to determine what will define my ongoing practice. The time spent here, I must consider within the context of my life ongoing. I feel drawn to continue elements of the practice overall, though I may not walk the labyrinth every day. Of course, I have the raw material for my intended book, obtained through the experience— though this is not the sole reason for this undertaking. It's not just about a feel-good activity in the morning. I have experienced in my life absolute mental/emotional and spiritual bankruptcy, and certainly marked physical decline along with it. I seek spiritual transformation at depth—my life is at stake here (at the very least, the *quality* of my life)— this all forms part of a desire to experience Spirit in me and through me, and to discover and bring the best I have to offer into the service of humanity.

This has nothing to do with the current popularity of spirituality, given by some the same treatment as the next trendy class at the fitness studio (having said that, I have no way of knowing what approach or path might lead to an opening in the life of another). So, though it need not become a dire search, I do take this seriously (but, just to add a little paradoxical twist, I don't take myself nearly as seriously). I also emphasize that this is my perspective only, and is not meant to dictate how anyone else approaches self-exploration or even that they do. I do presume that anyone reading this book has at least some curiosity.

No assurance exists that following the dictates of my heart and soul will always feel good, will prove easy (often, it seems anything but), that it will be convenient, or will bring on fame or fortune. Neither does it assure career success, nor that I will walk hand-and-hand into the sunset—after all, Hollywood hasn't written my soul path. Sometimes, apparently, "I don't get the girl." Instead, it would seem, I'm meant to determine how I continue the next day without surrounding my heart in armour. So, I don't want to cast any air of specialness based on the spiritual focus, and neither do I want to hide from the world in it. I seek to find the keys within to bring into being the best of my humanity. I may be able to "act as if" for a while, but the time will come when I can't buy my own B.S. any longer, and a surrender occurs (which doesn't mean I give up on life). It does mean that, frequently, I need a broader perspective than my current view, so I may need to surrender the limitations of my current thinking. Albert Einstein said, "A problem can't be solved at the same level at which it was created." Often, I become far too invested in my point of view to allow for another possibility, which might be okay if whatever that is continues to invest a source of satisfaction in my life, but what if it doesn't?

The situation doesn't always need to change; sometimes it's my view that must change or my attitude—it can then seem as though there occurs a transformation to the situation itself. At other times, maybe I do need to move on; either way, where does the impetus to change my perspective or give up a familiar and, therefore, comfortable situation come from? What generates that inner push? (Or, perhaps, I could better describe it as a spiritual malaise.) I can create the resistance to the prodding—even some well thought out and articulated reasons not to change—nothing says I have to. However, actions have consequences, and this proves equally true for inaction.

A crutch, a weakness, a dependency, many would say of the spiritual path; however, my personal experience is that it demands a reckoning with self that requires courage I don't always feel sure I possess, yet it appears there when required. I don't know how others arrive on this path; for me, I had found that everything I had depended on (as well as those things it seemed that most others I observed depended on) became no longer dependable. It felt a lonely, desolate, and barren wasteland that consisted of nothing but various shades of dark. From there, I decided that I could grow willing to consider reaching for something I couldn't guarantee existed, or if so, that it could benefit me. I also believed that I had nothing to lose. Now, I hold on with both hands because while to move forward is certainly not without fear, neither standing still nor turning back offers an option.

Day 39 Questions
(Truth)

01) It has been said that the truth will set you free. Consider that for yourself and journal what it means to you.

02) What does self-honesty mean to you?

03) What does it mean to you to live authentically?

04) Do areas of your life lack this honesty/authenticity?

05) How easy (or challenging) do you find it to express your needs?

06) How aware are you of your needs?

07) Aristotle said, "Knowing yourself is the beginning of all wisdom." Consider this and journal what it means to you.

08) What (if anything) keeps you from expressing what is true for you?

09) Are you willing to stand alone in your truth?

10) Is there a cost to ignoring the truth? What does it (or has it) cost you personally?

11) Consider the amount of courage it takes to go against the grain.

12) Have you ever examined your core beliefs? (About yourself, God, relationships, money, etc.)

13) When searching for the truth, how do you manage the inner turmoil that arises when an idea gets presented that conflicts with your beliefs?

14) What is the payoff for keeping quiet and not rocking the boat?

15) Is the acceptance of others worth ignoring your truth?

16) Were you encouraged as a child to tell the truth? What happened when you did? How did this effect your relationship with honesty?

17) Are your relationships based on truth?

18) Have you considered how white-lies or half-truths might impact a relationship?

19) Do you have an awareness and practice of emotional honesty?

20) Are you aware of the links between emotional expression (versus repression) and overall wellness?

Sample Answer

Question 1—It has been said that the truth will set you free. Consider that for yourself and journal what it means to you.

Question 14—What is the payoff for keeping quiet and not rocking the boat?

With regard to this idea of truth as a key to freedom, I should begin by saying I'm not trying to present myself as the source of truth. I would say that truth could express through me, which also holds true for every other human being. It can only do so in alignment with my consciousness and what I feel willing to accept as true. It doesn't mean there isn't more to the story of truth, but my free-will choice allows me to operate in ignorance of the full truth (without diminishing it) even if it would serve me better to know and embrace it more completely. So, to begin, free (free from what?). Taken from a prayer from the circles of A.A., comes the line, "Relieve me of the bondage of self." What is it that is referred to as this bondage of self? If we get past the influence of theology and the grammar of antiquity, it is mistaken assumptions, limiting beliefs, and programming (familial, societal, religious, etc.) that I have made true about myself, or that I have unconsciously used to draw erroneous conclusions based on these external influences. And I discover that my life gets diminished by the continued adherence to what amounts to my dogma (about myself). In effect, it seems much like a prison because, as I move about in my life, I continually bump up against these self-created walls that as much as say, "That's far enough. Never mind what lies beyond the wall or, for that matter, if there is anything at all. This is where you find safety; these carefully constructed walls are in place for your good."

Except, despite there having been a place in history where the walls served a useful purpose, I have discovered that it is no longer the case, and that in fact, the wall is the reason nothing else has become possible. Infinite possibility always existed; however, these walls severely hinder my view. Imagine, if you will, the dismantling of some of these walls. I gain freedom in the form of expanded possibility, which is not just abstract but has brought about experiences, which previously proved impossible for me to bring into my life because of my beliefs.

Now, I'll grant you, the reckoning with my having responsibility for both the experiences I had and the denial of more life-affirming experience felt tough to swallow; however, as the necessary element of awareness within my process, it has become a gift in the grander scheme of things. Having said that, when I'm in the process of gaining this new self-awareness, I don't always wax so philosophical or even feel that grateful. Sometimes, it can come as an awakening of the rude variety. My experience of the reckoning with such awareness is that it absolutely is a time to practice as much self-love and empathy (as well as compassion and forgiveness) as I can bring to the table—certainly, it doesn't serve to subsequently berate myself for what I discover. It can't possibly help bring parts of me to light previously unconscious if, once they present, I make an atmosphere of non-loving and non-acceptance. That attitude is far more likely to drive them back under ground.

To shift the focus to the question about what might have me withhold the speaking of my truth, suffice to say that authenticity has often not just gotten relegated to the back seat, more like it rode in a different vehicle. I have discovered a number of influences operating below the surface that come up for release or transformation. Approval-seeking lies among them. Below, I discover shame and low self-esteem. Incessantly being agreeable and saying yes when I would rather say no and not giving my true viewpoint in a discussion. All of which places too much concern on being liked than on the truth.

The irony is that I can't feel good about myself if I continually sell out my truth, nor can I be known. Relationships become based on falsity, and this disconnection with self feeds a feeling of loneliness, as despite being surrounded by people, my voice falls silent and leaves my true values unspoken and needs unmet. The other side of the coin showed a propensity to care-take the feelings others—not wanting to offend or upset them. The thing about that is it's not my business to oversee the feelings and reaction of others. I needed to examine my control issues. The other thing came from the concern that the feelings of others had more to do with further attempts by me to avoid the pain of rejection. I had healing to do with respect to what I made that mean. A big difference exists between experiencing and feeling disappointment when rejection occurs (didn't get the job, the date, the dance, etc.). It proves quite another matter if energies lay within me that, when activated, result in me behaving as though it is I, myself, who is flawed, unworthy, unlovable, or incompetent. Not an ounce of truth in that, but nonetheless, the power of subconscious beliefs can, absolutely, wreak havoc in my life, and I can, absolutely, attest to that.

As I'm sure you can imagine, freedom of a most delightful variety can become the result of doing the work of self-discovery and bringing some permanent healing to bear on these non-loving ways of being. I can't speak highly enough about the rewards of doing this work. Yes, there are moments of reckoning, which necessarily feel disillusioning, but this rather brief discomfort definitely proves preferable to the pain of continued self-delusion and opens the door to the joyful appreciation of greater integrity and authenticity.

Day 40
(Inspired Action)

As the final day of the forty-day commitment came upon me, I felt amazed at how quickly the time seemed to have gone by, versus how daunting the original thirty days, which became forty days, had seemed in the beginning. In those early days, I had no idea what was about to unfold — probably just as well, as I might not have taken it on had I known. One day at a time — one step at a time — and I had arrived. Having said that, the arrival was not at a place where the journey ended. Even still, those past forty days would inform and influence the ongoing walk into what came next in my life. I no longer needed to wonder if I could do it — I did it!

Did that mean that forever more I could call myself a committed person? Not necessarily. It did demonstrate I had the capacity to uphold a commitment to myself. I recognized and reckoned with buried emotions and potentially sabotaging thoughts along the way. I would continue to need these tools in my life, and so, though this had been called a practice all along, it also represented my actual life. Challenges that presented showed up in other areas of my life. This practice did not occur in isolation (as though in a vacuum). So, any amount of love, compassion, empathy, and patience I managed to hold for myself during the practice reflected my current capacity to generate these qualities for myself. My perseverance in the face of the commitment not always feeling convenient or easy served well and illustrated the need to apply focused energy upon the goal to keep moving it toward realization and avoiding the numerous distractions that crept into the picture. Needless to say, this proved invaluable for my wellbeing and, of course, my relationships would all get fed by this growing capacity — particularly the relationship to myself.

Elevation of spirit, increased energy levels, greater sense of connection — I had experienced all during this journey. I knew the kind of results one could expect when these feelings stay missing or get diminished, and so, to feel as though I could gain access to expanded spiritual and energetic resources makes so much more possible. To begin to get more insight into the beliefs and behaviours that can side-track (or derail altogether) was, indeed, valuable information. In turn, I could use it to devise strategies to continue on the intended path.

The walking of the labyrinth had provided an excellent vehicle for this exploration, and the form in itself gave a good reminder to keep my feet on the ground, as well as the need to keep putting one foot in front of the other to continue to move forward. The completion gave cause for acknowledgement and even celebration. Just the same, I must keep it in the perspective of the bigger picture — it represented a new beginning. The insights and illuminations had the potential to become life changing, but only if I combined them with action based on the expanded perspectives. To rest on my laurels, or worse, slip into complacency, would not bring about any change or bring anything into being beyond the etheric realm of potential. The experience described throughout this book would not have happened if I'd sat at home and wondered what it would be like to walk a labyrinth regularly—even if I dreamed of doing just that and, in the doing, experienced the elation of a dream that touched my heart—this alone would not have proven enough. In this example, it became necessary that I get up and show up (day after day). It became necessary to do the legwork. Then, and only then, did the vision become real.

Without question, the flights of fancy of the imagination entice, and it can feel tempting to spend an inordinate amount of time there. The old saying goes, "It's fine to build castles in the sky, as long as you don't move in." I can't say that I resided in the castle full-time; however, I grew familiar with the false sense of security gained by living behind its walls—surely nothing could breach its moat, towers, and bastions. In part, this remained true; however, it turned out that it kept all my allies at bay as well, rather than just the perceived adversaries. The longer the walls remained, the more estranged I became from such acquaintances as joy, adventure, and fulfillment.

The young prince Siddhartha found true contentment (in fact, enlightenment) outside the physical walls of his palace and the circumstances of his human birthright—to have settled for the security of his inheritance may have crushed his heart and spirit, not to mention his destiny of becoming the Buddha. The point being that the single-minded pursuit of safety might likely not satiate the yearning of my heart, nor would the mere pondering or talking about dreams bring them into reality.

As the forty days drew to an end, I recognized that it was more accurate to say that I had now arrived upon a plateau, and the view from here seemed quite different from that which I had experienced before climbing to this vantage point. However, now that I stood here, the objective became to enjoy the view but not become attached to it because it would soon come time to begin another climb—each summit becomes the base camp for the next frontier. As such, the wisdom to enjoy the journey becomes more meaningful, as does the realization that the climb to the next beautiful viewpoint will prove considerably easier without all that excess baggage.

Day 40 Questions
(Inspired Action)

01) It has been said that actions speak louder than words; what is your current awareness of the relationship between your words and your actions?

02) Have you ever experienced having a great idea, and maybe you even shared it with some friends or just kept it to yourself? Either way, one day, there it is, out there in the world, your idea. What might prevent you from acting on your inspired visions?

03) Are you aware of any disconnect between the feel-good energy of inspiration (whether that may come from a workshop, a book you read, TED talk video, etc.) and getting your hands dirty bringing your inspired idea into the world?

04) Do you have an action plan?

05) Do you plan to take action?

06) What sort of things become distractions from your action plan (or having an action plan)?

07) Does the idea that many people are over-read and under acting bring up anything for you?

08) What do you view as some of the more pressing issues in your community (country, the world)? What could you do in response?

09) Are you inclined to think that somebody needs to do something about _____? (Could that someone be you?)

10) What of procrastination? What forms may that take in accomplishing your vision?

11) What do you suppose lies behind procrastination? What do you suppose might cause you to run interference with your success?

12) Do you see others as more capable of getting it done than you?

13) What does it take to bring something successfully into being?

14) Consider some of your lifetime accomplishments — what qualities can you identify of your own that you possess or that you developed along the way?

15) Consider some of what you deem as failures (failure to start, failure to finish, etc.). What were the contributing factors? Does the failure to realize the idea make the idea unworthy of reconsideration?

16) What did you learn from such so-called failures?

17) Why would you continue to call them failures if they brought about valuable learning and subsequent wisdom?

18) Did you subsequently utilize new strategies when approaching your next vision, which you learned from the previously unsuccessful endeavour?

19) Could that then be seen as a success in regard to your personal development?

20) Sometimes, waiting is called for (to gather more information, etc.). Consider that if you tell yourself that you can't make a decision, you have made a decision — you have decided to delay making a definitive choice and then acted on that choice (which is both a choice and a decision). What lies behind any fears of making a new start?

Sample Answer

Question 11 — What do you suppose lies behind procrastination? What do you suppose might cause you to run interference with your success?

Question 20 — Sometimes, waiting is called for (to gather more information, etc.). Consider that if you tell yourself that you can't make a decision, you have made a decision. You have decided to delay making a definitive choice and then acted on that choice (which is both a choice and a decision). What lies behind any fears of making a new start?

I shall weigh in on the last question first, and then, perhaps, flow into some of the other questions. If I haven't already said so, I have not written this book from any real or imagined hilltop and, therefore, stake no claim on having everything handled. Neither do I see myself teaching everyone else how to make their life work.

The questions I've included throughout the book are, indeed, questions that I need to continue to ask of myself. The answers reflect various snapshots (if you will) of my awareness, evolution, challenges, and pratfalls along the way. I also acknowledge that I am not without my blind spots and walk upon the playing field of life that forever shifts and changes so that I, continually, get called to examine what I hold as true and, therefore, how I see the world and me within it.

I don't have the monopoly on indecision but have attained a significant degree of mastery at procrastination (ah, there we go, brought in question

11 without even trying). So, I speak pointedly and specifically to myself when I point out the distinction that not to decide is to decide, and not to act is to act. The irony is that I believe the long-term impact of holding back on my opportunity to know and be successful is just as painful, if not more than, any pain I might encounter if I set out to achieve something and encounter a setback (or a dozen). Fear holds me back. To become effective at releasing these blocks to my getting into action, I have found it useful to get specific with regard to awareness (the naming of these fears and the forms they take). It has both been said, "Know Your Enemy," and, "Love Your Enemy." I suggest that the two get undertaken together. I must know what lies within me that brings about the results I no longer wish to experience. Upon making this discovery, I don't want to endlessly beat myself up for what I find.

I think of it as though I am both teacher and student. I don't know about you, but I have never responded well to someone chastising me as their approach to trying to teach me something. If anything, such chastisement might leave me more inclined to do the opposite. It might well be that what they present would prove of great value to me, but if delivered upon a vehicle of hostility, I am not apt to stay receptive. I can't see that it is any different when working at bringing new ways of being into my life. I must do it with love, understanding, and compassion or, in effect, I shutdown to myself.

When I think about it, it is not the decision itself that presents the barrier. I have concern for the outcome, which of course, I can't know at the outset. Examined more closely, I find fear of humiliation, getting it wrong, and the real wrench-in-the-gears, shame-based perfectionism. I would find it difficult to describe, in any comprehensive way, how extensively I have sought preparation in order to believe myself competent and credible enough to start. What I discovered was an ego-trap. It wouldn't matter how much preparation, education, or experience I brought to the table; there would never be enough. It became necessary to reveal and heal the mistaken beliefs that I was not enough, and I would continue to pursue enough endlessly (i.e. not enough = can't start). It never occurred to me that I would continue to gain more expertise, wisdom, and experience along the way once I made a start. In fact, that perception remained invisible to me from the mindset of not enough.

Shame and fear can become such immobilizing energies. The presence of shame invites more fear to avoid further shame, and so it goes. I can suggest with no authority that they exist for everyone; however, I can say that they are more widespread than we might imagine. This is due to the unspoken cultural agreement to keep shame veiled in secrecy, which feeds it and allows it to remain entrenched. A culture and consciousness that often relies on shame as a way to mistakenly convey everything from error (omission or commission) and requests for recognition of needs to attempts at conflict resolution accomplishes nothing more than to drive shame further underground.

I have come to know these things as a result of examining such obstacles within me. As has always been true for me, when the student is ready, the teacher will appear. Either through a further awareness of myself, which in itself is a powerful teacher, or through a willingness to learn, I am guided and directed to the sources of just the right information or means to bring about healing and transformation. Here is where a decision proves integral—I must decide that I have the willingness to see that which previously remained invisible to me. I can choose to remain ignorant; however, I will continue to get the same results I have always gotten, which stands to reason, as I would utilize the same old approach.

For me, I have come to realize that I have handled a wide variety of life events and circumstances. I am still here, after all. So, really, I have no good reason not to believe that whether I achieve my desired outcome with any given endeavour, or something completely unexpected and undesirable were to occur, I can and will handle it.

Believe me, I understand the avoidance of pain, so I certainly do not sit in judgment of those stuck in a cycle of false starts or incompletion. I have done it all. I do say that there are ways to go about getting unstuck, and state from personal experience that unrealized potentials calling to get embraced will not remain ignored, and they will produce their own unique variety of angst.

Epilogue

In the process of bringing this book into being, I now sit using my third laptop computer. This gives neither a reflection on the resiliency of electronic devices nor the longevity. Some corresponding lessons came attached to the demise of the previous two computers; one having been stolen, and the other, subject to the non-ordinary wear and tear of my lack of due care and attention. My beginning this postscript in this fashion provides a little background to the statement that I have infinite gratitude to back-up technology that carried the bulk of my work forward from one computer to the next. The only thing I lost was the original Epilogue.

So, this book, then, got written well after the Forty-Day Practice. It also occurred a significant period of time after the original journal notes got massaged into what became the book's forty chapters.

Does it make any difference that what I now write as a conclusion, I didn't source directly from the place in time that I had freshly embraced the successful completion of the practice?

In a word — no.

As the above-mentioned computer saga indicates, the end of one part of the journey invariably leads to the beginning of the next leg.

As revealed over the course of my experience here, I met with myself in many different lights. I experienced myself having various forms of success and victories. I also got introduced to myself as "he who considered, at times, taking me out!"

The insights gained from the process itself became invaluable pathways to recognize some of the ways I limited myself, held myself back, and sabotaged myself; knowing these things offers immeasurable relief and freedom. The limiting beliefs, thoughts, and behaviours made visible opened the doors to the discovery and enjoyment of hidden potentials.

The whole thing could have ended at any time during the forty days. Subsequent to that, the ongoing issues with computers might have been allowed to derail my will to complete this project, or I might have seen it as a sign foretelling my fate as a writer.

Any of the various life circumstances that had occurred since I began the original practice (just over five years ago) could have become reasons to abandon ship. I don't suggest that this is the typical timeframe for one to complete a book (I don't even feel sure what complete looks like), but I can certainly attest that life situations continue to present.

My declaring that I would embark on a journey of self-discovery (which included my first attempt to produce a book) didn't stop both my parents passing in one year, some long-term disruption of income, and challenges arising in resuming stable employment. Not the least of which was considering whether I resumed within a career path that I had thought I had left behind permanently.

While I walked the labyrinth, I learned a thing or two about how I had done (and was doing) life. Of course, I found plenty to celebrate as well. I can assure you that the path of self-inquiry is not one of never-ending dower indictment.

Still, the metaphor prevails—one step, one foot in front of the other, and the walk continues. The physical layout of the labyrinth is without impediment. Just the same, the walker can dig cavernous canyons and impenetrable walls on an otherwise clear path.

I envision a walk of discovery that reveals for me how I can best reach the next plateau while dreaming and continuing to achieve greater pinnacles. As I make that real for myself, I want nothing more than to provide testimonial that reveals and inspires others to new heights on their path.

78387095R00229

Made in the USA
Columbia, SC
15 October 2017